Macassan History and Heritage
Journeys, Encounters and Influences

Edited by Marshall Clark and Sally K. May

Macassan History and Heritage
Journeys, Encounters and Influences

Edited by Marshall Clark and Sally K. May

E PRESS

Published by ANU E Press
The Australian National University
Canberra ACT 0200, Australia
Email: anuepress@anu.edu.au
This title is also available online at http://epress.anu.edu.au

National Library of Australia Cataloguing-in-Publication entry

Author: Clark, Marshall Alexander, author.

Title: Macassan history and heritage : journeys, encounters and influences / Marshall Clark and Sally K. May.

ISBN: 9781922144966 (paperback) 9781922144973 (ebook)

Notes: Includes bibliographical references.

Subjects: Makasar (Indonesian people)--Australia. Northern--History.
Fishers--Indonesia--History
Aboriginal Australians--Australia, Northern--Foreign influences.
Aboriginal Australians--History.
Australia--Discovery and exploration.

Other Authors/Contributors:

May, Sally K., author.

Dewey Number: 303.482

All rights reserved. No part of this publication may be reproduced, stored in a retrieval system or transmitted in any form or by any means, electronic, mechanical, photocopying or otherwise, without the prior permission of the publisher.

Cover images: Fishing praus and cured trepang in the Spermonde Archipelago, South Sulawesi. Source: Marshall Clark.

Cover design and layout by ANU E Press

This edition © 2013 ANU E Press

Contents

1. Understanding the Macassans: A regional approach 1
   Marshall Clark and Sally K. May

2. Studying trepangers 19
   Campbell Macknight

3. Crossing the great divide: Australia and eastern Indonesia . . . 41
   Anthony Reid

4. Histories with traction: Macassan contact in the framework
   of Muslim Australian history 55
   Regina Ganter

5. Interpreting the Macassans: Language exchange in historical
   encounters 69
   Paul Thomas

6. Unbirri's pre-Macassan legacy, or how the Yolngu became
   black 95
   Ian S. McIntosh

7. 'An Arnhem Land adventure': Representations of Macassan–
   Indigenous Australian connections in popular geographical
   magazines 107
   Rebecca Bilous

8. Rock art evidence for Macassan–Aboriginal contact in
   northwestern Arnhem Land 127
   Paul S. C. Taçon and Sally K. May

9. Drug substances introduced by the Macassans: The mystery
   of the tobacco pipe 141
   Maggie Brady

10. Tangible heritage of the Macassan–Aboriginal encounter in
    contemporary South Sulawesi 159
    Marshall Clark

11. Traditional and 'modern' trepang fisheries on the border of
    the Indonesian and Australian fishing zones 183
    Dedi Supriadi Adhuri

12. Travelling the 'Malay Road': Recognising the heritage significance of the Macassan maritime trade route 205
    Sandy Blair and Nicholas Hall

Contributors 227
Index 229

1. Understanding the Macassans: A regional approach

Marshall Clark and Sally K. May

Introduction

This volume addresses the history and heritage of the 'Macassan' fishers who made the long and sometimes dangerous maritime journey from the port town of Makassar in southern Sulawesi to the coastline of Arnhem Land and the Kimberley, northern Australia, from before European settlement in Australia until the early twentieth century.[1] The essays of this collection present an interdisciplinary perspective on the maritime journeys of the Macassans, as well as their encounters with Aboriginal communities in the north and the ongoing impact this exchange has had on Aboriginal languages, societies and cultures. The primary reason for the Macassan visits to the northern Australian waters each year was the collection of trepang (*teripang* in Indonesian), edible holothurians also known as sea cucumbers, bêche-de-mer or sea slugs. This volume addresses various aspects of the historical development and impact of the trepang trade as well as the enduring encounters between the Macassans and the Indigenous communities of northern Australia. Contemporary heritage iterations and reappropriations are also examined, including heritage listing possibilities, present-day trepang fisheries and Australia–Indonesia bilateral marine cooperation and management.

The history and heritage of the Macassan fishers form an important chapter of Australia's history. They have also played a role in the history of Indonesia and the Southeast Asian region, not to mention East Asia. The Macassan trepang or bêche-de-mer fishery dates back to at least the 1700s, when fishers from the trading port of Makassar and its environs, in the southwestern arm of the island of Sulawesi, made an annual journey to the coasts of the Kimberley and Arnhem Land, known as Kayu Jawa and Marege' respectively. It is quite possible that other voyagers from elsewhere in Indonesia, such as the Bajo (Bajau), also known as the Sama Bajau or Bajau Laut, may have visited Australia even earlier (see Fox 1977). Although the later Macassan crews may have included Sama Bajau and indeed fishers from a variety of ethnic groups such as the Butonese,

---

[1] We would like to thank various colleagues for reading and commenting on an earlier version of this chapter, which has been greatly improved as a result. This includes Campbell Macknight, Kate Lloyd, Ian McIntosh and Paul Taçon. We take full responsibility for any remaining errors or shortcomings.

the majority of the crew and their vessels were from Makassar and spoke languages used by the main ethnic groups based there—namely, the Bugis and the Makassarese. In large and regular fleets of wooden sailing vessels, known as prau (also spelled in Indonesian and the lingua franca of the region, Malay, as '*perahu*'), the Macassans sailed to Australia with the northwest monsoon each December and returned to their home port of Makassar with the southeast trade winds around March or April each year (Macknight 1976; Chaloupka 1993). The trepang catch and trade goods such as pearl shell, beeswax and ironwood were brought back to Makassar and sold to Chinese traders supplying the market of southern China, where trepang were highly sought (Macknight 1976; Clarke 2000). During their visits, the Macassans developed social and economic ties with local Indigenous groups, though the extent of these relationships is still being debated (Macknight 1976; Chaloupka 1996; Clarke and Frederick 2006; Mitchell 1994).

In general, for the Indigenous people of Arnhem Land and the Kimberley, the Macassans were among the first foreigners they had ever come across, provoking a great deal of interest in the various material cultures they subsequently introduced. These items include canoes, sails, hooks, fishing lines, beads and metals, to name just a few. The broader socio-cultural impact of this will be discussed in much greater detail in this volume. Besides introducing various items of material culture, the Macassans employed Indigenous people to help gather and process the trepang catch. Dozens, if not hundreds, of Aboriginal sojourners are said to have sailed on the return voyage to Makassar, settling there and beginning families with local women. Activity in the Macassan trepang industry declined from 1880 onwards due to the taxes and charges being imposed on the visiting trepangers. The last Macassan voyage to Australia took place during the 1906–07 season (see Macknight, this volume), before the South Australian Government effectively refused to grant fishing licences to non-Australian operators (Macknight 1976).

The timing of the earliest Asian visits remains an important and controversial debate in the archaeology and history of northern Australia. There are a number of contrasting views relating to the chronology based on documentary and/or archaeological evidence. As mentioned in his chapter (this volume), Macknight (1976, p. 97; 1986, p. 69) initially placed the origins of the Macassan trepang industry between 1650 and 1750 AD. He later revised his evaluation, arguing the industry was not in full swing until the 1780s, with some possible earlier excursions to northern Australia occurring from the 1750s. Macknight's initial evaluation was based on a number of written sources that date the industry to the eighteenth century, including historical accounts, personal journals and government records, while his re-evaluation (Macknight 2008) is based on evidence presented by Knapp and Sutherland's (2004) study of detailed trade data for Makassar. At the same time, a number of archaeologists have questioned Macknight's document-based theory and point to his own archaeological work as evidence for earlier visits. Radiocarbon dates on wood charcoal found in the remains of trepang boiling fireplaces returned dates several hundred years older than ages inferred from documentary evidence. These three geographically separate sites (at Anuru Bay, Entrance Island and Groote Eylandt) returned radiocarbon dates with ages ranging from 1170 to 1520 AD (Macknight 1976, pp. 98–9). Due to the discrepancy between these dates and historical accounts, Macknight argued that there must be a source of error in the archaeological dates. Indeed, Mitchell (1994) argued that the radiocarbon dates were unreliable and that they result from technical problems with radiocarbon analysis of mangrove wood.

In addition to the work of Macknight, a pottery shard at Dadirringka rock shelter on Groote Eylandt was found below where a calibrated radiocarbon date of between 904 and 731 BP was obtained (Clarke and Frederick 2011, p. 151). Clarke (1994, 2000) argues that she found further evidence to support earlier contact from an analysis of material excavated at Malmudinga. Importantly, however, Clarke maintains that 'this initial contact was not necessarily of the order of magnitude of the later trepang industry, organised from the city of Macassar and may have been both sporadic and small scale' (Clarke 1994, p. 470).

Recent rock art and archaeological work undertaken in northwestern Arnhem Land has contributed to the ongoing debate. This includes the radiocarbon dating of a beeswax figure overlaying a painting of a Southeast Asian sailing vessel in the Wellington Range (Taçon et al. 2010; see also Taçon and May, this volume). Results indicate this sailing vessel, most probably a prau, was painted prior to 1664 AD, and there is a 99.7 per cent probability that the overlying beeswax figure was made between 1517 and 1664 AD. Recent archaeological excavations and re-evaluation of earlier excavated materials at the Anuru Bay site have also provided insights into the timing of Macassan visits (Theden-Ringl et al. 2011). The team analysed two skeletons excavated by Macknight in the 1960s and confirmed Macknight's argument that the skeletons were of Southeast Asian origin (Theden-Ringl et al. 2011, p. 41). They also suggest that one of the individuals died before 1730 AD (Theden-Ringl et al. 2011, p. 45). Overall, we are entering an exciting new era of archaeological research into Macassan sites and new findings will almost certainly rewrite our understanding of the timing and the nature of early Asian contact with Australia.

Yalangbara and *Trepang*

What has become one of the most celebrated chapters in Australia's history continues to attract great interest. For instance, in the Australian spring of 2011 there were two museum exhibitions highlighting the historical impact of the encounters between the Indigenous people of Arnhem Land and the 'Macassans' of Sulawesi. The first exhibition of the two, *Yalangbara: Art of the Djang'kawu*, was held at the National Museum of Australia in Canberra. *Yalangbara* showcases artworks by the Marika family from northeast Arnhem Land, depicting the journey of the Djang'kawu ancestors. The Djang'kawu are believed to be the 'first ancestors' of northeast Arnhem Land, the first people who were born or created there. The paintings illustrate the events associated with the *Wanggarr*, the 'ancestral dimension' or creative period when the Djang'kuwu undertook their journeys (Morphy 2008). The members of the Marika family are highly regarded as prolific artists, influential teachers, cultural ambassadors, environmentalists and activists. Mawalan 1 Marika, for example, was a key guide and informant for Campbell Macknight, who travelled to the region in the 1960s in preparation for his groundbreaking doctoral research on the history of the Macassan trepang fishers, or trepangers. This research has since been published in the classic book in the field, *The Voyage to Marege': Macassan trepangers in northern Australia* (Macknight 1976).

The *Yalangbara* exhibition focuses on the Marika family's most significant clan estate at Yalangbara, or Port Bradshaw, south of Yirrkala in northeast Arnhem Land. Yalangbara, distinguished by its great sand dunes and pristine beaches, is a focal point for ancestral activity. It is the site where the first ancestors, the Djang'kuwu, landed: 'people as far away as western Arnhem Land and south down to Lumbulwar refer to Yalangbara as the place of the first people, the first people who were born or created there' (Marika 2008, p. 8). The *Yalangbara* collection consists of works produced at the Yirrkala mission in the 1930s as well as rare crayon drawings commissioned by the anthropologist Ronald Berndt, who worked closely with Mawalan 1 Marika and Wandjuk Marika at Yirrkala in 1946–47. Other works include bark paintings from the 1950s and a series of contemporary prints, fibre items, barks and carvings. In terms of themes, the exhibition explores issues such as heritage and land rights as well as the interrelationship between people, their art and the land. For those interested in the centuries-long Macassan–Aboriginal encounter, the *Yalangbara* works are notable for a recurring element: motifs depicting the legendary 'Bayini', widely believed to be a mythical group of white or golden-coloured Asian seafarers who voyaged to Arnhem Land, before the arrival of the Macassan fishing fleets.

Who are the Bayini? Some scholars such as Macknight have argued that Indigenous Australian ancestral memories of the Bayini or pre-Macassans originate from Indigenous Australian visits to the homeland of the Macassans, the port of Makassar (Macknight 2008). Alternatively, Fox (1977) has suggested that the scattered fishers known as the Bajo (Bajau) or Bajau Laut ('Sea Gypsies') were the first fishers and trepangers from Indonesian waters to voyage to northern Australia. Could the Bajo (Bajau) and the Bayini be the one and the same? McIntosh (1995) has argued that the identity of the pre-Macassans as a historical phenomenon has always been something of a conundrum, and will continue to be the case, despite the Bayini occupying centre stage in Yolngu cosmology. McIntosh (2011) has argued that until very recently—1988 to be precise—the Yolngu deliberately concealed the true identity of the Bayini. In the stories that have been disclosed, it appears that, in McIntosh's words, 'the Bayini are seafarers who, at the dawn of time, make their way from points south of Numbulwar in the Gulf of Carpentaria, around Dholtji and Cape Wilberforce, and into Arnhem Bay and Gurrumurru, where their journey ends as mysteriously as it began' (McIntosh 2011, p. 352). In any case, the Bayini iconography of the *Yalangbara* collection foreshadows another recurring narrative element in their artwork: the ubiquitous presence of the Macassan trepangers in the region, with their distinctive praus, and their hearths, pots, pans and other cooking utensils for boiling, smoking and drying trepang.

In the *Yalangbara* collection it could be argued that each painting tells a story. Most of the works are a variation on the same theme—that is, the origins of the Djang'kawu ancestors. One of the paintings, *Map of Yalangbara* (1947), a crayon on paper work by Mawalan Marika, is worth describing in some detail. It is a magnificent topographical work, tracking the intersecting journeys of the Djang'kawu and other travellers in the region, including the Bayini, the adventurer and trepanger Fred Gray, and Macassan trepangers. The painting takes the form of a map of Port Bradshaw. Yellow tracking with a red outline depicts the journeys of the Djang'kawu and the mythical Bayini. A red track with blue outline depicts the route of the Macassan trepangers. The latter track traces their maritime route into Port Bradshaw as it leads to a vegetated granite island in the middle of Lalawuy Bay, Wapilina, which was used as a base and campsite for processing the trepang catch. The footprints of the Djang'kawu intermingling with the trepang in the hearth ashes of the trepangers' camp symbolically reflect the close interaction between the Aboriginal ancestors of the region and the Macassans. The island itself has provided much archaeological evidence for the activities of the Macassans.

The second exhibition of spring 2011 relating to the history and heritage of the Macassans was held at Melbourne Museum. The title of this exhibition was *Trepang: China & the story of Macassan–Aboriginal trade*. The exhibition combines historical artefacts, paintings, maps and photographs with new works of art by classically trained Chinese artist Zhou Xiaoping and highly respected artist John

Bulunbulun. According to the exhibition notes, the aim of the exhibition is to explore the long history of cultural exchange and trade between the Chinese, the Macassan trepangers and northern Australian Aboriginal people. Compared with the *Yalangbara* exhibition, *Trepang* places a greater emphasis on the role of China in the Macassan–Aboriginal encounter. This should not be surprising given that Rio Tinto, a large Australian mining company with a long history of commercial ties with China, was a major sponsor of the exhibition. But as this volume of essays will reveal, the role of China in the history and heritage of the Macassans should not be understated. It was the eighteenth-century boom in China that drew in products from Southeast Asia, including the trepang from northern Australia. Thus despite, or even because of, its China-centric focus, the *Trepang* exhibition is a welcome addition to the overall Macassan narrative. It certainly helps make the trepang industry less 'unknown'. As one visitor to the exhibition's web site remarked, somewhat optimistically, 'maybe the time will come again where cucumbers of the sea become the new food'.

This collection of essays aims to re-examine not only the history and heritage of the Macassans, but also the broader history of the trepang fishery and trade in the region. In one sense, 'the region' can be taken to mean the coastline of northern Australia. In a broader sense, it can also mean Southeast Asia, given that the Macassan trepangers played an important role in the history of colonial Makassar and therefore the development of what has become the Indonesian nation-state (Sutherland 2000). To this day a number of the leading political leaders in the region, including Indonesia's former president B. J. Habibie, Indonesia's former vice-president Yusuf Kalla and the current Malaysian Prime Minister, Najib Razak, trace their ancestry directly back to southern Sulawesi. Beyond this, the Macassan trepang foodway extended to southern China. These days, a good proportion of Indonesia's contemporary trepang industry continues to be centred in present-day Makassar. The islanders of the Spermonde Archipelago offshore from Makassar, for instance, continue to process and supply trepang for the Chinese market. The same can be said for the contemporary trepang fishery in northern Australia, which boasts a modest trade with the Chinese restaurants of Melbourne and Sydney and a multimillion-dollar trade with China itself. It is for these reasons that this collection of essays—combining the expertise of scholars working in the fields of Aboriginal studies, Indonesian studies, archaeology, history, anthropology, human geography, marine resource management, and art and material cultures—literally examines Macassan history and heritage from both sides of the Arafura and Timor seas.

Trepang in Australia's 'Top End': Contemporary issues

Before outlining the content of each chapter and the underlying themes of this volume, it is perhaps worth addressing in more detail the status of the contemporary trepang fishery, particularly in the maritime border zone between Indonesia and Australia, which includes the many reefs and islands in the Timor Sea. Of course, we cannot avoid the fact that in present-day Australia the once close trading ties between the trepang fishers of eastern Indonesia and the Indigenous communities of Arnhem Land and the Kimberley have well and truly ceased. There are various reasons for this. On the one hand, the Indigenous communities of northern Australia are now Australian citizens subject to Australian federal and State and Territory laws and, on the other, the trepang fishers of Sulawesi and elsewhere are now Indonesian citizens and thus subject to strictly enforced laws relating to fishing in Australia's northern waters. The politics of refugees, asylum-seekers and people smugglers operating in Australia's northern maritime border zone have ensured that while vessels from the Indonesian archipelago throughout the eighteenth and nineteenth centuries were positively welcomed as a general ragbag source of the unusual, in the contemporary era vessels arriving from the north are generally regarded with suspicion.

In practical terms, if perchance fishers from Sulawesi, or any other part of eastern Indonesia for that matter, were to seek to reclaim their centuries-old tradition of trepang fishing in Australian waters they would be, and quite often are, apprehended, imprisoned and sentenced as 'illegal fishermen' or 'poachers'. This has been the general pattern over the past decade in particular (Fox and Sen 2002; Francis 2006; Ganter 2006).[2] Why such a harsh stance? In a practical sense, the trepang fishery in Australia, which is still a small-scale operation, cannot absorb the costs associated with poaching. Australia's primary trepang licence holder, Tasmanian Seafoods, has heavily invested in the 'Top End' trepang fishery, which is subject to strict government regulations. Tasmanian Seafoods is also under constant pressure to demonstrate the sustainability of the trepang fishery. Poaching, therefore, is extremely damaging. According to a Tasmanian Seafoods manager: 'We only catch up to 100 tonnes of wet catch each year [in Western Australia] and it wouldn't take much to knock this on its head. There are reefs further afield where illegal poaching has over-fished some areas for trepang and they are closed to commercial wild catch' (Francis 2006).

---

2 An exception to this is the provision for 'traditional' Indonesian fishers to fish using 'traditional' vessels and fishing techniques in the Australian Fishing Zone (AFZ). This zone is also known as the MoU Box, which was established after a memorandum of understanding (MoU) was signed between the Australian and Indonesian governments in 1974 (see Adhuri, this volume).

Besides experiencing detainment and, ultimately, deportation, illegal vessels, including fishing gear and catch, are also systematically confiscated by Australian authorities (Fox and Sen 2002; Stacey 2007). Since the 2007 election of the Labor government and the demise of the former conservative government's so-called 'Pacific solution' (offshore detention of asylum-seekers in Pacific Island states), the resurgence in the number of Indonesian vessels transporting asylum-seekers and refugees to Australian shores has added to the sensitive nature of this issue. This has been exacerbated by the failure of the current Labor government's so-called 'Malaysia solution' to its asylum-seeker problem (a bilateral agreement to return asylum-seekers arriving by boat to Malaysia in exchange for already processed refugees). Subsequently, the problem of asylum-seeker boat arrivals has become a serious political one for the Labor government and, for many, the fine line between 'illegal fishermen' and 'people smugglers' along northern Australia's porous border zone has been blurred. In the eyes of naval, fisheries and customs personnel actually dealing with both parties, however, the distinction is still quite clear.

In any case, trepang still attracts stray Indonesian fishing vessels to Australian shores, despite the great costs associated with detection and apprehension. But what is trepang and how is this ongoing attraction best explained? Trepang belongs to the phylum Echinodermata, class Holothuroidea, of which some 900 species have been identified. As noted earlier, the term trepang is also widely interchangeable with bêche-de-mer. While the Indonesian term *teripang* certainly refers to the live animal in Indonesian, both trepang and bêche-de-mer can refer to the processed body-wall of sea cucumbers, which are dried, boiled or smoked. In non-technical terms, sea cucumbers are soft-bodied marine animals with a leathery skin and an elongated body and they inhabit the sea floor of all seas, at all depths. Historically, trepang has had a distinct commercial niche in the commodity market of Southeast and East Asia, particularly as it has been used in Chinese traditional cooking since the seventeenth century as a delicacy and as a male sexual-enhancement product. Trepang is also used as a dietary supplement throughout Asia for treating a range of ailments, including ulcers, skin lesions, high blood pressure and quite a few more besides. According to one Chinese source, the medical function of trepang 'is to invigorate the kidney, to benefit the essence of life, to strengthen the penis of man and to treat fistula' (see Macknight, this volume). Besides the ailments already listed, in the northern and eastern coastal states of Peninsular Malaysia ethnic Malays often use trepang, which is known as *gamat* or *gamat emas*, as a traditional ointment for skin conditions. In present-day Kuala Lumpur it is also possible to purchase over-the-counter bottles of cough mixture containing traces of trepang.

Chinese traders have long been alert to the 'cure-all' and aphrodisiac qualities of trepang and, as mentioned earlier, it was the demand from China that spurred on the Macassan fleets to the shores of northern Australia. Even after the Macassan fishing fleets made their last annual journey to Arnhem Land in 1907, Indonesian trepangers continued to fish in Australian waters, in the Timor Sea in particular, for decades afterwards, illegally. There was a period during the Japanese occupation of East Asia during World War II when the trade ceased altogether (Fox and Sen 2002). But low-level trepang gathering began again in the offshore islands and reefs in the Timor Sea, continuing until very recently, when the Australian Government, under the conservative leadership of prime minister John Howard in particular (1996–2007), demonstrated its determination to clamp down on illegal fishing for trepang and other marine products. The establishment of a Darwin office of the Australian Fisheries Management Authority (AFMA), with the associated hiring of 20 additional compliance officers, was a significant gesture in this regard (AFMA 2006). AFMA's foreign compliance budget was significantly boosted, from $10 million to $33 million between 2004–05 and 2006–07 (AFMA 2007). AFMA's increased funding, coupled with a marked increase in the support AFMA received from the Australian Defence Force (ADF) and Customs, had an immediate impact. In 2005–06 at least 368 vessels were detained, which was the peak amount over the past decade (AFMA 2007). Between July 2007 and July 2008, 186 boats were apprehended, of which 141 were Indonesian owned (Howlett 2011). The crews were arrested and transferred to immigration detention centres, and their boats towed to the nearest port, most often Darwin, and burnt. Between July 2008 and December 2011, just 71 vessels in total were destroyed (Howlett 2011), and between July 2010 and April 2011 only 11 foreign boats were caught fishing illegally in northern Australia (Gibson and Razak 2011).

In Australia's northern waters, trepang still appear in relatively abundant numbers, especially in areas where naturally occurring stock have been boosted by ranching. But like the Australian fishing industry in general, the Top End trepang fishery is chronically under-utilised. There are numerous reasons for this, many of them inter-related. Key factors for under-fishing include strict quotas and a business decision by the sole trepang-fishing operator to focus on trepang ranching rather than open-sea harvesting. To some extent the sole licensee is also a victim of the key problems affecting the entire Australian fishing industry—namely, a shortage of experienced fishing and deck crew and, with declining numbers of vessels in operation each year, diminishing fleet capacity (Commonwealth Fisheries Association 2012; Lloyd 2012; Cleary 2010). In response to this, over the past decade the Commonwealth Fisheries Association and various fishing operators have held talks with the Australian Department of Immigration and Citizenship (DIAC) about bringing in foreign workers under the 457 Visa, which is targeted specifically for temporary foreign workers. Moves to outsource fishing quotas to subcontracted foreign fishing fleets are also afoot, as demonstrated by the decision to allow the Dutch-owned trawler the FV *Margaris* to operate out of Devonport, Tasmania, with a licence to catch red bait and mackerel; however, due to public pressure, the Australian Government rescinded this permission and by all accounts changes in legislation will be needed for this sort of thing to occur in the future (Cleary 2010). In the meantime, the demand from China is insatiable and the rest of the world, including Australia and many other nations of the Asia-Pacific, is scrambling to keep up.

The chapters of this volume

Although a great deal of knowledge has emerged on the history of various trepang fisheries throughout the world, this is the first edited collection of essays on the Australian contribution to the trepang trade, which we believe should not be viewed in isolation from trepang production, trade and consumption elsewhere in the region. The chapters of this volume were first presented at a two-day research symposium hosted by the Institute for Professional Practice in Heritage and the Arts (IPPHA) at The Australian National University, Canberra, in early February 2012. The symposium and this subsequent publication were supported financially by The Australian National University's College of Arts and Social Sciences.

This book, like the symposium that gave birth to it, primarily revolves around a most unassuming creature: the sea cucumber. For centuries, the humble holothurian has emerged as an endless source of curiosity, fascination and trade, arousing a great deal of transnational interaction. Reflecting this, the first few chapters of this volume approach the question of trepang, and Australia's early trepang industry in particular, from a broad regional perspective. We begin with a 'state of the field' chapter by the doyen of Australian 'Macassan' trepang industry research, Campbell Macknight. This chapter aims to collate the various bodies of knowledge devoted to the trepang industry of Australia. It soon becomes apparent that because of the significance of Australia's trepang industry in terms of size, duration and consequence, a great deal of research has emerged. This includes the scattered references to trepang in a series of literatures from China, the Dutch East Indies and colonial Australia, the last of which is largely written in an ethnographic vein. Tindale's study in the 1920s of the effects of contact between the trepangers and local Aborigines is a good example of this genre. In Macknight's words, 'he recorded what he saw and what his informants told him, giving this information an internally consistent form and structure, but not testing it against other sources or approaches'. The ethnographic approach ruled supreme over the next 50 years, with numerous fieldworkers and historians recording a wealth of information about the effects of first contact. Significantly, the informants were all Aboriginal and the focus of interest was on Aborigines, not trepangers and the trepang industry. The ethnographic approach to the history and heritage of Australia's early trepang industry persists to this day, but to some extent it has been broadened by efforts to understand the background from which the trepangers came.

Given the greater measure of scholarly attention directed to the trepangers in recent times, it is perhaps unsurprising that Macknight lodges a belated admonition on 'the wild use of the unfortunate term "Macassan"'. Although Macknight's chapter does not elaborate on the matter, we think it is important to briefly consider this point. Viewed from the perspective of the trepangers themselves, the term 'Macassan' would seem to be very odd indeed. No-one from Makassar, either in the current era or in centuries past, would identify themselves as a 'Macassan'. As Macknight (2011, p. 129) observes, 'the term "Macassan" (or "Makassan") has no currency in an Indonesian context'. Nonetheless, most of the trepangers voyaging to Australia's north regarded Makassar as their home port, and because the trade in trepang was centred in Makassar, for better or worse, scholars, including Macknight in his earlier publications, have embraced the term. Yet, as mentioned earlier, these fishers were of diverse ethnicity. Besides the ethnic Makassarese who are predominantly located on the western coast of the South Sulawesi peninsula, the most prominent Sulawesi-based populations involved in trepang gathering were the Bugis (or Buginese), the Butonese and the Bajau. Nonetheless, the 'Macassan' term has firmly lodged itself in the popular consciousness, including the next generation of scholars writing on the impact of the trepang industry, many of whom are archaeologists working on trepanging sites, albeit with an ethnographic bent. With acute insight, Macknight examines a number of the key archaeological puzzles, including the perennial question: when did the trepangers first set foot on Australian soil? Asking such a question is a good indication of the focus of the more recent scholarly trends in the literature on trepang, including a greater focus on the biological and economic aspects of trepang and, as mentioned, a newfound fascination with the trepangers themselves.

Although Reid's chapter diverges somewhat from a direct focus on the so-called 'trepang trail', to some extent his chapter is a manifestation of what Macknight acknowledges is the dominant trend in the current literature on the trepang industry. That is, an examination of the Macassan trepang industry in terms of the broader picture, including the world of the trepangers, who were among the first seafarers to brave the Arafura Sea, which, because it straddles the deep troughs between the Sunda and Sahul tectonic plates, 'has formed the world's greatest divide throughout human history'. Reid argues that the 'Great Divide' of the Arafura has ensured that the world of Makassar has been largely separated from the world of Marege', even in the modern era. Despite early trading links, the overarching narrative of Australia's relations with its northern neighbours has been one of mutual incomprehension. It didn't have to be this way. For instance, as Reid describes, Australia's military and diplomatic engagement with the region, particularly in the World War II period, was followed in the postwar era by Australia playing a potentially decisive role in the postwar Asian order. This was particularly so in the case of Indonesia, which was determined to shrug off its colonial shackles. Australian unions, which refused to facilitate the postwar return of the Dutch colonial masters, played a key role in Indonesia's assertion of independence. These initial tentative forays into the region, however, were preceded and to some extent overshadowed by the *Immigration Restriction Act*, which dates, in Commonwealth legislation, from 1901. This led to the flagrantly xenophobic White Australia Policy and a subsequent disavowal of the early history and heritage of the trepangers and others like them, such as the Aboriginal and then Indonesian, Filipino and Japanese divers of pearl and pearl shell. It should be a source of great shame that Australia's collective ambivalence, if not outright hostility, towards its historical links with Asia—links that were bravely forged in the face of the deep geographic divide of the Arafura Sea—persists.

The chapters by Ganter and Thomas nuance the notion that Australia is somehow threatened by or evasive of its history of Asian engagement. Although both authors recognise the fact that certain Asia-related histories have, in Ganter's words, 'sailed below the wind of popular attention', both of these chapters demonstrate how Australians have, on occasion, successfully understood and responded to Asia. Ganter's chapter, for instance, examines the link between the arrival of the Macassan trepangers and the early history of Islam in Australia. In particular, Ganter highlights the engagement of Indigenous people with their 'mixed histories' in relation to Asians, Pacific Islanders and Muslims, the last of which includes 'Afghan' cameleers, 'Malay' pearl divers and 'Macassan' trepangers. In one sense this chapter echoes Reid's broader consideration of other, less well-documented aspects of the contact between northern Australia and its neighbours on the other side of the Arafura. Just as others have attempted to 'write' the Afghan cameleers back into Australian history, Ganter aims to 'write back in' the groundbreaking role of the Macassan trepangers in bringing Islamic influence to the Yolngu and neighbouring Aboriginal communities of Arnhem Land. Thomas's chapter also aims to reinsert several forgotten figures into Australia's early history—namely, three interpreters of Indonesian background who assumed the roles of intermediaries between the early European pioneers and the Indonesian trepangers. After discovering the trepang industry in 1803, the European pioneers were keen to understand as much as they could about it in order to incorporate it into the colonial trading network. To do this effectively, they needed the services of interpreters and translators. The three figures Thomas examines—namely, Abraham Williams, Oodeen and Tingha de Hans—were exemplary in this regard. Thomas's chapter demonstrates that like so many of the actors involved in the Macassan era, these three men, although subject to their conditions of engagement, were free agents, disinclined to serve their colonial employers in a subservient way. By emphasising the fact that these men are, above all, interpreters, Thomas demonstrates how they have played a crucial role in ensuring that the voice of the various Indonesian fishers and traders working along Australia's northern coast was heard, understood and recorded for posterity. Reflecting on their unique skills, in the case of Oodeen and Tingha, for example, Thomas asserts that 'they were clearly intelligent and determined individuals, characteristics that need to be considered when assessing them as adaptable linguists, capable of going beyond their own language and culture'.

The chapters by McIntosh and Bilous squarely focus on the impact of the Macassans on the Indigenous communities of northern Australia. In a chapter finetuning his previous research on the pre-Macassans mentioned earlier, McIntosh shares a pre-Macassan story told to him by David Burrumarra, a Yolngu elder. He draws some conclusions on why the story was shared, shining light on what 'coming home' means in terms of contemporary relations between Yolngu and outsiders such as the Macassans and pre-Macassans. The aim of this chapter is to show how some Yolngu view the history and legacy of trepanging not just through the narrow lens of tamarind trees, pottery shards and the years 1780–1907, but, rather, through an entirely different and sacred lens. The chapter by Bilous takes a more analytical approach to analysing general public engagement with Macassan heritage in Australia. Through an analysis of *Walkabout*, *National Geographic* and *Australian Geographic* articles from the 1930s to the present, Bilous questions the ways in which stories of Macassan–Indigenous Australian connection are represented to a non-academic, popular audience. The links between political discourses of the time and these popular magazine articles are clearly drawn, including attitudes to landownership and *terra nullius* and the idea of Arnhem Land as a 'frontier' landscape. Perhaps most intriguing in her findings is the persistence, despite significant evidence to the contrary, that Indigenous Australians were an unchanging people—across time and place. As Bilous states,

> The representation of Macassan and Indigenous Australian contact stories—where Indigenous Australians were an integral part of an informal international trade network—would presumably disrupt some of these discourses. Instead, these same discourses are used to tell contact stories in a way that strengthens and reinforces the stereotypes and geographical marginalisation of Arnhem Land and the people who live there.

The next chapter in this volume, by Taçon and May, presents findings from new archaeological research taking place in northern Australia and relating to

Macassan–Indigenous Australian contact. It focuses on the search for evidence of Macassan contact in rock art from northwestern Arnhem Land. As Taçon and May state, 'Contact rock art provides us with some of the only contemporary Indigenous accounts of interactions that were taking place over hundreds of years. In this regard, it is a unique archive of Australian history, providing insight into the relationships formed between local Aboriginal groups and visitors.' This chapter presents specific information on new sites documented as part of an Australia-wide contact-period rock art study and evaluates previously published statements on 'Macassan' rock art in Australia.

The next two chapters turn an anthropological gaze on Macassan contact and material culture. Brady, for instance, explores the introduction of drug substances to Australia by the Macassans. She argues for a re-examination of our longstanding assumptions relating to the introduction and adoption of new drugs in Australia as well as the processes and adaptations to material culture used to consume such substances. As Brady observes in her chapter, it has been universally assumed that the Macassans were the ones who introduced the smoking of tobacco to coastal Aboriginal peoples using long 'Macassan' pipes. Strangely though, according to Brady, there is little evidence that the Macassans themselves ever used the pipes in this way for tobacco alone. As well as tobacco, Brady explores the use and spread of arrack (a spirit often made from the fermented sugars and sap of particular plants and trees) and betel nut (the nut or seed of the areca palm chewed together with the leaf of the betel pepper and lime with tobacco added as flavouring).

The chapters by Clark and Adhuri shift the focus of this volume away from Marege' to squarely address the historical legacy of the Macassan trepang industry in contemporary Indonesia and its environs. In these two chapters there is a particular focus on the 'living history' epitomised by Makassar's rich maritime heritage and the contemporary trepang fisheries of South Sulawesi and the Australian MoU Box (an area of Australian water in the Timor Sea where Indonesian traditional fishers, using traditional fishing methods only, are permitted to operate). Clark's chapter initially examines what could be understood as examples of tangible 'Macassan heritage' in contemporary Makassar: authentic monuments, historical objects and sites with distinctive connections to the fishers and entrepreneurs involved in the Macassan trepang industry. Unfortunately, it soon becomes evident that there is very little remaining in the way of tangible Macassan heritage, either in Makassar itself or in South Sulawesi in general. But this should not mean that there is no Macassan heritage in Sulawesi—far from it. This is especially the case if the Macassan heritage of South Sulawesi is understood as an ongoing cultural process with associated intangible values. Similarly, Adhuri's chapter examines the contemporary trepang fisheries along the border area of the Indonesian and Australian fishing zones as a site of continuous and ongoing history, with close historical links to the Macassans. Adhuri achieves this by comparing the characteristics of a so-called 'traditional' trepang fishery (practised by the Oelaba trepang fishers of Rote Island) with a contemporary or supposedly 'non-traditional' trepang fishery (practised by the Oesapa trepang fishers, also of Rote), both of which are based in the MoU Box region. Ironically, Adhuri's chapter suggests that the relative newcomers to the trepang industry, the so-called 'non-traditional' Oesapa fishers, many of whom can directly trace their ethnic heritage to the various ethnic groups of South Sulawesi, are closely connected to the Macassan pioneers of centuries past.

The final chapter of this volume, by Blair and Hall, raises the possibility of seeking greater global recognition for the heritage of the Macassan trepang foodway. They consider its potential to be recognised as a cultural route of outstanding universal value under the UNESCO World Heritage Convention. This chapter's underlying argument is innovative, timely and important. In 1992 the World Heritage Convention became the first international legal instrument to recognise and protect cultural landscapes of outstanding universal value. In 2005, the concept was widened to include cultural routes and itineraries, and an international scientific committee has been established to promote research and World Heritage inscriptions in this area. The new cultural routes category highlights long-distance routes and journeys, such as those associated with trade or pilgrimage, which have linked people, countries, regions or even continents for long periods. Little work has been done to date on the recognition of maritime trading routes on a regional or global scale or on communicating their values as universal cultural heritage. In many respects the Macassan trepang pathway—extending from southern China in the north and the Kimberley and Arnhem Land in the south—is a worthy contender for the world's first UNESCO-listed maritime cultural route. Much more work will need to be done to ensure such a nomination sees the light of day, potentially involving complex exchanges and collaborations between local groups as well as numerous national and international entities. This collection is but one small step in this process.

References

Australian Fisheries Management Authority (AFMA) (2006) *Annual Report 2005–2006*, Canberra: Australian Fisheries Management Authority.

Australian Fisheries Management Authority (AFMA) (2007) *Annual Report 2006–2007*, Canberra: Australian Fisheries Management Authority.

Department of Sustainability, Environment, Water, Population and Communities (2011) *Assessment of the Northern Territory Trepang Fishery*, Canberra: Department of Sustainability, Environment, Water, Population and Communities.

Chaloupka, G. (1993) *Journey in Time: The 50,000 year story of the Australian Aboriginal art of Arnhem Land*, Chatswood, NSW: Reid.

Chaloupka, G. (1996) 'Praus in Marege: Makassan subjects in Aboriginal rock art of Arnhem Land, Northern Territory, Australia', *Anthropologie*, 34 (1–2), pp. 131–42.

Choo, P. (2008) 'Population status, fisheries and trade of sea cucumbers in Asia', in V. Toral-Granda, A. Lovotelli and M. Vasconcellos (eds), *Sea Cucumbers: A global review of fisheries and trade*, Rome: Food and Agriculture Organization of the United Nations, pp. 81–110.

Clarke, A. (1994) Winds of change: an archaeology of contact in the Groote Eylandt archipelago, Northern Australia, Unpublished PhD thesis, The Australian National University, Canberra.

Clarke, A. (2000) 'The "Moorman's trousers": Macassan and Aboriginal interactions and the changing fabric of Indigenous social life', in S. O'Connor and P. Veth (eds), *East of Wallace's Line: Studies of past and present maritime societies in the Indo-Pacific region*, Modern Quaternary Research in Southeast Asia 16, Rotterdam: A. A. Balkema, pp. 315–35.

Clarke, A. and U. Frederick (2006) 'Closing the distance: interpreting cross-cultural engagements through Indigenous rock art', in I. Lilley (ed.), *Archaeology in Oceania, Australia and the Pacific Islands*, Malden, Mass.: Blackwell, pp. 116–33.

Clarke, A. and U. Frederick (2011) 'Making a sea change: rock art, archaeology and the enduring legacy of Frederick McCarthy's research on Groote Eylandt', in M. Thomas and M. Neale (eds), *Exploring the Legacy of the 1948 Arnhem Land Expedition*, Canberra: ANU E Press, pp. 135–55.

Cleary, P. (2010) 'Local fishers to opt out to foreign boats', *The Australian*, 27 December, <http://www.theaustralian.com.au/news/nation/local-fishing-fleet-to-opt-out-to-foreign-boats/story-e6frg6nf-1225976467846>

Commonwealth Fisheries Association (2012) New maritime laws to increase fishing industry labour shortages, Media release, 16 March, Deakin, ACT: Commonwealth Fisheries Association, <http://comfish.com.au/wp-content/uploads/2012/03/CFA-Media-Release-New-maritime-laws-to-increase-fishing-industry-labour-shortages-16-March-2012.pdf>

Fox, J. J. (1977) 'Notes on the southern voyages and settlements of the Sama-Bajau', *Bijdragen Tot de Taal-, Land- en Volkenkunde (BKI)*, 133, pp. 459–65.

Fox, J. J. and S. Sen (2002) *A study of socio-economic issues facing traditional Indonesian fishers who access the MoU box*, Canberra: Department of Sustainability, Environment, Water, Population and Communities.

Francis, A. (2005) 'Expanding the Territory's oldest export business', *ABC Rural: Northern Territory*, 30 May, <http://www.abc.net.au/rural/nt/stories/s1380107.htm>

Francis, A. (2006) 'Trepang poachers fined in Kimberley', *ABC Rural: Northern Territory*, 5 June, <http://www.abc.net.au/rural/nt/content/2006/s1655553.htm>

Ganter, R. (2006) *Mixed-Relations: Asian–Aboriginal contact in north Australia*, Crawley, WA: University of Western Australia Press.

Gibson, J. and I. Razak (2011) 'Illegal fishing captures fall in Top End waters', *ABC News*, 29 April, <http://www.abc.net.au/news/2011-04-29/illegal-fishing-captures-fall-in-top-end-waters/2701078>

Howlett, C. (2011) 'Fishing without borders', *ABC Environment*, 13 December, <http://www.abc.net.au/environment/articles/2011/12/13/3389001.htm>

Knapp, G. and H. Sutherland (2004) *Monsoon Traders: Ships, skippers and commodities in the eighteenth century*, Leiden: KITLV Press.

Lloyd, G. (2012) 'Cast out', *The Weekend Australian Magazine*, 17–18 March, pp. 15–18.

McIntosh, I. (1995) 'Who are the Bayini?' *The Beagle: Records of the Museums and Art Galleries of the Northern Territory*, 12, pp. 193–208.

McIntosh, I. (2011) 'Missing the revolution! Negotiating disclosure on the pre-Macassans (Bayini) in north-east Arnhem Land', in M. Thomas and M. Neale (eds), *Exploring the Legacy of the 1948 Arnhem Land Expedition*, Canberra: ANU E Press.

Macknight, C. C. (1972) 'Macassans and Aborigines', *Oceania*, 42, pp. 283–321.

Macknight, C. C. (1976) *Voyage to Marege': Macassan trepangers in northern Australia*, Carlton, Vic.: Melbourne University Press.

Macknight, C. C. (1986) 'Macassans and the Aboriginal past', *Archaeology in Oceania*, 21 (1), pp. 69–75.

Macknight, C. C. (2008) 'Harvesting the memory: open beaches in Makassar and Arnhem Land', in P. Veth, P. Sutton and M. Neale (eds), *Strangers on the Shore: Early coastal contacts in Australia*, Canberra: National Museum of Australia, pp. 133–47.

Macknight, C. C. (2011) 'The view from Marege': Australian knowledge of Makassar and the impact of the Trepang industry across two centuries', *Aboriginal History*, 35, pp. 121–43.

Marika, B. (2008) 'Foreword', in M. West (ed.), *Yalangbara: Art of the Djang'kawu*, Darwin: Charles Darwin University Press, pp. 8–9.

Mitchell, S. (1994) Culture contact and Indigenous economies on the Cobourg Peninsula, northwestern Arnhem Land, Unpublished PhD thesis, Northern Territory University, Darwin.

Mitchell, S. (1997) 'George Sunter, trepanger', in G. H. Sunter (ed.), *Adventures of a Trepang Fisher*, Carlisle, WA: Hesperian Press, pp. i–iii.

Morphy, H. (2008) 'Yalangbara: the paintings', in M. West (ed.), *Yalangbara: Art of the Djang'kuwu*, Darwin: Charles Darwin University Press, pp. 65–76.

Stacey, N. (2007) *Boats to burn: Bajo fishing activity in the Australian fishing zone*, Canberra: ANU E Press.

Sutherland, H. (2000) 'Trepang and wangkang: the China trade of eighteenth-century Makassar c. 1720s–1840s', *Bijdragen tot de Taal-, Land- en Volkenkunde (BKI)*, 156, pp. 451–72.

Taçon, P. S. C, S. K. May, S. J. Fallon, M. Travers, D. Wesley and R. Lamilami (2010) 'A minimum age for early depictions of Macassan praus in the rock art of Arnhem Land, Northern Territory', *Australian Archaeology*, 71, pp. 1–10.

Theden-Ringl, F., J. Fenner, D. Wesley and R. Lamilami (2011) 'Buried on foreign shores: isotope analysis of the origin of human remains recovered from a Macassan site in Arnhem Land', *Australian Archaeology*, 73, pp. 41–8.

2. Studying trepangers

Campbell Macknight

Trepang has been collected, processed, traded or consumed by diverse groups of people, largely in East and Southeast Asia, but also, importantly, in northern Australia. The producers of trepang, however, have not usually traded their product beyond the initial sale, and the consumers have been different again. This has meant that those who have studied and written about trepang and trepangers have often done so in relative ignorance of other parts of the overall story and the separate literatures that have developed are divided not just by geographical coverage, since there are also distinct differences of discipline and approach. As one continues to explore aspects of the subject, more and more unsuspected vistas open up, especially as the consequences of the activities associated with the industry and of those involved in it are pursued. It is difficult, therefore, to find a central focus in any study of trepang and those involved with its exploitation and use. A fruitful way to analyse our knowledge is to distinguish various literatures—as set out in what follows—and this has the benefit of throwing up some inconsistencies and gaps that invite further research. The contrasts between the research done within different disciplines and fields of study provoke many questions about the organisation of knowledge.

The first body of literature to consider is a negative case. The collecting, processing and trading of trepang all involve the sea and have thus been open to the view of those who also come and go in ships. Moreover, trepang has only rarely been for the consumption of those who collect and process it, but is usually for trade; there is money in trepang and that drew the interest of observers. This visibility of the getting and trading of trepang is relevant when considering the complete absence of any mention of the industry in the abundant records left by the servants of the Portuguese Crown, or of the Dutch and English trading companies, in island Southeast Asia in the sixteenth and seventeenth centuries. Within a year or two of the Portuguese capture of Malacca in 1511, Tomé Pires was assiduously gathering information for his king on the whole trading world of the Indian Ocean and seas beyond as far as Japan (Cortesão 1944). His work is a remarkable compilation and its final publication in 1944 transformed our understanding of trade in this period; it contains no mention of trepang. Even closer to the eventual centre of the trade, in 1670 Cornelis Speelman, who had just conquered Makassar for the Dutch East India Company, completed a massive report on South Sulawesi for the company, spelling out in detail all the information he had been able to amass on the history, politics and economic affairs of the area. He was, naturally enough, particularly thorough on trade; but again there is no mention of trepang (Noorduyn 1983). These are but two examples—even if particularly persuasive ones—of the silence of the early sources on the subject of trepang.

It is easy to assume that a commodity that came to have such a major place in the trade between the Indonesian archipelago and China had long been sought and traded. I remember talking about this with the late Mrs Meilink-Roelofsz, the authority on early Southeast Asian trade; she thought trepang must have been there, and pulled a copy of her masterwork from the shelf to consult the hugely detailed index. It does not contain an entry for trepang (Meilink-Roelofsz 1962). All the records of the first two centuries of direct European involvement in the trade of Asia are silent on the question of trepang, whether its collection, processing or trade.

The Chinese sources explain why this should be so. Although there is one reference to trepang in the sixteenth century, the consumption of trepang only began in any quantity in the seventeenth century. Its use seems to have originated in northern China, though there are also early references to inferior types of trepang from the south coast. The question was kindly investigated for me in the 1960s by Wang Gungwu and reported in Macknight (1976, pp. 7–8). More recently, in a separate study, Dai Yifeng could find no record of trepang earlier than a book written in the reign of Wanli (1573–1620) by a man who had been a candidate in the imperial examinations in 1602 (Dai Yifeng 2002, p. 21).

Not unexpectedly perhaps, there is no lack of later comment on trepang in Chinese. As Dai Yifeng remarks, 'Starting from the Qing Dynasty [1644–1912], records about trepang in Chinese literature were more and more extensive' (Dai Yifeng 2002, p. 23). This interest covers its biology, its culinary uses and its sources, both in China, especially from northern waters, and as imported from Japan and Southeast Asia.[1] It had particular medicinal uses; as a source from 1757 says, 'The best trepang live in Liaohai [northern China]…The medical function of trepang is to invigorate the kidney, to benefit the essence of life, to strengthen the penis of man and to treat fistula' (quoted in Dai Yifeng 2002, p. 25). I suspect that there is much more to be done with the Chinese sources.

This brings us back to the discussion of the affairs of island Southeast Asia. Even if trepang was not an item of immediate interest to Europeans, the eye of traders and administrators has been on trepangers from the outset of the industry there and this has resulted in a remarkably detailed body of records. Here is another literature, or perhaps more accurately, series of literatures. The first known reference to trepang in Southeast Asia comes from June 1710 when a

---

1   Although trepang had been known in Japan as early as the eighth century, its actual use at that period is not clear. Export from Japan, as from Korea, Taiwan and Vietnam, to China only began from the middle of the seventeenth century (Akamine 2004).

Bugis, Toissa, was granted a pass by the Dutch East India Company in Makassar to collect trepang on Buton (Sutherland 2000, p. 460; Nagel 2003, p. 500).[2] The trepang trade through Makassar to China, often via Batavia, grew somewhat unsteadily through the eighteenth century, but by 1800 was substantial. This growth in the import of trepang and other sea products into China is presumably linked to the vast expansion of the Chinese economy through the eighteenth century.

The demand for trepang in Makassar drove the search for suitable collecting grounds. As early as 1728, 40 small Bajau Laut praus were looking for trepang off the southwestern coast of Rote and, when driven off by local people, then moved on to Kupang from where the Dutch East India Company official reported the matter (Fox 1977, p. 460). Even if that attempt to open up new grounds was unsuccessful, numerous official and private reports over the next century and more describe Bajau and others collecting and processing trepang throughout the islands to the south and east of Makassar.

The earliest reference to trepang being collected in Australia dates from 1754 when the Dutch authorities in Batavia reported that, as far as they knew, the 'Southland' southeast of Timor produced nothing but trepang and wax. It was visited 'now and then' from Timor and Makassar (Macknight 1976, p. 95). I believe that this is a reference to the Kimberley coast. The reference to wax is puzzling; what exactly was it and how was it obtained? This report had been prompted by earlier news that a Chinese trader had set out from Timor—that is, Kupang—to look for 'turtle-horn', presumably tortoise shell, on islands south of Rote. Given what we now know about eighteenth-century trade, there is no surprise in any of this.

Such knowledge was not restricted to Dutch observers and officials. In the 1760s, Alexander Dalrymple, planning the extension of British trade, heard that sailors from Sulawesi had reached Australia. In the 1780s, Thomas Forrest collected more accurate and detailed information about the trepang industry being carried on in northern Australia to supply the Makassar market (Macknight 1976, pp. 95–6).

In the nineteenth century, the major focus of the trepang industry in Australian waters was the Arnhem Land coast and adjacent areas—that is, Marege'. I now accept the evidence recorded by Flinders and Brown that the abundant resources of trepang in this area only began to be exploited from about 1780 and this date

---

2 One claim for an earlier date needs correcting. Schwerdtner Máñez and Ferse (2010, p. 3) claim that Pieter Pieterzoon in the Aru Islands in 1636 reported a trepang industry. They seem to have misread the remarks by Earl in his Translator's Preface to Kolff's *Voyages of the Dourga* (1840). (They have confirmed in personal communication that they should have referred to their reference 13, not the reference 9 as in their text.) The original report of Pieterzoon's visit to the Arus from 12 May to 9 June 1636 is to be found in Colenbrander (1899, pp. 227–8); though full of interesting information, the report has no mention or hint of trepang.

is confirmed by a marked rise in the quantity of trepang passing through the Makassar market.³ For the nineteenth century, the reports of numerous observers and various official records allow us to understand the activities in Australia of the trepangers from Makassar in some detail, though the material for Arnhem Land is better than that for the Kimberley coast. I have estimated that in the first half of the century between 30 and 60 praus visited the Northern Territory coast each year, bringing 1000 or more men. The numbers declined somewhat later and by the end of the century only about half a dozen praus were coming, though they still brought some hundreds of men. A single, final prau—at least for the trepangers from Makassar working the Northern Territory coast—the *Bunga Ejaya*, under the command of Using Daeng Rangka, came for the 1906–07 season (Macknight 1976). Trepang has been one of various maritime products taken from the reefs and islands in the Timor Sea, and occasionally from the Kimberley coast, by vessels from the Indonesian archipelago throughout the twentieth century, but the quantities seem to have been relatively small and the groups engaged in these activities have been very various.⁴

The Australian contribution to the trade, even if considerable, needs to be seen in relation to production elsewhere in the Indonesian archipelago, in the Pacific and in various other parts of the colonial world. Everywhere officials and observers recorded what they could and it is from these accounts that the main outline of the history of the industry can be reconstructed. At one level, the sources seem various: the Dutch East India Company records, the journals of British—and a few French—explorers, the annual reports and other papers of Dutch colonial officers, the diaries of British officials in the early settlements in northern Australia, and the later records of the colonial and federal governments in Australia. At another level, however, these are the products of outsiders, written in European languages. Whatever the problems of access, language or handwriting, historians are used to dealing with documents of this type.

A quite different discourse has its origin in oral accounts from people affected by the industry. Within Australia, trepang was collected and processed on the beach in a series of sites from the Cobourg Peninsula to the Wellesleys, though there was also some slight contact with the Tiwi Islands. This activity involved,

---

3   A further argument for a date later in the eighteenth century, which I have not seen before, arises from thinking about the 1756 voyage under Gonzal to the Gulf of Carpentaria. This expedition appears to have been in response to the 1754 report from Kupang. Admittedly, it was a poorly managed business and not to the area visited by the trepangers, but it is hard to believe that, were there a flourishing trepang industry in Arnhem Land in 1756 and given the reason for the voyage, this would not have been noticed somewhere in the records. As I have previously observed, no earlier Dutch account of contact with the Australian coast mentions the industry or its effects, especially the material from the 1705 expedition that spent some time around the Cobourg Peninsula and had extensive contact with Aborigines (Macknight 1976, pp. 96–7).

4   Much has been written about these activities from various perspectives, but they are not of much significance for the trepang trade as a whole. Crawford (2001, pp. 68–94), Fox (1998) and Dwyer (2001) provide helpful discussions.

necessarily, meeting local people and there was much interaction, including Aboriginal people travelling on the praus back to Makassar and even further afield. Though a few other items were collected, the essential purpose of those who sailed from Makassar to the Australian coast was the trepang industry. This was an industrial process, not a trading exchange.[5]

Although there were a few contemporary observers who commented on the effects of contact between the trepangers and local Aborigines, the first significant study was by Norman Tindale on Groote Eylandt in 1921 and 1922. Exercising a 'proper breadth of interest', as was so typical of all his work, Tindale fell into studying local people and that led to an interest in the effects of contact with the trepangers. His reports, published with admirable speed, remain useful sources (Tindale 1925–28). With the notable exception of his reference to a picture of a late sixteenth-century sailing vessel from South Sulawesi (Macknight 2011, p. 128), Tindale knew little of the history of Makassar or Southeast Asia in general. His account was ethnographic—that is, he recorded what he saw and what his informants told him, giving this information an internally consistent form and structure, but not testing it against other sources or approaches.

Over the next 50 years, a series of very distinguished fieldworkers recorded a wealth of information about the effects of contact—to name only the most prominent: Rose, Worsley, Moyle and Turner on Groote Eylandt; Warner and Thomson in northeastern Arnhem Land; Ronald and Catherine Berndt all over Arnhem Land; Mountford and McCarthy on the 1948 expedition. With the exception of some of the Berndts' work, this body of ethnographic record shared, in the main, four characteristics. First, the focus of interest was on Aborigines, not trepangers and the trepang industry. Second, the various accounts relied almost exclusively on information provided, in one way or another, by Aboriginal informants. Third, there was little knowledge or understanding of the world from which the trepangers came. Last, there was a tone of scientific detachment with a studied absence of any moral judgments.

My 1972 article in *Oceania*, entitled 'Macassans and Aborigines', which was based on a chapter in my doctoral thesis from 1969, serves as a summary of this ethnographic literature, together with a modest contribution in the same vein, which, I was surprised to discover in the field, could still be made. The article is distinguished from previous work, however, by an awareness of the need to know more about the sources of influence. As I said then:

> One major difficulty with virtually all this previous work by Australian ethnographers has been the failure to look for the models which the

---

5 This is an important point in the interpretation of early European contacts with the continent. See the discussion in Macknight (2008b).

> Aborigines are supposed to have imitated…Enough is now known about the Macassans to set some limit to their usefulness as a general ragbag source of the unusual. (Macknight 1972, p. 291)

This is a call to move from one body of literature to another. In particular, I was able to show the helpfulness of the Makasar[6] dictionary and supporting ethnographic atlas of B. F. Matthes, the Bible translator who was working in Makassar from the middle of the nineteenth century, exactly the most relevant period for providing background to the trepangers. I also had the considerable assistance of the 1952 articles by two Dutch scholars, A. A. Cense (1952) and H. J. Heeren (1952), who had taken the ethnographic data available to them at the time and analysed them in the light of their good knowledge of South Sulawesi languages, history and society. They had also read the most obvious historical sources such as Flinders' account of his meeting with the trepanging fleet in 1803. Since then, there has been, of course, much more work done that is relevant to understanding the background from which the trepangers came. Anthony Jukes (2006) has provided a detailed account of the Makasar language, which he refers to as 'Makassarese'; Gene Ammarell (1999) has demonstrated how it was possible to navigate on such a voyage as that to Australia, both across the open sea and around a coast; Christian Pelras (2000) has explored the patron–client relationship that was undoubtedly critical for any such cooperative enterprise undertaken by men from South Sulawesi.

While I would modestly claim that there is some value in re-reading my 1972 article, further work, still essentially in the ethnographic mode, has gone well beyond it (Macknight 2011, pp. 135–7). In particular, I admire the work of Ian McIntosh on the 'bayini' (most recently, McIntosh 2008, 2011), Scott Mitchell (1994, 1995, 1996) on the economy—though this relies on very elegant analysis of archaeological data—and Alan Walker and David Zorc (1981) on language. Nicolas Evans (1992, 1997) has sought to add time depth to the question of linguistic borrowings. There is clearly room for further work of this kind. One matter that would be worth exploring is an analysis of the *wuramu* or 'crookman' wooden figures and stories from northeast Arnhem Land. These are associated with Makassar in some way, as well as featuring in local ceremonies. I take *wuramu* to be an Indigenous word meaning something like 'crazy' or 'unpredictable' for which 'crookman' is a gloss. The concept represents an Aboriginal perception of the actions of Dutch colonial officials, including harbour officials, and perhaps financiers and owners who took money from returning trepangers for no reason apparent to Aborigines. The theme of collection has then been transferred to the

---

6 Makasar is the language spoken in the area around the city of Makassar. It is sometimes referred to as Makassarese, both forms having many variant spellings. See the chapters by Ganter, Thomas and Brady later in this volume.

local ceremonies. Perhaps *wuramu* just means people acting in incomprehensible ways for any reason. The key sources, but not the only ones, are the reports of R. M. and C. H. Berndt (1949; 1954, pp. 60–3).

Regrettably, my admonition on the need to understand the sources of influence still applies to much of the literature, most notably in the wild use of the unfortunate term 'Macassan'. A few puzzles also remain: why do Aborigines refer to Makassar as 'Yumainga'?[7] A rather more diffuse question is to understand the purpose of the many illustrations of praus and other items of material culture associated with the trepangers in the rock art of Groote Eylandt and western Arnhem Land, or for that matter the two stone picture sites in eastern Arnhem Land (Macknight and Gray 1970).

A very different approach to studying the trepang industry, in Australia at least, has been through archaeology, and a distinct body of knowledge has gradually built up around this. It began, however, with the ethnographers. The approach goes back to Warner's excavations of the middens around Macassar Well at Milingimbi in the 1920s, and, in the 1940s, the Berndts obtained shards and some other materials from the Mungaruda sandbank off South Goulburn Island—collected mainly by Lazarus Lamilami—and from Wobalinna Island in Port Bradshaw. Macknight (1969, sites 8[b] and 25[a]) gives details of these sites. The first proper archaeological work was done in 1948 by McCarthy and Setlzer (1960). In the early 1960s, John Mulvaney visited several sites and saw the potential for further work (1966). This led directly to my survey and excavations in 1966 and 1967 (Macknight 1969). Ian Crawford (1969) was slightly ahead of me in the Kimberley. More recently, Morwood and Hobbs (1997) have followed up Crawford's work and found further sites.

Archaeology has, I think, answered two questions quite well. The first is the geographical range of the industry. Thus, in the Gulf of Carpentaria, the lack of trepang preparation sites in Limmen Bight suggests that this area was not much visited, though there are important sites in the Pellew Group. Further on, the Wellesley Islands were certainly visited, but there has been no thorough survey looking for trepanging sites. In the Kimberley, all the sites are west of Cape Londonderry and there may have been sporadic contact as far down the coast as the Pilbara. The second matter we now understand in some detail is the actual working of the beach preparation sites. There is a very clear pattern for the location of boiling fireplaces, burying trenches and smoking huts (Macknight 1976, pp. 48–82).

One question that it was hoped the archaeology would answer, but which, I believe, it has not, is the question of the date at which the industry began. The

---

7   I do not now accept the identification with Jongaya as suggested in Macknight (1972, p. 304).

only artefacts recovered from trepang preparation sites whose manufacture can be securely dated before 1800 are several Dutch coins, but even then there are problems, such as the long-continued use of the date of 1790, to say nothing of the issue of the time between minting and deposition. The earliest example appears to be a coin of the Dutch East India Company probably dated to 1742 and found on the Lyaba site off Groote Eylandt (Macknight 1969, pp. 305–6; 1976, p. 73). Ceramics from southern China have been found on many sites, but there are many problems with dating these wares on stylistic grounds. The much more abundant earthenware can certainly be shown to come mainly from South Sulawesi, but again cannot be usefully dated by means of its decoration or form (Bulbeck and Rowley 2001). Attempts to apply fission track and thermoluminescence dating to glass, ceramics and earthenware produced inconclusive results (Macknight 1976, pp. 162–3). This brings us to the problem of the radiocarbon dates of which a number have been obtained by various people from various sites, giving results strung out over the past thousand years or so.[8] Whatever is being dated and whatever the issues of taphonomy or other factors may be that produce these results, the historical evidence, especially the complete silence of the sixteenth and seventeenth-century sources throughout Southeast Asia on any trade in trepang, make it impossible to accept such radiocarbon dates as indicating the existence of the industry in northern Australia before some time in the eighteenth century, and I repeat my judgment that it began in Arnhem Land about 1780.

There is a clear tendency in much of the archaeological writing on the industry to want to push its origin as far back as possible. Why should this be so? There seem to be four factors, in various combinations with different authors, though given that the claims are rarely explained, it is often hard to tell which factors count most. These are: a desire to separate the industry from European initiative and activity—even if Makassar in the eighteenth century was a port dominated by the Dutch East India Company and most of the Australian coast had been on company charts since at least 1650; a romantic, Orientalist image of the 'ageless Indies', sometimes allied with a vague sense of the antiquity of anything to do with China; the prestige of age itself and the virtue of having been around for a long time; and a reliance on the apparently 'hard science' nature of radiocarbon and a failure to engage with the totality of evidence. A corollary of this attitude is often a judgment on the trepang industry as somehow 'a good thing', which is morally desirable in some way that other industries or activities might not be.

Moreover, much of the more recent archaeological work on trepanging sites has been directed towards elucidating the role of Aborigines on the sites and the effects of their contact with the trepangers. Scott Mitchell's work, mentioned

---

8   The discussion by Bulbeck and Rowley (2001, pp. 59–60), drawing on the work of Mitchell (1994) in particular, is important for this question, though further dates are now available.

above, was on middens, not trepanging sites, but Carmel Schrire (1972), working in the Port Bradshaw area, and Annie Clarke on Groote Eylandt (1994, 2000)—and more recently at Caledon Bay—have dug on processing sites. Clarke, in particular, has been concerned to stress Aboriginal initiative. Daryl Wesley has recently been working along the same lines at Anuru Bay and in the Wellington Range. I remain slightly sceptical as to the possibility of answering questions about the nature of interaction between trepangers and Aborigines by means of archaeology.

One interesting archaeological puzzle remains. This is the purpose of the circular stone arrangements in the intertidal zone, of which the best example has been discovered off South Goulburn Island. There seem to be some others a little further east and others again off Bentinck Island and Albinia Island in the South Wellesley Group. One tenuous link with the trepang industry is that item 33 at the Wurrawurrawoi stone picture site near Yirrkala, where all other items seem related to the industry, looks very like a stone picture of such a feature (Macknight and Gray 1970, pp. 22–3). Since we do not understand what these rings of stones were for or when they were built—and they do not seem to be of recent Aboriginal or European origin—they are perhaps best described as 'Dobson rings' after Graeme Dobson who discovered them.[9] The best guess as to their function seems to be that they were some kind of holding area for trepang that had been collected, but not yet processed.

When one comes to look at the way in which historians of Australian experience have treated trepang and trepangers, there are some strange silences, despite the abundant and varied documentary sources mentioned above. Again, the starting point must be with the ethnographers. In 1954, R. M. and C. H. Berndt published their book *Arnhem Land: Its history and its people*. This is a book with shortcomings (Macknight 2011, pp. 128–30), but it deserves to be better celebrated as the first major work in the now crowded field of Aboriginal history. Who else, at that time, was integrating oral accounts from Aboriginal informants with published sources and detailed archival research? Who else could provide illustrations such as the spectacular maps drawn with crayon on brown paper that they had sponsored? Naturally, given its focus and the experience of its authors, the book shares some of the characteristics of the ethnographic literature I have described above.

This interest in the consequences of the industry for Aboriginal societies was taken up in the work of John Mulvaney as he pioneered the study of Australian prehistory. In his first great survey, Mulvaney briefly mentions the trepangers under the heading of 'Proto-historic influences' (Mulvaney 1961, p. 99), and this was followed by his enthusiastic account of archaeological fieldwork in Arnhem

---

9   I am grateful to Graeme Dobson and Grant Leeworthy for photographs of these features.

Land and deeper reading in the nineteenth-century sources (Mulvaney 1966). As mentioned above, Mulvaney's work spurred the archaeological investigation of the industry. In the first chapter of *The Prehistory of Australia* (1969), Mulvaney continues to devote considerable space to the matter, though its salience in the literature on Australian prehistory has gradually faded, perhaps as interest has grown in the deep past.

A quite different approach to the subject is found in the first volume of Manning Clark's *A History of Australia*. Although Clark glimpsed the possibility of a long human past on the continent, he was too early to benefit from Mulvaney's work. He was more concerned with the grand geopolitical context within which outsiders first came to know of Australia, and it is within this that he gives his account of the industry (Clark 1962, pp. 37–8). Even if there are some shortcomings in his account, it has the great merit of acknowledging the need to place the industry in its archipelagic context and he makes use of the Dutch articles by Cense (1952) and Heeren (1952).

Over the past 50 years, most historians working in the category of 'Australian history' have written within a model that is essentially Anglocentric and anglophone. The dominant narrative begins with the settlement of New South Wales in 1788 and traces the development of the several British colonies and, after 1901, the federated nation-state. The focus is largely on southern and eastern Australia and the story concentrates on success, or at least on enduring features of the society and economy.

More recently, some other voices have been heard and consideration of the trepang industry arises in various ways. The effects of contact with the trepangers is a theme in Aboriginal history and particularly in relation to the question of the introduction of the smallpox epidemics that devastated Aboriginal Australia in the eighteenth and nineteenth centuries.[10] The unusual nature of the archaeology has also attracted attention (Connah 1993). There is, naturally, more interest in the industry in works dealing with northern Australia, such as Alan Powell's excellent history of the Northern Territory (2009), and especially

---

10 For the original evidence on this, see Macknight (1986, pp. 72–4). For my current view, see Macknight (2011, p. 137). In his final word on the subject, Noel Butlin seems to have shifted somewhat from his opposition to the case for northern introduction. He writes: 'But one disease can be regarded as having certainly been delivered to parts of northern Australia and possibly more widely from Macassan praus. This was smallpox' (Butlin 1993, p. 198). Accepting a date of about 1780 for the origin of substantial contact by trepangers, as the presumed source of the infection, with people in Arnhem Land also removes one of the many difficulties that troubled Butlin; this would make the assumed 1780s epidemic that reached Sydney in 1789 a completely virgin field event, without the effect of previous epidemics. Resistance to accepting non-European agency lingers in the strangest places. Bill Gammage, in his recent paean for Aboriginal agency, after acknowledging that '[s]ome researchers think the disease came from the north', can then go on to suggest that Tench's denial of European introduction may be 'deliberately ironic'. Poor Tench! Reading his remarks fairly and in context, it is clear that he is genuinely puzzled and very sensibly casting around for explanations—and finds none of those he can imagine sufficient to explain what he has observed (Gammage 2011, p. 152; Tench 1979, p. 146).

when they deal with issues of race, such as Regina Ganter's *Mixed Relations* (2006) and Peta Stephenson's *The Outsiders Within* (2007). This is, however, by no means general, and Henry Reynolds' *North of Capricorn* (2003) has relatively little on the trepangers from Makassar. Even more surprising perhaps, given its interest in projected contacts between north Australia and Asia, there is little on the trepang industry in Jack Cross's *Great Central State* (2011). Steve Mullins (1992), writing about north Queensland, makes the important point that there was a break between the trepanging activity on the Great Barrier Reef in the 1840s and that in Torres Strait in the 1860s and later. That break, Mullins believes, marks a shift from an industry with links westwards towards the Indonesian archipelago to one looking to the Pacific, and that made a crucial difference for the later history of Torres Strait. The fact that the trepangers from Makassar were Muslim has given them a place in a new flurry of writing on the history of Islam in Australia. Peta Stephenson rightly places them at the front of her survey of the subject (Stephenson 2010, pp. 21–34), drawing heavily on the detailed work of Ian McIntosh (1996a, 1996b).

A feature of virtually all the Australian literature mentioned so far has been that the trepangers come from over the horizon towards Australia and its people. They are the other, the unfamiliar. The perspective changes, however, if one moves from seeing the trepangers coming to the Australian coast to seeing them as setting out from Makassar to Marege', as they called Arnhem Land and the adjacent coast (Macknight 1976). Does this, however, remove the subject from 'Australian history'? At any event, the move is fundamental, if not entirely original. After all, off the coast of Arnhem Land in 1803 the Englishmen Flinders and Brown made the move from *Investigator*'s deck to the deck of the trepanging prau captained by Pobassoo from Makassar; they moved across and that is perhaps why they were able to gather so much information. Very few other Europeans, if any through the nineteenth century, set foot on the deck on a trepanging prau other than to exert authority. The point has a special salience for me; the first version of the title of my book *The Voyage to Marege'* came to me on 28 July 1969, while sailing on the *pajala Galesong*, master Muis Daeng Tarrang, off the coast of South Sulawesi.[11] It is revealing that many have had difficulty in classifying the book. In the first chapter of the book particularly, I outline the social, political and economic contexts of the industry, distinguishing the various kinds of voyage that came and went out of Makassar.

This is a field that has received a great deal of attention recently. The trade records of Makassar, both in the eighteenth century under the Dutch East India Company and in the nineteenth century during the colonial period, have been

---

11   At that time, I had not yet read John Smail's classic 1961 article analysing the many senses of the phrase 'point of view' (now most easily available in Smail 1993), but this is a good instance of one matter he discusses. A careful reading of this chapter will show how much else I owe to Smail.

intensively studied by historians. The sources discussed above have begun to reveal an overall picture of the trade. Gerrit Knaap and Heather Sutherland's *Monsoon Traders* is subtitled *Ships, skippers and commodities in eighteenth-century Makassar* (2004). It is based on the amazingly detailed records that survive on the trade and shipping of Makassar throughout this century and is quite as much, if not more, concerned with goods going to China as it is with the trade within the archipelago, and, like the harbourmaster's records that form its main source, it looks at 'private'—that is, non–Dutch East India Company—trade. It builds, also, on Sutherland's research into the social history of Makassar (in particular, Sutherland 2000, 2001). In these records, trepang is a major item of import and export, and a clear picture emerges of slow growth from just before 1720 to a boom in the 1780s when it was the main item of export, especially to China. The industry was important in other ways too; Knaap (2001, p. 96) estimates that the total adult male population of Makassar in 1730 was no more than about 2500. Even with some recruitment of crews from surrounding areas, this shows the significance of the estimate of around 1000 men in the trepanging fleet in northern Australia in the early nineteenth century (Macknight 1976, p. 29).

By strange coincidence, at the same time as Sutherland and Knapp were working, Jürgen G. Nagel was preparing a massive thesis from very similar sources: *Der Schlüssel zu den Molukken: Makassar und de Handelsstrukturen des Malaiischen Archipels im 17. und 18. Jahrhundert: Eine exemplarische Studie* (2003). Its purpose is to show the history of Makassar as 'exemplary' of the process of interaction between European trade and local or regional trading structures. The trepang trade fits into this picture in a most interesting and unusual way. Nagel's conclusions on trepang mirror those of Knaap and Sutherland and are set in a very extensive discussion of Makassar and its history. While some quibbles and difficulties remain with the figures in these sources and with the figures I have provided from my own work on these eighteenth-century trade records (Macknight 1986), that is only to say that there is the potential for further work.[12]

One can even find a slight mention of the trade in South Sulawesi in indigenous records. When, in 1803, Pobassoo told Flinders of a fleet of 60 praus 'belonging to the Rajah of Boni', he was referring to Sultan Ahmad as-Salih, whose extensive diaries have recently been studied in some detail, though I do not know of any specific reference to trepanging. In a diary of his predecessor, however, Sultan

---

12   I am very tempted to argue that the consistent gap between the import and export figures for trepang and other items is to be explained by the failure to record imports from places outside the Dutch East India Company's control or interest, including Australia. If we can infer that considerable quantities of trepang were coming from such areas, of which Marege' would rank as a prime area of production, this helps greatly to explain the considerable gap between import and export. In any case, I believe that the export figures are likely to be more accurate (Macknight 2011, pp. 134–5). The question invites further research.

Abdurrazak Jalaluddin, on 16 December 1752, a certain Ance Kia buys from the ruler what sounds like an annual licence for the trepang market on Bonerate. On 25 December, I Kacoa buys a similar licence for Bajoe, while six years later, on 14 December 1758, La Tenro hires the Bajoe trepang market. In each case, the fee seems to have been 200 reals (Asmat and Jamaluddin 2007, pp. 46, 85).[13] The diary also allows us to know that Sultan Abdurrazak was living in the vicinity of Makassar when these transactions took place. I suspect that further work on the mass of available Bugis and Makasar diaries would turn up similar references. Various later contracts in the Makasar language are discussed in Macknight (1976 pp. 19–24), but I doubt that there are more of these to be found.

Within the history of maritime trade between Southeast Asia generally and China in the later eighteenth and early nineteenth centuries, trepang naturally features as a major item in the trade, though indications of the quantity of trepang are rare. Thus, for example, Tagliacozzo (2004) provides a broad overview, which is of particular use since it deliberately avoids much mention of Makassar. This gap is filled by Edward Poelinggomang's fine study (2002), though even here there is more emphasis on shipping than on the quantities of goods. Much more work remains to be done in searching out and analysing relevant statistics. For example, in the early 1840s, trepang was still the most important item of export from Makassar, according to a careful survey (Macknight 2008a, p. 138), and judging from an excess of roughly Dfl. 500 000 in the total export over import for the period from 1847 to 1870, this probably continued well into the century (Poelinggomang 2002, p. 157). Yoshiharu Abe (1995), who discusses the trepang industry in Fiji, Queensland, Sulu and Arnhem Land, provides one of the few comparative studies.

A major step forward in our understanding is Dai Yifeng's publication of some figures for the import of trepang into China. There seem to be no systematic Chinese records to match the eighteenth-century statistics from Makassar and elsewhere, but Dai estimates that each year from 1723 to 1820 'several hundred to more than one thousand *dan* of trepang were imported from Southeast Asia' (Dai Yifeng 2002, p. 28).[14] Given annual export figures from Makassar in the 1780s of 6000 to 7000 piculs (Knaap and Sutherland 2004, p. 99; Nagel 2003, p. 501), that looks like a conservative estimate. I have also estimated an annual Australian production figure of more than 5000 piculs for the early nineteenth century (Macknight 1976, p. 38). In the late nineteenth century, Chinese imports boomed, reaching 44 142 *dan* (about 2600 t) in 1896 (Dai Yifeng 2002, p. 29). Xiamen (Amoy) and Shanghai were always the most important ports in the trade. It would be interesting to examine the trade statistics in more detail with a view to estimating the reliability of these figures based on the Chinese

---

13   I thank Faried Saenong for showing me this book.
14   A *dan* is 60 kg or almost the same as a picul.

Maritime Customs records. Given the growth in Chinese trading networks around the South China Sea and into maritime Southeast Asia generally, one wonders about the completeness of such records. Various other figures are available through the nineteenth century, many quite unbelievable, as I have discussed elsewhere (Macknight 1976, pp. 15–16, 145–6). While further work might bring considerable refinement to the figures, I believe that my estimate that through the nineteenth century north Australia supplied in the order of one-quarter of the Chinese market remains reasonable. With the addition of other sources of supply, the contribution through Makassar was a considerably larger share.

Recent public interest in the history of the industry takes many forms and produces a scattered literature. There is a steady flow of media articles and reports in both Indonesia and Australia—often claiming that the subject is little known or surprising. There are excellent museum exhibits both in the Museum and Art Gallery of the Northern Territory and in the National Museum of Australia. Many other museum and art gallery displays, especially of relevant bark paintings, refer to trepangers and their praus in captions and other material. The recent major exhibition in the Melbourne Museum entitled *Trepang: China & the story of Macassan–Aboriginal trade* played up—perhaps overplayed—the link with China (see Clark and May, this volume). In addition, there are celebratory events such as the wonderfully ironic voyage in 1988 of a replica prau, the *Hati Marege*, from Makassar to Arnhem Land to celebrate the bicentenary of European settlement, or the staging in Sulawesi and northern Australia of the opera *Trepang*, or other recent visits of various groups in both directions (see Ganter, this volume).

Interest in trepang itself has also endured; indeed, the industry flourishes as never before (see the chapters by Clark and Adhuri, this volume). This produces two kinds of literature. The first is the strictly biological, with particular attention to the complex taxonomy of the many genera and species, but there is also interest in the animal's unusual physiology and ecology. Hamel et al. (2001, p. 131) claim to have reviewed 14 theses and 352 technical reports and scientific papers relating to *Holothuria scabra*, and research continues to refine our knowledge.

This biological interest has been more than matched by the economic. As Hamel et al. say, again in relation to *Holothuria scabra* alone, 'The accumulated knowledge about the biology of the species has paved the way for sustainable management of remaining populations through restocking and stock enhancement, and also offers the potential for increasing production through farming' (Hamel et al. 2001, p. 201). The past decade has seen a great deal of effort put into both these areas—that is, sustainable management of 'wild' populations and aquaculture—and much information on the current status of the industry is now available. A series of volumes published by the Food and Agriculture Organization draws much of this together (Lovatelli et al. 2004; Toral-Granda et al. 2008; Purcell 2010). It is interesting to note, for example, the continuing importance of Indonesian production and the role of the island of Barrang Lompo in trepang aquaculture (Tuwo 2004). The importance of understanding the history of the industry for evaluating sustainability is brought out in a recent paper by Kathleen Schwerdtner Máñez and Sebastian Ferse (2010). Until recently, Australia contributed little to this modern aspect of the industry, but this is changing with the development of some aquaculture projects (Giraspy and Ivy 2005), and Howard (2009) provides a lively account of much recent activity.

The symposium that inspired the chapters of this edited collection was the chance for scholars coming from different backgrounds to talk with each other. There was also some listening and mutual solving of problems. This chapter is intended to widen the discussion even further. Who would have guessed that such an apparently humble creature as the sea slug would hold such significance in human history, especially the past of East and Southeast Asia, to say nothing of northern Australia? Perhaps, as the Chinese economy rises again, it has a glorious future as well.

References

Abe, Y. (1995) The trepang industry in the Pacific and Southeast Asia: an anthropological and historical study, Unpublished MA thesis, University of Melbourne, Melbourne.

Akamine, J. (2004) 'The status of the sea cucumber fisheries and trade in Japan: past and present', in A. Lovatelli, C. Conand, S. Purcell, S. Uthicke, J.-F. Hamel and A. Mercier (eds), *Advances in Sea Cucumber Aquaculture and Management*, Rome: Food and Agriculture Organization of the United Nations, pp. 39 48.

Ammarell, G. (1999) *Bugis Navigation*, New Haven, Conn.: Yale University Southeast Asia Studies.

Asmat Riady Lamallongeng and H. A. Jamaluddin (eds) (2007) *Catatan Harian Raja Bone*, Makassar: La Macca Press.

Berndt, R. M. and C. H. Berndt (1949) 'Secular figures of northeast Arnhem Land', *American Anthropologist*, 51, pp. 213–22.

Berndt, R. M. and C. H. Berndt (1954) *Arnhem Land: Its history and its people*, Melbourne: Cheshire.

Butlin, N. G. (1993) *Economics and the Dreamtime: A hypothetical history*, Cambridge: Cambridge University Press.

Bulbeck, D. and B. Rowley (2001) 'Macassans and their pots in northern Australia', in C. Fredericksen and I. Walters (eds), *Altered States: Material culture transformations in the Arafura region*, Darwin: Northern Territory University Press, pp. 55–74.

Cense, A. A. (1952) 'Makassaars-Boeginese prauwvaart op Noord-Australië', *Bijdragen tot de Taal-, Land- en Volkenkunde*, 108, pp. 248–64.

Clark, C. M. H. (1962) *A History of Australia. Volume I: From the earliest times to the age of Macquarie*, Parkville, Vic.: Melbourne University Press.

Clarke, A. (2000) 'The "Moorman's trowsers": Macassan and Aboriginal interactions and the changing fabric of Indigenous social life', in S. O'Connor and P. Veth (eds), *East of Wallace's Line: Studies of past and present maritime cultures of the Indo-Pacific region*, Modern Quaternary Research in Southeast Asia 16, Rotterdam: A. A. Balkema, pp. 315–35.

Clarke, A. F. (1994) Winds of change: an archaeology of contact in the Groote Eylandt archipelago, northern Australia, Unpublished PhD thesis, The Australian National University, Canberra.

Colenbrander, H. T. (1899) *Dagh-Register gehouden int Casteel Batavia vant passerende daer ter plaetse als over geheel Nederlands-India Anno 1636*, 's-Gravenhage: Martinus Nijhoff.

Connah, G. (1993) *The Archaeology of Australia's History*, Cambridge: Cambridge University Press.

Cortesão, A. (1944) *The Suma Oriental of Tomé Pires: An account of the East, from the Red Sea to Japan, written in Malacca and India in 1512–1515 and The Book of Francisco Rodrigues*, [2 vols], Hakluyt Society Second Series, vols 89 and 90, London: Hakluyt Society.

Crawford, I. (1969) Late prehistoric changes in Aboriginal cultures in Kimberley, Western Australia, Unpublished PhD thesis, University of London, London.

Crawford, I. (2001) *We Won the Victory: Aborigines and outsiders on the north-west coast of the Kimberley*, Fremantle, WA: Fremantle Arts Centre Press.

Cross, J. (2011) *Great Central State: The foundation of the Northern Territory*, Kent Town, SA: Wakefield Press.

Dai Yifeng (2002) 'Food culture and overseas trade: the trepang trade between China and Southeast Asia during the Qing dynasty', in D. Y. H. Wu and S. C. H. Cheung (eds), *The Globalization of Chinese Food*, Richmond, Surrey: Curzon, pp. 21–42.

Dwyer, D. (2001) 'Fishers of people: from reef fishing to refugees, the changing role of Indonesian sailors and their *perahu* at Ashmore Reef, north Australia', in C. Fredericksen and I. Walters (eds), *Altered States: Material culture transformations in the Arafura region*, Darwin: Northern Territory University Press, pp. 31–54.

Evans, N. (1992) 'Macassan loanwords in Top End languages', *Australian Journal of Linguistics*, 12, pp. 45–91.

Evans, N. (1997) 'Macassan loans and linguistic stratification in western Arnhem Land', in P. McConvell and N. Evans (eds), *Archaeology and Linguistics: Aboriginal Australia in global perspective*, Melbourne: Oxford University Press, pp. 237–60.

Fox, J. J. (1977) 'Notes on the southern voyages and settlements of the Sama-Bajau', *Bijdragen tot de Taal-, Land- en Volkenkunde*, 133, pp. 459–65.

Fox, J. J. (1998) 'Reefs and shoals in Australia–Indonesia relations: traditional Indonesian fishermen', in A. Milner and M. Quilty (eds), *Australia in Asia: Episodes*, Melbourne: Oxford University Press, pp. 111–39.

Gammage, B. (2011) *The Biggest Estate on Earth: How Aborigines made Australia*, Sydney: Allen & Unwin.

Ganter, R. (2006) *Mixed Relations: Asian/Aboriginal contact in north Australia*, Perth: University of Western Australia Press.

Giraspy, D. A. and G. Ivy (2005) 'Australia's first commercial sea cucumber culture and sea ranching project in Hervey Bay, Queensland, Australia', *SPC Beche-de-mer Information Bulletin*, 21, pp. 29–31.

Hamel, J.-F., C. Conand, D. Pawson and A. Mercier (2001) 'The sea cucumber *Holothuria scabra* (Holothuroidea: Echinodermata): its biology and its exploitation as bêche-de-mer', *Advances in Marine Biology*, 41, pp. 129–223.

Heeren, H. J. (1952) 'Indonesische cultuurinvloeden in Australië', *Indonesië*, 6, pp. 149–59.

Howard, P. A. (2009) Past and present: an ethno-historical and archaeological study of the north Australian trepang industry, Unpublished Honours thesis, School of Earth and Environmental Sciences, University of Wollongong, Wollongong, NSW.

Jukes, A. (2006) Makassarese (*basa Mangkasara'*): a description of an Austronesian language of South Sulawesi, Unpublished PhD thesis, University of Melbourne, Melbourne.

Knaap, G. (2001) 'Manning the fleet: skippers, crews and shipowners in eighteenth-century Makassar', in E. Sedyawati and S. Zuhdi (eds), *Arung Samudra: persembahan memperingati sembilan windu A. B. Lapian*, Depok: Pusat Penilitian Kemasyarakatan dan Budaya & Lembaga Penelitian Universitas Indonesia, pp. 83–97.

Knaap, G. and H. Sutherland (2004) *Monsoon Traders: Ships, skippers and commodities in eighteenth-century Makassar*, Leiden: KITLV Press.

Kolff, D. H. (1840) *Voyages of the Dutch Brig of War Dourga*, (G. W. Earl trans.), London: James Madden & Co.

Lovatelli, A., C. Conand, S. Purcell, S. Uthicke, J.-F. Hamel and A. Mercier (eds) (2004) *Advances in sea cucumber aquaculture and management*, FAO Fisheries Technical Paper 463, Rome: Food and Agriculture Organization of the United Nations.

McCarthy, F. D. and F. M. Setzler (1960) 'The archaeology of Arnhem Land', in C. P. Mountford (ed.), *Records of the American–Australian Scientific Expedition to Arnhem Land. Volume 2: Anthropology and nutrition*, Parkville, Vic.: Melbourne University Press, pp. 215–95.

McIntosh, I. (1996a) 'Allah and the spirit of the dead: the hidden legacy of pre-colonial Indonesian/Aboriginal contact in north-east Arnhem Land', *Australian Folklore*, 11, pp. 131–8.

McIntosh, I. (1996b) 'Islam and Australia's Aborigines? A perspective from north-east Arnhem Land', *Journal of Religious History*, 20, pp. 53–77.

McIntosh, I. S. (2008) 'Pre-Macassans at Dholtji? Exploring one of north-east Arnhem Land's great conundrums', in P. Veth, P. Sutton and M. Neale (eds), *Strangers on the Shore: Early coastal contacts in Australia*, Canberra: National Museum of Australia, pp. 165–80.

McIntosh, I. S. (2011) 'Missing the revolution! Negotiating disclosure on the pre-Macassans (Bayini) in north-east Arnhem Land', in M. Thomas and M. Neale (eds), *Exploring the Legacy of the 1948 Arnhem Land Expedition*, Canberra: ANU E Press, pp. 337–54.

Macknight, C. (2008a) 'Harvesting the memory: open beaches in Makassar and Arnhem Land', in P. Veth, P. Sutton and M. Neale (eds), *Strangers on the Shore: Early coastal contacts in Australia*, Canberra: National Museum of Australia, pp. 133–47.

Macknight, C. (2008b) 'A useless discovery? Australia and its people in the eyes of others from Tasman to Cook', *The Globe: Journal of the Australian Map Circle*, 61, pp. 1–10.

Macknight, C. (2011) 'The view from Marege': Australian knowledge of Makassar and the impact of the trepang industry across two centuries', *Aboriginal History*, 35, pp. 121–43.

Macknight, C. C. (1969) The Macassans: a study of the early trepang industry along the Northern Territory coast, Unpublished PhD thesis, The Australian National University, Canberra.

Macknight, C. C. (1972) 'Macassans and Aborigines', *Oceania*, 42, pp. 283–321.

Macknight, C. C. (1976) *The Voyage to Marege': Macassan trepangers in northern Australia*, Carlton, Vic.: Melbourne University Press.

Macknight, C. C. (1986) 'Macassans and the Aboriginal past', *Archaeology in Oceania*, 21, pp. 69–75.

Macknight, C. C. and W. J. Gray (1970) *Aboriginal Stone Pictures in Eastern Arnhem Land*, Canberra: Australian Institute of Aboriginal Studies.

Meilink-Roelofsz, M. A. P. (1962) *Asian Trade and European Influence in the Indonesian Archipelago between 1500 and about 1630*, The Hague: Martinus Nijhoff.

Mitchell, S. (1994) Culture contact and indigenous economies on the Cobourg Peninsula, northwestern Arnhem Land, Unpublished PhD thesis, Northern Territory University, Darwin.

Mitchell, S. (1995) 'Foreign contact and Indigenous exchange networks on the Cobourg Peninsula, northwestern Arnhem Land', *Australian Aboriginal Studies*, 1995 (2), pp. 44–8.

Mitchell, S. (1996) 'Dugongs and dugouts, sharptacks and shellbacks: Macassan contact and Aboriginal marine hunting of the Cobourg Peninsula, north western Arnhem Land', *Bulletin of the Indo-Pacific Prehistory Association*, 15, pp. 181–91.

Morwood, M. J. and D. R. Hobbs (1997) 'The Asian connection: preliminary report on Indonesian trepang sites on the Kimberley coast, N. W. Australia', *Archaeology in Oceania*, 32, pp. 197–206.

Mullins, S. (1992) 'The Torres Strait beche-de-mer fishery: a question of timing', *The Great Circle*, 14 (1), pp. 21–30.

Mulvaney, D. J. (1961) 'The Stone Age of Australia', *Proceedings of the Prehistoric Society*, 27, pp. 56–107.

Mulvaney, D. J. (1966) 'Beche-de-mer, Aborigines and Australian history', *Proceedings of the Royal Society of Victoria*, 79 (2), pp. 449–57.

Mulvaney, D. J. (1969) *The Prehistory of Australia*, London: Thames & Hudson.

Nagel, J. G. (2003) *Der Schlüssel zu den Molukken: Makassar und de Handelsstrukturen des Malaiischen Archipels im 17. und 18. Jahrhundert: Eine exemplarische Studie*, [2 vols], Hamburg: Verlag Dr Kovač.

Noorduyn, J. (1983) 'De handelsrelaties van het Makassaarse rijk volgens de Notitie van Cornelis Speelman uit 1670', *Nederlandse Historische Bronnen*, 3, pp. 96–123.

Pelras, C. (2000) 'Patron–client ties among the Bugis and Makassarese of South Sulawesi', *Bijdragen tot de Taal-, Land- en Volkenkunde*, 156, pp. 393–432.

Poelinggomang, E. (2002) *Makassar abad XIX: studi tentang kebijakan perdagangan maritim*, Jakarta: Kepustakaan Populer Gramedia bekerjasama dengan Yayasan Adikarya IKAPI dan The Ford Foundation.

Powell, A. (2009) *Far Country: A short history of the Northern Territory*, (5th edn), Darwin: Charles Darwin University Press.

Purcell, S. W. (2010) *Managing sea cucumber fisheries with an ecosystem approach*, (A. Lovatelli, M. Vasconcellos and Y. Yimin eds), FAO Fisheries and Aquaculture Technical Paper 520, Rome: Food and Agriculture Organization of the United Nations.

Reynolds, H. (2003) *North of Capricorn: The untold story of the people of Australia's north*, Crows Nest, NSW: Allen & Unwin.

Schrire, C. (1972) 'Ethno-archaeological models and subsistence behaviour in Arnhem Land', in D. L. Clarke (ed.), *Models in Archaeology*, London: Methuen, pp. 653–70.

Schwerdtner Máñez, K. and S. C. A. Ferse (2010) 'The history of Makassan trepang fishing and trade', *PLoS ONE*, 5 (6), e11346, pp. 1–8.

Smail, J. R. W. (1993) 'On the possibility of an autonomous history of modern Southeast Asia', in L. Sears (ed.), *Autonomous Histories, Particular Truths: Essays in honor of John R. W. Smail*, University of Wisconsin Center for Southeast Asian Studies Monograph Number 11, Madison, Wis.: University of Wisconsin, pp. 39–70.

Stephenson, P. (2007) *The Outsiders Within: Telling Australia's Indigenous–Asian story*, Sydney: UNSW Press.

Stephenson, P. (2010) *Islam Dreaming: Indigenous Muslims in Australia*, Sydney: UNSW Press.

Sutherland, H. (2000) 'Trepang and wangkang: the China trade of eighteenth-century Makassar c. 1720s–1840s', *Bijdragen tot de Taal-, Land- en Volkenkunde*, 156, pp. 451–72.

Sutherland, H. (2001) 'Money in Makassar: credit and debt in an eighteenth century VOC settlement', in E. Sedyawati and S. Zuhdi (eds), *Arung Samudra: Persembahan memperingati sembilan windu A. B. Lapian*, Depok: Pusat Penilitian Kemasyarakatan dan Budaya & Lembaga Penelitian Universitas Indonesia, pp. 713–43.

Tagliacozzo, E. (2004) 'A necklace of fins: marine goods trading in maritime Southeast Asia, 1780–1860', *International Journal of Asian Studies*, 1 (1), pp. 23–48.

Tench, W. (1979) *Sydney's First Four Years: Being a reprint of A Narrative of the Expedition to Botany Bay and A Complete account of the settlement at Port Jackson*, (with an introduction and annotations by L. F. Fitzhardinge), Sydney: Library of Australian History.

Tindale, N. B. (1925–28) 'Natives of Grooote Eylandt and of the west coast of the Gulf of Carpentaria, parts I and II', *Records of the South Australian Museum*, 3, pp. 61–134.

Toral-Granda, V., A. Lovatelli and M. Vasconcellos (eds) (2008) *Sea cucumbers: a global review of fisheries and trade*, FAO Fisheries and Aquaculture Technical Paper 516, Rome: Food and Agriculture Organization of the United Nations.

Tuwo, A. (2004) 'Status of sea cucumber fisheries and farming in Indonesia', in A. Lovatelli, C. Conand, S. Purcell, S. Uthicke, J.-F. Hamel and A. Mercier (eds), *Advances in Sea Cucumber Aquaculture and Management*, Rome: Food and Agriculture Organization of the United Nations, pp. 49–56.

Walker, A. and R. D. Zorc (1981) 'Austronesian loanwords in Yolngu-Matha of northeast Arnhem Land', *Aboriginal History*, 5, pp. 109–34.

Walter, K. R. (1988) The proper breadth of interest Norman B. Tindale: the development of a fieldworker in Aboriginal Australia 1900–1936, Unpublished MA thesis, The Australian National University, Canberra.

3. Crossing the great divide: Australia and eastern Indonesia

Anthony Reid

Introduction

The enterprise of understanding 'Macassan history and heritage' is one of valorising the many crossings of the gulf between northern Australia and eastern Indonesia. To do justice to those crossings, however, we must first of all clarify the immensity of the gulf itself, which I will call 'the Great Divide'. Viewed in the long term, it is a divide more fundamental than that between any other two neighbours in the world, and the crossings of it were no mean feat. Once humans extended the use of efficient sailing craft into the waters north of Australia some thousands of years ago, that divide would have been expected to be bridged, but it was not. I will end my story by seeking to explain the depth of the mutual incomprehension as late as the 1930s, on the very eve of the violent collision of the two neighbouring peoples in the crucible of war in the 1940s.

Sunda and Sahul

Looked at over the long term, the Arafura Sea has formed the world's greatest divide throughout human history. As we know, some hundreds of millions of years ago Australia, or more accurately the broader Sahul plate it formed together with the island of New Guinea, was united with the other southern continents in what geologists call Gondwana. Africa, South America and the Indian subcontinent in turn tore themselves off from Gondwana and began their journey northward, a journey that would ultimately join them with the great northern landmass of Laurasia, or today's Eurasia and North America. Sahul was the last plate to be torn from Antarctica, only 50 million years ago, to begin its journey northward towards what we now know as Southeast Asia. But instead of joining up with the northern plate, as South America did at Panama and Africa at Suez, Sahul created a great rumpling in the space between Sahul and Sunda, the deep troughs that form Wallacea, with its Wallace and Weber lines, and with Sulawesi in the middle, itself composed of two disparate pieces of plate thrust awkwardly together. These rifts between Sunda and Sahul remained so profound that even the most extreme ice ages of the past million years could not lower sea levels enough to make it crossable by the humans of the major northern continent; whereas at various times it was possible to walk across the Bering Strait to America. Hence the extreme difference of Australia's fauna and flora from those of the Eurasian landmass, and the virtual impossibility for primates and our human ancestors to reach the world's only truly isolated liveable continent.

But somehow *Homo sapiens* did make this crossing, arriving at a time now thought (since 2011's genome analysis of a lock of hair) to be as much as 70 000 years ago, before northern Asia or Europe were populated at all. They thereby became the only fully isolated human population for the next 60 000 years or so before boats became part of human equipment. How they could have done this remains a great conundrum, as is the issue of what happened to their relatives who stayed behind in the closer parts of Sunda, where of course they had to cope with intrusions from the north, or much earlier from the west, if we believe the Sundaland hypothesis of Steven Oppenheimer (1999), of people who had developed tools and agriculture that they lacked. I think this issue is the most fundamental part of the agenda of this collection, and indeed of much Australian scholarship. It is the question that drove John Mulvaney to begin archaeological work in South Sulawesi in 1969, and for later Australian prehistorians to extend their work to the eastern Indonesian islands closest to Sahul, and to develop the most fruitful (if often difficult) of the scholarly cooperations between Australia and (eastern) Indonesia. The most spectacular result so far was the unexpected discovery in 2003 of *Homo floresiensis* (Flores man, nicknamed 'the hobbit' for his diminutive stature), who also somehow crossed the Wallace Line at a remote time, though not the much wider gulf to Sahul. The cooperation between Australian prehistorians (with some advanced technology and funding), Indonesian scholars and the local knowledge of the people of Nusa Tenggara Timur was essential to this progress, and needs to be extended.

Adding to the complexity of this human history across the Great Divide is the unusual dynamism of this region geologically. Because it forms a complicated and highly active part of the Ring of Fire, the landforms may have been dramatically altered by eruptions, earthquakes and tsunamis as well as the rise and fall of sea levels. We now know that massive eruptions such as those of Long Island (Papua New Guinea) in ±1660 (Blong 1982), Tambora (Sumbawa) in 1815 and Krakatau (between Sumatra and Java) in 1883 cast a massive ash deposit over hundreds of kilometres to their west, and caused darkness and climatic cooling around the planet, and the failure of agriculture within their own region for a year or two.

But since most of our knowledge of the 70 000 years of possible human contact between Sahul and Sunda is crammed into the past 500 years, let me focus the remainder of the chapter on that. What follows is a review of some of the contacts we do know about across this divide in relatively recent times.

Tracing shadows before the nineteenth century

Once the Austronesians arrived in the southern islands some 5000 years ago with their efficient outrigger sailing vessels, which could sail as far as Easter Island and Madagascar, the depth of the sea was no longer an adequate reason for the sporadic nature of the contact. From a maritime trading perspective, one might have expected the northwest coast of Australia to become part of a kind of 'Arafura zone' centred on one of the busy commercial hubs of those seas, just as James Warren (1981) identified a 'Sulu zone' of interaction in the Sulu Sea, around the small-island trading and raiding centre of Sulu, which in turn depended for its wealth on the visits of Chinese traders. Tidore provided such a hub for the western regions of Papua, ensuring that by the sixteenth century coastal west Papua, manifestly part of the Sahul geological plate, was also incorporated into the great Eurasian trading world.

That world did not peter out slowly in the southeast, but extended vigorously as far as the spice islands of Maluku. The cloves of Ternate and Tidore and the nutmeg of the Banda Archipelago were both items of Eurasian trade throughout the Common Era, having been found both in ancient Rome and in Han China. They became indispensable to the European pharmacopeia in the late Middle Ages, and the lust to obtain them without dependence on Muslim trading routes was what had united the world in Europe's age of discovery. In the sixteenth century Banda became another small-island trading hub, relatively safe from predatory rulers and dominated by a cosmopolitan group of traders from around the archipelago. Its conquest and depopulation by the Dutch in 1623 required free merchants to find other centres—in the first instance in other small islands to the east of Ceram, particularly Goram (Knaap 1987, pp. 53–8). By the early nineteenth century, Dobo in the Aru Islands (see below) had become the small-island free port closest to Australia, and a classic exemplar of the genre, though there were others, like Bawean in the Java Sea and Bonerate further east.

In the sixteenth century the rival sultanates of Ternate and Tidore, each based on a tiny clove-producing volcanic island within sight of the other, became little Sulus seeking to coordinate multi-ethnic fleets that could raid or trade for slaves and sea produce as far as Aru, Kei, Tanimbar and Papua. Their languages were Papuan rather than Austronesian, and their myths confirmed ancient connections of trade, warfare and ritual to Papua in the east. Andaya (1993, pp. 49–55, 100–12) includes 'the king of the Papuas' as one of the complementary four pillars of his 'World of Maluku' delineated by origin myths. Dutch sources in the seventeenth century show Tidore as the most active claimant to primacy throughout the islands to its east, with major centres of its influence in the Papuan offshore islands of Misool and Raja Ampat, and contacts with the Onin Peninsula on the mainland. Further south, the sandalwood-trading network linked Timor and its nearby islands into the great Eurasian trading world. Rote, the island call for many latter-day Indonesian voyages to Australia, was in trade and treaty relations with the Dutch from 1662 and largely Christianised in the following century.

Why was the Australian coast so much less visited? Of course the distance across the Timor Sea (though not the Torres Strait for coast-huggers) was several times the distance of any sector on the route to western Papua. But the more important point seems to have been that visitors found almost nothing of value on the Australian northwest coast, and moved quickly away. As Dampier (1981, p. 149) complained in 1699, this coast 'was not very inviting, being but barren towards the sea, and affording me neither fresh water, nor any great store of other refreshments, nor so much as a fit place for careening'. Accidental Austronesian navigators who visited this inhospitable coast would have been little different from the seventeenth-century Dutch in spending as little time as possible on it.

Nineteenth-century contacts

I said *almost* nothing of value, but that almost is the entry to what contact there was. Australia offered no trade goods on the scale of cloves, nutmeg or sandalwood, and no staple cereals such as rice. For the long-distance traders to know about the potential trade wealth of a place, that wealth had already to be exploited by the locals, as was the case with the products of the Indonesian islands. The native Australians were not miners who valued gold or iron, to present a point of entry to the gold or iron ore that would have attracted Chinese, Indonesian or European traders to the northwest; nor were they agriculturalists who could provide recognisable food sources (except seafood). But they were coastal scavengers of apparently a very high order. The question even more enticing than the trepang trail is that of pearls and pearl shell. Whereas the historical demand for trepang has been well documented as beginning only in the eighteenth century (Knaap and Sutherland 2004), the pearls of tropical Asia were desired trade commodities for 2000 years, often mentioned in Chinese sources as among the trade and tribute items from Southeast Asian maritime centres. If female Aboriginal 'naked divers' of the Kimberley area were as exceptionally good as some of the European pioneers reported in the 1850s, it seems unlikely that they only began diving at European behest. If there is a longer history of contact across the Great Divide, it should be sought in the coastal marine resources for which the Arafura region was well known—in the first place pearls and pearl shell, but also tortoise shell, valued in China for many centuries.

Dobo, a tiny island in the Aru archipelago, appears to have flourished as a typical small-island entrepot free of political interference from any state, Indonesian or Dutch, and useful as a collecting point for sea produce. The Makassar kingdom was in contact with Aru as early as 1624, and a Dutch report then advised that there were already seven mosques in the archipelago because of the importance of this commercial and political link (Coolhaas, vol. I, p. 166). But the pearl industry may not have developed there until the third quarter of the nineteenth century. John Crawfurd insisted in his 1820 *History of the Indian Archipelago* that pearls 'are found no where but in the Suluk [Sulu] Islands' in Indonesian waters, and that it was from there that they were exported in vast quantities to China. He reckoned 25 000 Spanish dollars worth of pearls, and 70 000 of pearl shell, were sold in Sulu every year for the China market (Crawfurd 1820, vol. III, p. 415). But in his later 1856 *Descriptive Dictionary*, Crawfurd described the whole eastern coast of Aru as being 'rich in the shell-tortoise, two kinds of mother-of-pearl shells, and in pearl oysters, with the tripang'. Every year in the season there came '100 small square-rigged vessels and large native craft with Chinese junks', bringing rice, cloth and provisions in exchange for the sea produce and exotic birds (Crawfurd 1971, p. 24). What had happened in between was a movement south and east of Sama Bajau divers and scavengers from Sulu waters to Maluku and eventually Aru, driven in part by the greater opportunities of virgin fields, but perhaps also by the great increase of Iranun raiding in the latter part of the eighteenth century, which made the whole Sulu zone unsafe (Warren 1981, pp. 160–5; Andaya 1993, pp. 230–3).

Best known, of course, was the evocative description of Dobo in 1857 by the creator of the Wallace Line, naturalist Alfred Russell Wallace:

> Every house is a store, where the natives barter their produce for what they are most in need of. Knives, choppers, swords, guns, tobacco, gambier, plates, basins, handkerchiefs, sarongs, calicoes, and arrack, are the principal articles wanted by the natives; but some of the stores contain also tea, coffee, sugar, wine, biscuits, &c., for the supply of the traders; and others are full of fancy goods, china ornaments, looking-glasses, razors, umbrellas, pipes, and purses, which take the fancy of the wealthier natives. Every fine day mats are spread before the doors and the trepang is put out to dry, as well as sugar, salt, biscuit, tea, cloths, and other things that get injured by an excessively moist atmosphere. In the morning and evening, spruce Chinamen stroll about or chat at each other's doors, in blue trousers, white jacket, and a queue into which

red silk is plaited till it reaches almost to their heels. An old Bugis hadji regularly takes an evening stroll in all the dignity of flowing green silk robe and gay turban, followed by two small boys carrying his sirih and betel boxes...

I daresay there are now near five hundred people in Dobbo of various races, all met in this remote corner of the East, as they express it, 'to look for their fortune'; to get money any way they can. They are most of them people who have the very worst reputation for honesty as well as every other form of morality,—Chinese, Bugis, Ceramese, and half-caste Javanese, with a sprinkling of half-wild Papuans from Timor, Babber, and other islands, yet all goes on as yet very quietly. This motley, ignorant, bloodthirsty, thievish population live here without the shadow of a government, with no police, no courts, and no lawyers; yet they do not cut each other's throats, do not plunder each other day and night, do not fall into the anarchy such a state of things might be supposed to lead to. It is very extraordinary...Think of the thousands of lawyers and barristers whose whole lives are spent in telling us what the hundred Acts of Parliament mean, and one would be led to infer that if Dobbo has too little law, England has too much.

Here we may behold in its simplest form the genius of Commerce at the work of Civilization. Trade is the magic that keeps all at peace, and unites these discordant elements into a well-behaved community. All are traders, and know that peace and order are essential to successful trade, and thus a public opinion is created which puts down all lawlessness. (Wallace 1869)

By Wallace's time the trading interest in pearls and pearl shell had spread to the northwest Australian coast, though the existing literature on it appears all to be from the British/Australian side. At first Aboriginal divers were used, but in the 1870s Indonesians began to be recruited, providing the most important economic connection across the Great Divide. The first eight Indonesians were brought from Batavia to Shark Bay in the northwest in 1871, but immediately thereafter 44 'Malays' were brought in from Makassar by Francis Cadell. This rose quickly to almost 1000 in 1875, the year when Cadell's harsh treatment of his work force caused a scandal, the intervention of the Netherlands Indies Government, and the virtual collapse of this site for the industry. The centre of activity shifted to the Broome area, where diving suits were introduced and in consequence the preferred divers became those more familiar with the technology. Aboriginal divers disappeared, and Filipinos and Japanese became more numerous. Two of the Filipino (Visayan) divers, Francisco del Castillo and Candido Iban, were responsible for probably Australia's most important contribution to Southeast Asian history before 1942, by devoting much of their earnings in Broome, enhanced by a lottery win, to the underground Katipunan society of Bonifacio in 1895. This enabled the society to buy a printing press, on which it launched its revolutionary newspaper, *Kalayaan* (*Freedom*)—banned after the first issue. All these events are now sanctified in the historiography of the Philippine Revolution of 1896, in which for all its exploitation of Southeast Asian labour, the pearl fisheries of Broome can be said to have played their part (Zaide 1931).

Broome was by 1910 the largest pearling centre in the world, and its diving force included people from Timor, Makassar and Ambon as well as the Philippines and Japan. I believe further research into the earlier history of pearling would be rewarding, even more perhaps than in the case of trepang, to understand connections across the Arafura Sea. Better known, however, thanks to Campbell Macknight and his successors, is the trepang trade that developed in response to growing demand in China in the eighteenth century, mediated through Sulu and later Makassar. The active sea scavengers who collected it were most frequently Sama Bajau, it appears, though working closely with Bugis, Butonese and other traders with bigger ships and more access to capital. Matthew Flinders encountered them on the Australian coast, and understood that they had shifted their operations progressively further south, to the Aru Islands, Rote, Ashmore Reef and finally the northwest Australian coast towards the end of the eighteenth century. He describes the kind of accidental process that must often have happened in the past, whereby a boat was driven off course onto the coast. But whereas earlier accidental visitors could not get away soon enough, the Bajau sea scavengers found exactly what they were looking for, and came back for more (Flinders 1814, vol. II, p. 257, cited in Fox 2005).

Twentieth-century separations

The twentieth century, however, brought a distinct deepening of the Great Divide, as new concepts of exclusive sovereignty defined and enforced a national boundary along it. On the one hand, the Dutch succeeded in knitting their scattered island domain together with a network of shipping routes through their Royal Packet Line (KPM), which linked all their islands to each other but not to northern Australia. On the other hand, Australia began its history as a collective federal state with a burst of exclusive regulations forbidding or discriminating against any intrusion or recruitment from the north. The *Immigration Restriction Act* of 1901 put an end to the use of Indonesian labour for northern fisheries or Queensland plantations, and had many other negative effects on the normal relationships of neighbours.

Australia and Indonesia grew steadily further apart from each other, though closer to their respective imperial capitals on the opposite side of the world. Dutch and Malay languages, media and education systems, and Netherlands Indian currency, law and exchange networks spread throughout the eastern islands, tying them into the archipelagic political economy that would give birth to Indonesia. Their English/Irish/Australian equivalents did the same for the Australian continent, ensuring that the coastal northwest would become a peripheral frontier of Australia, not of the tropical archipelago. Although in some respects the economies of Indonesia and Australia should have been complementary, imperial preference as well as simple laziness and unfamiliarity ensured that interaction of any kind became minimal. In the 1930s (and perhaps indeed into the 1960s), both Indonesians and Australians knew far more about Europe than about each other.

The Pacific War: Encounter without preparation

It was the rise of a threatening Japan that shook the whole colonial order in eastern Asia, including the back-to-back non-relationship between Australia and Indonesia. One early consequence of the rising tension had already occurred in 1934, when a trade delegation sailed from Sydney to Batavia, leading to the appointment of Australia's first trade commissioner in Batavia (Jakarta) the following year. The journalist Richard Moorehead was aboard and published a book about this 'goodwill' voyage (Moorehead 1934). The delegation also visited Makassar, and Moorehead must have been particularly struck by its exoticism, mystery (in the sense of widespread ignorance) and perhaps by the puzzlingly dynamic but hierarchic nature of South Sulawesi society. He subsequently wrote what I presume was the first Australian novel about it, an appalling boy's own adventure about a swashbuckling Australian hero who meets a mysterious but thoroughly 'white' woman among the Torajan death-statues (*tau-tau*). *The Mists of Macassar* was published only in 1946, when perhaps its relevance to the hundreds of diggers in Sulawesi was thought to compensate for its dreadful racial fantasies (Moorehead 1946).

As war approached in Europe, and particularly once Hitler occupied the Netherlands (May 1940), Indonesia and Australia were obliged to pay more attention to each other in strategic terms. By 1939, 5 per cent of Indonesia's trade was with Australia, and 14 per cent of the small numbers of Bali tourists were Australians (Reid 1995, p. 4). Nevertheless, the military connections that began at the end of 1940 came in a relative vacuum. Once Holland had fallen Australian assistance looked essential to Netherlands Indies strategists, though they did not want to look weak before their Indonesian subjects by admitting it publicly. It was agreed secretly that Australians would reinforce Timor, Ambon and Java as soon as war came to the Pacific. Preparations were also made secretly, and the men were on their way within a week of Pearl Harbor in December 1941, without any chance for education about where they were headed. About 1100 Australians went to Ambon, where most died in a heroic defence of the strategic port and airport against the Japanese in February 1942. Another 1400 landed in Timor, where the majority were killed or captured in February, though 400 held out in the interior with the support of the local population until they could be taken off by ship. About 3000 were sent to Java where most were taken prisoner at the Dutch surrender. Their memories, therefore, may have been more of cruel Japanese prison guards and ineffective Dutch allies than of Indonesians.

At the end of the war on 14 August 1945, what was at stake was no longer the defence of a colonial system but its restoration under radically changed conditions. The unexpectedly sudden Japanese surrender, following two horrendous nuclear bombs, found newly liberated Holland in no position to take charge. Its Netherlands Indies Government was based in Australia, and having increasing difficulty controlling its Indonesian employees, let alone the political prisoners evacuated to Australia from internal exile in Digul (Papua) and long since freed under Australian union pressure. A popular nationalist movement had been encouraged and publicised by the Japanese during their last desperate year of occupation, and it declared Indonesian independence on 17 August.

At the surrender, Australia already had 50 000 men on the soil of Kalimantan (Indonesian Borneo) and East Indonesia, after its massive bombardment and invasion of the oil towns of Tarakan (May 1945) and Balikpapan (July 1945). As a member of the victorious Allied Forces with specific East Indonesian responsibilities, Australia had a potentially decisive role in the post-war order. Would Allied commitments to restore the prewar (colonial) legal order be honoured, or would the democratic values for which the war had nominally been fought be held to apply also to the Asian colonies?

Fortunately, the story best remembered both in Australia and in Indonesia is that memorably immortalised in the film *Indonesia Calling*, chronicling the activity of independence activists among the Indonesians in Australia, and the support for them in the Australian Communist Party, the unions and to a lesser extent the postwar Labor government. Through these means, Indonesia and Australia became sympathetically aware of each other for the first time, and a small but idealistic cohort of young Australians responded to the excitement of an embattled new nation. The story has been well told in the books of activists of the time, including Rupert Lockwood (1975) and Molly Bondan (1992), as well as academic Margaret George (1980).

Figure 3.1 **Australian military occupation of Borneo and East Indonesia, 1945–46**

Source: ANU Cartography Unit

The largest-scale encounter of the two peoples was of a quite different kind, however, as tens of thousands of young Australians suddenly found themselves as occupying troops responsible for a population of east Indonesians in excess of Australia's. That occupation was woefully under-prepared. For the most part, Australian political and military leadership had accepted colonial-era assumptions that expertise in dealing with 'native populations' belonged with the colonial regimes, and that difficult postwar problems would be left to Britain and the Netherlands to sort out. There was resistance to colonial arrogance on the part of Australia's mercurial foreign minister H. V. (Doc) Evatt and some of the young intellectuals thrown into positions of influence at the end of the war, but insofar as this had practical planning results it was chiefly at the expense of the British. Alf Conlon had established a 'Directorate of Research' within the wartime government early in 1945, and this spawned a 'British Borneo Civil affairs Unit' on 30 April of that year, as planning was under way for the Australian occupation of Sarawak and Sabah. The *Borneo Book for Servicemen* was prepared to assist the occupying troops. It contained only four paragraphs on the Dutch East Indies, which briefly summarised the prewar colonial structure but never mentioned nationalism or the strange word 'Indonesia'. The most useful advice was contained in the words: 'The native, whether Mohammedan, Pagan or Christian, has no reason to love the white man any more than he does the Jap. If he gets a better deal from the Jap than he does from you—well, what then?' (AMF 1945, p. 23).

This was at least an improvement on the advice contained in the only previous guidance offered, in the few hundred copies of a simple Malay vocabulary prepared in 1944 for Royal Australian Air Force (RAAF) personnel shot down in Indonesia/Malaysia. This began with four pages of racial stereotypes deriving from some old hand from colonial Malaya—namely, that the Malays were 'an easy-going and rather lazy race', but would 'in most cases show respect for, and willingly assist the white man' (cited in Reid 1990, p. 33).

Despite widespread irritation with Dutch officials on the ground, not even Conlon's group appeared to have the confidence that they could replace Dutch expertise on Indonesia. The Australian military had been accustomed to operating under General Douglas McArthur's Southwest Pacific Command. When suddenly entrusted by McArthur in August 1945 with the task of taking the Japanese surrender and restoring prewar Dutch rule in Borneo and eastern Indonesia, they received no instructions from Canberra that might have nuanced this. Their ignorance of that prewar order was in general a grave handicap, but could also be an asset in imaginative hands. There were plenty of cases where diggers were required to protect and enforce the early Dutch steps to reclaim authority, while protesting nationalists were shot by Australian troops. Whereas in Sumatra and Java the responsible British forces under Mountbatten felt obliged to remain neutral between the Dutch and the newly proclaimed Indonesian Republic, the Australians did fulfil the task assigned them of restoring Dutch authority throughout Borneo and eastern Indonesia. The main test for the Australians was South Sulawesi, where there was an active independence movement comparable with that in Java and Sumatra. After some hesitation under the initial commander, Ivan Dougherty, a new commander from October forced the local rajas to accept the Netherlands Indies Civil Administration (NICA) and arrested the Indonesian-appointed Governor of Sulawesi, Dr Ratulangie (Reid 1986, 1990).

Despite this, Australians were relatively well remembered in the region. Part of the reason is the national-level story of Australian support for the Republic, and part the obvious fact that Australians arrived well supplied with goodies after a time of terrible hardship, and made it obvious they did not want to stay but to get home as soon as possible. But there was also the extraordinary role of some individual young men who sympathised with the Indonesians either passively or actively. Most active were the handful of members of the Australian Communist Party, largely concentrated in the Army Education Unit, who managed to smuggle in pro-independence pamphlets prepared by the Indonesian committee in Melbourne, and distribute them to surprised Indonesians in the occupied cities of Kalimantan. The principal Indonesian chronicler of the independence movement in Kalimantan's largest city, Banjarmasin, noted what a powerful impact these had. 'People were overjoyed and thought that these pamphlets were officially authorised by Australia, since they were distributed by members of its military' (Basry 1962, p. 17). One member of this group was impressed enough by the independence movement to volunteer to serve in Makassar, where he knew the movement was strongest. This was John Cohen, Jewish and German-born, who became almost a disciple of the nationalist leader Ratulangie. They shared the German language (Ratulangie had his doctorate from Zurich) and passionate interests in both politics and culture. Cohen was one of the few who had the openness and the intellectual equipment to respond enthusiastically to the eastern Indonesia he encountered (Reid 1990, p. 38).

The war brought Indonesians to Australia, and Australians to Indonesia, crossing the Great Divide in their tens of thousands for the first time. Much was learned on both sides, but it was too early to break down barriers. White Australia was still enforced, and even the couples who married across the Divide could not live in Australia. Much progress has been made since, but the Great Divide remains, now more heavily policed than ever, waiting for more constructive bridges to be built.

References

Andaya, L. (1993) *The World of Maluku*, Honolulu: University of Hawai'i Press.

Australian Military Forces (AMF) (1945) *The Borneo Book for Servicemen*, Australia.

Basry, H. (1962) *Kisah Gerila Kalimantan*, Banjarmasin.

Blong, R. J. (1982) *The Time of Darkness: Local legends and volcanic reality in Papua New Guinea*, Canberra: ANU Press.

Bondan, M. (1992) *Spanning A Revolution: The story of Mohamad Bondan and the Indonesian nationalist movement*, Jakarta: Penerbit Sinar Harapan.

Coolhaas, W. Ph. (ed.) (1960) *Generale Missiven van Gouverneurs-Generaal en Raden aan Heren XVII der Verenigde Oostindische Compagnie*. Volume I, The Hague: Nijhoff.

Crawfurd, J. (1820) *History of the Indian Archipelago*, [3 vols], Edinburgh: Constable.

Crawfurd, J. (1971 [1856]) *A Descriptive Dictionary of the Indian Islands and Adjacent Countries*, Kuala Lumpur: Oxford University Press.

Fox, J. J. (2005) 'In a single generation: a lament for the forests and seas of Indonesia', in P. Boomgaard, D. Henley and M. Osseweijer (eds), *Muddied Waters: Historical and contemporary perspectives on management of forests and fisheries in island Southeast Asia*, Leiden: KITLV Press, pp. 43–60.

George, M. (1980) *Australia and the Indonesian Revolution*, Melbourne: Melbourne University Press.

Knaap, G. J. (1987) *Kruidnagelen en Christenen: De Verenigde Oost-Indische Compagnie en de Bevolking van Ambon 1656–1696*, Dordrecht: Foris for KITLV.

Knaap, G. J. and H. Sutherland (2004) *Monsoon Traders: Ships, skippers and commodities in eighteenth-century Makassar*, Leiden: KITLV Press.

Dampier, W. (1981 [1729]) *A Voyage to New Holland*, (J. Spencer ed.), Gloucester: Alan Sutton.

Lockwood, R. (1975) *Black Armada*, Sydney South: Australasian Book Society.

Moorehead, R. J. (1934) *The Cruise of the Goodwill Ship*, Melbourne: Ruskin Press.

Moorehead, R. J. (1946) *The Mists of Macassar*, Melbourne: National Press Club.

Oppenheimer, S. (1999) *Eden in the East*, Phoenix, Ariz.: Orion.

Reid, A. (1986) 'Australia's hundred days in South Sulawesi', in *Nineteenth and Twentieth Century Indonesia: Essays in honour of Professor J. D. Legge*, Melbourne: Monash Centre for Southeast Asian Studies, pp. 201–24.

Reid, A. (1990) 'The Australian discovery of Indonesia, 1945', *Journal of the Australian War Memorial*, 17 (October), pp. 30–40.

Reid, A. (1995) 'Australia and Indonesia's Struggle for Independence', in A. Reid and M. O'Hare *Australia and Indonesia's Struggle for Independence*, Jakarta: Gramedia, 1995.

Wallace, A. R. (1869) *The Malay Archipelago*, London: Harper.

Warren, J. (1981) *The Sulu Zone, 1768–1898: The dynamics of external trade, slavery, and ethnicity in the transformation of a Southeast Asian maritime state*, Singapore: Singapore University Press.

Zaide, G. F. (1931) *Documentary History of the Katipunan Discovery*, Manila: Gregorio Zaide.

4. Histories with traction: Macassan contact in the framework of Muslim Australian history

Regina Ganter

Introduction

Australia's pre-British contact with the Indonesian archipelago is one of the most intriguing chapters of Australian history.[1] These early Indonesian visitors, long referred to in the introductory byline of standard Australian histories as 'Macassans', once came and went without a trace. But they have now become a staple part of the Australian story, no longer considered incidental and inconsequential.

The pockets of awareness of the histories of 'Afghans', 'Macassans' and 'Malays' in Australia—none of which is a strictly ethnic appellation—have been forged into a cohesive historical narrative by the 'War on Terror', which redefined all of these groups by the religion they held in common. They have now become interesting historical subjects and in the past 10 years Australia's major cultural institutions have engaged with these histories. They have now become well entrenched in the Australian historical narrative and they have become useful histories for a range of socio-political purposes in Australia. The 'Macassan' history now has political traction.

Muslim organisations in Australia have long grasped the importance of remembering the long genealogy of Muslim contact in Australia, which began with the Macassans. Many of their publications referred to the Macassan trepangers and the later Afghan cameleers as the historical anchors of their presence in Australia. Rather than emphasise conflict and disempowerment—as white-authored histories of ethnic minorities have tended to—they underlined the long and predominantly harmonious accommodations with white and black Australia. Indigenous people, too, have shown a palpable sense of engagement with their mixed histories with Asian, Pacific and Muslim people, as I discovered during my fieldwork in northern Australia between 1986 and 1996. This is particularly the case with Macassan contact history, which anthropologists and

---

[1] Thank you to Campbell Macknight and an anonymous reviewer for incisive comments on an earlier version of this chapter.

archaeologists had started to recover. The Macassan contact history was also used by Yolngu people as a paradigm of accommodative rather than conflictive ethnic relations.

Muslims in Australian public history

The groundwork for a reappraisal had been laid during the 1980s, a decade of historical introspection, with large and well-funded nationwide history projects leading up to the bicentennial celebrations in 1988. The history profession was determined not to write 'history as usual', but to undertake a bottom-up approach, where ordinary lives mattered and cultural diversity was celebrated. This created an impulse to write Asians back into Australian history, including a series of books and films on Afghans in Australia.

Australian institutions started to become more interested in such histories, responding to new waves of migrants and emerging signs of ethnic tension. Museum Victoria sponsored a collection of essays on Muslims in Australia in 1992, which pointed out that one-third of all Muslims in Australia were born in the country, and the Australian Government Publishing Service published a survey of Muslim settlement in Australia in 1994 (Jones 1992).

The War on Terror, declared in 2001, sparked a redesignation of ethnic groups according to religion and reignited an interest in historiographies of Muslim presence. Some Muslim organisations have drawn on their own historians to rework the history of Islam in their State. The Islamic Council for Victoria published a history of Muslims in Australia by Bilal Cleland of the Australian Federation of Islamic Councils in 2003, which forms the basis for the comprehensive historical treatment in the Islam Australia network and the Islamic Council of New South Wales (Cleland 2003). In 2007 Almir Colan premiered his documentary *Muslims in Australia Since the 1600s*, accompanied by a web site. Queensland has had its own Muslim Historical Society since 2008, and in May 2010 an Islamic Museum of Australia was initiated in Melbourne. This will certainly bring together what have long appeared as disparate themes in Australian historiography into a history of Muslim presence, including Macassan, Malay, Afghan and later ethnic enclaves.

The *Wikipedia* entry on Islam in Australia, begun in May 2005, tackles the old popular conception straight on:

> Although Islam's presence in Australia is often perceived to be recent by Australian non-Muslims, adherents of Islam from what is today Indonesia had in fact been visiting the Great southern land prior to colonial era settlement of European Christians. For several centuries these Muslims

had traded with coastal Aboriginal peoples of the north. The common misconception among Australian non-Muslims that Islam is new to Australia is due mostly to knowledge of Islam and Muslims limited only to the recent migratory waves. (*Wikipedia*, 'Islam in Australia')

Now part of a narrative on Muslims in Australia, as a defensive strategy against the xenophobia directed at Muslims in Australia since 2001, the Macassan contact history has moved from the margin to the core of Australian historical understanding. During Kevin Rudd's prime ministership, the Department of Foreign Affairs and Trade web site had an elegant diplomatic pointer to a shift in attitude since the demise of the Howard government, with this lead paragraph in English and Indonesian: 'Muslims in Australia have a long and varied history that is thought to pre-date European settlement. Some of Australia's earliest visitors were Muslim, from the east Indonesian archipelago. They made contact with mainland Australia as early as the 16th and 17th centuries' (DFAT n.d.).

Australia's major institutions have made reference to Muslim histories of Australia, and many of them have started to include the Macassan history in this perspective. The National Gallery of Australia's *Crescent Moon* exhibition in 2006 on Islamic art in Southeast Asia included the Macassan traders in northern Australia. The National Museum of Australia added the Macassan contact history to its permanent *Australian Journeys* exhibition in 2008 and in 2011 Museum Victoria produced the *Trepang* exhibition and book (Langton et al. 2011).

For the most part, these histories are potted accounts that are general enough to be uncontroversial. But the details of the story are highly contested and any agreement is hard won by specialists. Most effort has been spent on debating the question of dates, particularly the question of first contact, in order to gauge how long the Indigenous people in the Macassan contact zone were exposed to foreign cultural influences. The topic of a Muslim legacy on Indigenous cosmology has always been treated with some circumspection. First, this is because Indigenous people are protective of their intellectual property and can use the full gamut of options from non-disclosure to legal proceedings. I have myself deleted certain things from my book drafts after consulting with my informants. Second, there is a degree of uncertainty over what portion of the 'Macassans' were Muslim, and to what degree they themselves were indigenous people of the islands with pagan beliefs, customs and rituals.

Islam and Indigenous cosmology

According to current knowledge, and following Macknight, the trepang trade to the north coast reached the Kimberley in the 1750s and Arnhem Land in 1780. It was in full swing around 1800, always just a few paces ahead of the British assault on the southern part of the continent.

Islam, having reached the Malay Archipelago remarkably early in the seventh century, progressed slowly and gradually, but gained pace in the sixteenth century, when the Portuguese competed for social dominance in the region. McIntosh notes that, like elsewhere on the globe, in the archipelago religious conversion was an important goal for Muslim traders in their commercial colonisation. The Kingdom of Gowa, with Makassar as its centre, formally embraced Islam in 1603–05, and by the end of that century there was little trace of an indigenous creed. It is assumed that the fishers who visited northern Australia in the eighteenth and nineteenth centuries were therefore predominantly Muslim (Tjandrasasmita 1978, cited by MacIntosh 1996a). The 'outward signs of conversion' were circumcision and the adoption of Arabic names such as Hussein.

As a result of this longstanding contact, Yolngu languages are tinted with Malay, Bugis and Makassarese inflections much like English is inflected with French, and in both cases this is more obvious to the non-native speaker who is familiar with the foreign language. The extent of the suffusion of Muslim elements into the traditional Yolngu culture of northeast Arnhem Land has been subject to some speculation. Even before the British colonisation of the Australian continent, the British East India Company hydrographer Alexander Dalrymple reported in 1762 that the Aborigines of New Holland visited by the trepang fleets were 'Mahometans'. Macknight thinks this impression may have arisen from the practice of circumcision among Yolngu and it was evidently an overstatement. But there is a remnant vocabulary in Yolngu rituals that is derived from Muslim prayer, and it has long been observed that their most important religious ceremonies are strongly inflected with Macassan influences. 'Macassan'—or rather a mixture of the trade languages of Malay, Bugis and Makassarese—was once a lingua franca to interact with outsiders, and continues to be used by ceremonial leaders, much like the Catholic Church held on to Latin longer than other learned circles, and a familiarity with that foreign language continues to be a mark of prestige and learning. With the arrival of Christian missions in the mid-twentieth century the Muslim allusions in Yolngu mythology were downplayed and often went unexplained. This may be why the Macassan connections appear so difficult to tease out of recorded statements. Ian McIntosh (2009) argues that a strategic decision was taken by Yolngu elders under pressure of rapid changes in the mid century to downplay some aspects of their cosmology (turning them inside) and allow others to be publicised (turning them outside). We appear to be left with shreds of evidence.

In the Manikay song-cycle genre of Yolngu songs, ethnomusicologist Peter Toner detects traces of classical Arabic religious music (Toner 2000). Yolngu singers improvise with sacred texts, and icons of Macassan contact like ships, anchors, swords and flags are among the important symbols. According to descriptions by Yolngu elders, prayer-men (or *imam*) accompanied the Macassan trepang fleets. These were the ceremonial leaders, a role referred to as 'sick-man' (*buwagerul*) in the Yolngumatha language of northeast Arnhem Land. One of them is still remembered by name as Deingaru, also known as Baleidjaka.[2] David Burrumarra remembered in the 1980s with amazing detail how an *imam* or 'sick-man' would climb to the top of the mast to chant when the fleet departed, and pray at sunset, resounding an '*ama!*' towards the setting sun, then bow his head to the ground and exclaim '*walata'walata!*' (McIntosh 1996a, p. 7).

The same term, '*Walitha'walitha*',[3] is also the name of the creation spirit, sometimes translated as 'the most high God' or Allah. We need to keep in mind that the people who recorded these stories did not speak Arabic or Malay or Makassarese, and did not always distinguish between these different languages embedded in accounts rendered in Yolngumatha or Kriol, so we are faced with phonetic approximations. The *Walitha'walitha* creation spirit belongs to the *Wuramu* song cycle of northeast Arnhem Land, which is a mourning ritual that Yolngu say they 'share with Macassans'. In this ceremony the words 'Oooo-a-hal-la' and 'A-ha-la' are exclaimed, and it contains appeals to the god in the heavens. These were transcribed as: 'si-li-la-mo-ha-mo, ha-mo-sil-li-li' and 'ra-bin-a-la la-ha-ma-ha-ma', and ending with 'Se-ri ma-kas-si' (McIntosh 1996b; Macknight 2011). The similar-sounding '*terima kasih*' means 'thank you' in Malay (and Indonesian).

The carved *Wuramu* figures usually depict a figure with a *songkok* (Muslim cap). Sometimes this cap is quite elongated, showing an earlier fashion. Historically this song cycle derives from an incident of a ritual performed by Macassans at Cape Wilberforce, reportedly for the burial of a group of Aborigines; however, its meaning has been reworked to blend Yolngu beliefs and Macassan rituals, and there are multiple layers of meaning attached to the *Wuramu* figure, so that each explanation is only partial. The ritual extends over several days, containing imagery reminiscent of exchanges with Macassans, such as a flag dance, a knife dance, a boxing dance, a smoking dance, an alcohol dance (where

---

2 It is a feature of many contact stories that the protagonist has both a Macassan and a Yolngu name, expressing relatedness and family connections to both sides.

3 I take '*Walitha'walitha*' to be the same as '*walata'walata*' in the line above, a difference that may arise from different phonetic conventions, just like the difference between Arrernte and Arunda, for example.

dancers feigning to be intoxicated try to wrestle and dance at the same time), a *lunggurrma* dance (referring to the northeast monsoon wind associated with the arrival of the trepang fleets) as well as storytelling elements brought back from Yolngu who had spent time in Makassar, such as reminiscences of rice paddies, shipbuilding and lily ponds (McIntosh 1996b).

McIntosh emphasises that Yolngu never embraced Islam as a faith; rather, they incorporated elements of what they observed from their Indonesian visitors into their own cosmology. It is tempting, however, to speculate where this development might have led theologically had not the British begun to conquer the same territory at the turn of the nineteenth century, ousted the Muslim visitors and introduced Christian missions. Evicting the Macassan trepang fleets in 1906 was a last-ditch attempt to claim a thriving trading opportunity with China for the European colonisers. It was just a few years before the Commonwealth took over the Northern Territory in 1911, after the anticipation of riches in the untapped north had dissipated into a string of disappointments. The competing claims are reflected in a duality of names for many sites: Ashmore Reef is known by Indonesians as Pulau Pasir, likewise Scott Reef is Pulau Datu and Cartier Reef is Pulau Baru. In the Yolngu territories, apart from Indigenous names for places, there are Lembana Panrea for Melville Bay, Tarrusanga for Bowen Strait, Lemba Moutiaria for Port Essington and Lemba Binangaja for Trepang Bay. In some cases Yolngu even accepted Macassan terms for sites, such as Gunyangarra for Ski Beach at Yirrkala, which derives from Kodingareng Lompo, the name of an island in the Spermonde Archipelago, offshore from Makassar (see Clark, this volume; Ganter 2006; Macknight 1976b).

At the turn of the twentieth century there were Yolngu people who were circumcised, polygamous, well-travelled, enmeshed in transnational trade and family relationships, who spoke using vocabulary used by the Macassans and carried Macassan names. The Yolngu had made room for Muslim ceremony in their own rituals and appear to have been on a path of natural, unforced conversion when the Christian missionaries arrived.

Since the mid 1980s, just as the last eyewitnesses were passing away, the Macassan contact stories have undergone a revival and mutual visits have recommenced. This is precisely what happened 10 years later in white Australia with the revival of the Anzac legend, which focused on the story of the disastrous Australian landing at Gallipoli, Turkey, during World War I. With the passing of the World War I veterans, the Anzac 'legend' transformed for the majority of Australians from being a story owned and enacted by old men to being a story about real places ready to be explored by a younger generation who were starting to travel overseas. With the participation of Turkish officials, Australian ceremonies were being held on Turkish soil.

Muslim history as empowerment

A revival of the Yolngu–Macassan contact history emerged in the 1980s in the wake of the 1976 *Northern Territory Land Rights Act*, which led the way in Australia to a national recognition of Indigenous rights over country and the statutory recognition of land councils. A strong sense of ownership emerged among Indigenous people in the Northern Territory, over their country, over their languages, over their histories. The Milingimbi Literature Centre recorded and published stories in Yolngumatha, among them stories of Macassan contact (Djawawungu 1979; Bopaniwungu 1988). In 1985 the first Barunga festival took place, facilitating an exchange of traditions and stories, art and culture, and in 1986 the highly respected Yolngu elder Wandjuk Marika recorded the story of Djaladjari, a Yolngu man who had been to Makassar several times, for a group of young Yolngu students at Batchelor College planning to visit Makassar.

The last phase of Macassan–Yolngu contact was still accessible to oral history when Campbell Macknight and Peter Spillett were conducting fieldwork in the 1960s and 1970s. Macknight, working under the supervision of the iconic Professor John Mulvaney, began to rediscover some of the names of Indonesian captains in the customs records, and matched them with names remembered in various stories told by Yolngu. He made contact with the family of Husein Daeng Rangka in Makassar, who was the last of the captains who came to Australia and whose career is practically reflected in the Australian customs records. A 1981 issue of *Aboriginal History* contained two important essays on the Macassan influence in the Yolngu languages, reflecting linguistic work then being undertaken (Urry and Walsh 1981; Walker and Zorc 1981).

Husein Daeng Rangka and members of his family appear in a range of Yolngu stories, though with different spellings, sometimes difficult to recognise. The Arabic name Husein becomes 'Using' or 'Oesing' in Indonesian. The 'Daeng' in his name devolves from an old honorific title from the ancient Kingdom of Gowa on Sulawesi and is widespread in Makassar (Macknight 1976b). It was also devolved to some of their Aboriginal relatives and trading partners in Australia where it appears as the prefix 'Dayn' in Yolngu names. Husein Daeng Rangka had at least two Aboriginal wives (Macknight 1976a). He is also reported to have abducted a wife of Ganimbirrngu, who was the leader at Melville Bay (Lembana Panrea in Yolngu territory). The Macassans referred to the latter as the 'raja of Melville Bay', and Husein Daeng Rangka bestowed on him the name of Dayngmangu (Macknight 1976b, p. 84). This was the father of David Burrumarra, informant for most researchers conducting fieldwork there until the 1980s. The family connections are closely woven.

Peter Spillett from the Northern Territory Museum instigated a bicentennial project to reconstruct a traditionally crafted *perahu padewakang*, the type of boat used in the trepang trade, to sail once more from Makassar to the Top End of Australia, known by the Macassans as Marege'. He accompanied the Batchelor College students on a visit to Makassar in 1986, at which time it was called Ujung Pandang. They were amazed at the similarity in language, expressions and names they encountered. They felt as if old legends were coming alive in front of them, to see the characteristic sails, men wearing the *songkok* caps, also known as *peci*, as well as all the iconography from the paintings at home. Based on discussions with several of these students, it was evident that they felt great amazement that the *Mangathara* (Yolngumatha for Macassans) of the old stories really existed (see also Spillett 1987). It was only a few years since the last of the known travellers to Australia had died, in 1978, Mangnellai Daeng Maro. As a boy of about ten, he had accompanied his father, Husein Daeng Rangka, to Australia.

The *Hati Marege* bicentennial project (see chapters by Macknight and McIntosh, this volume) caused a flurry of negative media reportage because the Northern Land Council had objected to the flying of the bicentennial flag on the prau, arguing that this history had nothing whatsoever to do with the bicentennial or the arrival of the British anywhere in Australia. The Indonesian and Australian diplomats involved were faced with the possibility of a hostile reception or a cancelled event. It became a tussle about who owns this history. The *Hati Marege* sailed into Yirrkala precisely 200 years after the First Fleet reached Botany Bay (16 January 1988), captained by Mansjur Muhayang, a great-grandson of Husein Daeng Rangka. He handed over a bag of rice like in olden times, and was greeted by Matjuwi Burrawanga from Galiwin'ku at Elcho Island as a family member. This bicentennial project was understood as a family reunion, and was surely the single most successful bicentennial project. With it, the Yolngu people broke the isolation that had severed them from friends and relations in 1906.

This project and the personal encounters it entailed brought about an immense reinvigoration of interest in the Macassan connection among Yolngu and neighbouring Aboriginal people and set off a series of mutual visits. A Maningrida dance troupe led by artist John Bulunbulun took the *Marayarr Murrukundja*—a ceremony of diplomacy lasting three nights—to Sulawesi in 1993, and with this the Indonesian village news-trucks announced with blaring loudspeakers the arrival of the *'orang aborijin dari Australia utara'* (Aborigines from northern Australia) (Garde 1993). On the Indonesian side there was also much amazement at the rekindling of contact. Peter Spillett, the organiser of the bicentennial project, was given the honorific name *Daeng Makulle* ('Mister Capability', according to Jukes 2005, p. 278). Bulunbulun spotted an old ceramic storage pot in one of the shops exactly the shape that he had always included in his paintings, but he had never actually seen one. He brought it home and it became one of the first items in the Djomi museum, opened in 1996 at Maningrida, which celebrates the Macassan–Yolngu connection.

The next big collaborative project was a trepang opera scripted by theatre director Andrish Saint-Clare. In 1994 he showed films of Yolngu dances in Makassar to arouse interest, and in 1996 he brought Mansjur Muhayang (referred to as Yotjing, or Otjing, as the descendant of Husein Daeng Rangka) to Elcho Island, to perform in an opera, *The Trepang Project* (see Blair and Hall, this volume). The following year the opera was staged in Makassar, on the foundation day of the city of Makassar (Hari Jadi Gowa) celebrations in front of a 9000-strong audience. By then, it was by a performance team consisting of six actors and musicians from Sulawesi and 10 artists from Galiwin'ku, performing 'the story of Matjuwi and Otjing who are brothers through the marriage of their grandparents'. Two years later the opera was performed at the Festival of Darwin (16–19 September 1999), and the Australian Broadcasting Corporation (ABC) recorded it for video release in 2000. For the Centenary of Federation, the opera came to Federation Square in Melbourne in 2001. From the margins of history, it was moving to the central celebrations of the nation.

At the opening of the 2000 Sydney Olympics, too, the long history of Macassan contact was mentioned, by Ernie Dingo, though he claimed a wildly exaggerated history for it, perhaps following the lyrics of the Sunrize Band from Maningrida whose 1993 title *Lembana Mani Mani* suggests a 20 000-year history of contact. The Wirrnga band from Milingimbi produced *My Sweet Takirrina* in commemoration of the bicentennial project in 1990, and in 1998 the Yothu Yindi Foundation commenced the Garma Festival at Gulkula in east Arnhem Land, at which the Macassan history has always been represented. Yothu Yindi released their *Garma* album in 2000, containing a song with the title 'Macassan Crew'.

In dance, song and also in paintings, the Macassan history underwent a revival. In 1993 Bulunbulun was starting to collaborate with painter Zhou Xiaoping from Hebei, China, who had become artist-in-residence at Maningrida. Their collaboration was to result eventually in a Chinese book by Xiaoping and exhibitions in Beijing and Melbourne in 2011 (see Clark and May, this volume; Xiaoping 2006, some of which is republished in Langton et al. 2011). Bulunbulun's series of 25 paintings reflecting Macassan stories in the Yirrtitja song cycle, one of them in Darwin Airport, received national acclaim. He revealed the clan totem *Lunggurrma* (north wind) as a symbol of the seasonal arrival of the Macassans.

Yolngumatha does not make a distinction between British and Indonesian foreigners, referring to both as *'balanda'* (derived from Malay/Indonesian words referring to the Netherlands or the Dutch, *'Belanda'* or *'orang Belanda'* respectively). But Yolngu do distinguish between the effects of Macassan contact and British colonisation. There are ample indications of violent conflict in their myths and in the historical record, but the Macassan contact is now so long ago that there are no eyewitnesses left and it has become remembered as a period of trade and exchange without compulsion, in contradistinction with the British colonisation. The telling of the Macassan stories has become an act of resistance. It refuses to allow a government decision to sever the link to Makassar. It also asserts that Yolngu have long engaged in contact with outsiders without surrender or colonisation. In 1998 a group of Croker Island people lent on this history to support a sea claim, arguing that the Macassans had obtained prior permission for using the seas controlled by Yolngu, and that they negotiated payments-in-kind. The judge rejected the claim (Russell 2004).

Despite the negative legal decision outlined above, the Australian Government has also gained some mileage in the mixed histories of the north. In 2008 the Department of Foreign Affairs launched its IN2OZ program of cultural exchange with Indonesia, and sent among its cultural ambassadors to Indonesia two Indigenous women who have Asian ancestry: *Australian Idol* star Jessica Mauboy, Darwin daughter of an Indigenous mother and a Timorese father, and novelist Alexis Wright, with Mornington Island/Gulf of Carpentaria family roots. Such figures personify the poly-ethnic past in Australia where Asians and Muslims are not 'outsiders'.

Finally, the Australian historical imagination has begun to embrace the idea that Australian history starts well before the arrival of the British, and the Macassan contact chapter is being written into the script because it is no longer seen as inconsequential. It is a history that has traction for a range of purposes: Yolngu people draw cultural pride from their transnational history, Aboriginal organisations deploy their history of trade in mounting legal arguments about native title, Muslim organisations point to their long anchor in the historical presence in Australia, and diplomatic circles support cultural exchange and the celebration of shared histories with Australia for geo-strategic reasons in what the Australian Government now calls the 'Asian century'. Schoolteachers have started to fit the Macassan story into the national history curriculum, showing a more transnational Australia interacting with its nearest neighbours. There is much that remains to be discovered about this story, and our challenge is to get the details right without becoming too doctrinaire for a wide audience.

References

Bopaniwungu (1988) *Daewu Dhuwal Gpiyawuywainguwuy. Ga Mangatharrawainguwuy*, Roneo, Milingimbi Literature Centre, Milingimbi, NT.

Cleland, B. (2003) *The Muslims in Australia: A brief history*, Melbourne: Islamic Council for Victoria, <www.islam.iinet.net.au/channel/near_north.html> [viewed November 2011].

Colan, A. (2007) *Muslims in Australia Since the 1600s*, (VHS and About Documentary Film), <http://muslimsinaustralia.com/about/> [accessed November 2011].

Denoon, D., P. Mein-Smith with M. Wyndham (2000) *A History of Australia, New Zealand and the Pacific*, Oxford and Malden, Mass.: Blackwell.

Department of Foreign Affairs and Trade (DFAT) (n.d.) *Muslims in Australia*, Canberra: Department of Foreign Affairs and Trade, <http://www.dfat.gov.au/facts/muslims_in_australia_in.html> [accessed October 2011].

Djawawungu (1979) Dhae-Dhuditjpuy Mangatharra (The last visit of the Macassans), Roneo, Milingimbi Literature Centre, Milingimbi, NT.

Dunn, K. M., A. Kamp, W. S. Shaw, J. Forrest and Y. Paradies (2010) 'Indigenous Australians' attitudes towards multiculturalism, cultural diversity, "race" and racism', *Journal of Australian Indigenous Issues*, 13 (4), pp. 31–40.

Ganter, R. (2006) *Mixed Relations: Asian/Aboriginal contact in north Australia*, Perth: University of Western Australia Press.

Garde, M. (1993) *The Marayarr Murrkundja Ceremony Goes to Makassar*, Maningrida, NT: Bawinanga Aboriginal Corporation.

Jones, M. (ed.) (1992) *An Australian Pilgrimage: Muslims in Australia from the seventeenth century to the present*, Melbourne: Victoria Press in association with Museum of Victoria.

Jukes, A. (2005) 'Makassar', in K. Alexander Adelaar and N. Himmelmann (eds), *The Austronesian Languages of Asia and Madagaskar*, New York: Routledge, pp. 647–82.

Langton, M., A. Duschatzky and S. Holt (eds) (2011) *Trepang: China and the story of Macassan–Aboriginal trade*, Melbourne: Centre for Cultural Materials Conservation, Museum Victoria.

McIntosh, I. (1996a) Can we be equal in your eyes? A perspective on reconciliation from north-east Arnhem Land, Unpublished PhD thesis, Northern Territory University, Darwin.

McIntosh, I. (1996b) 'Islam and Australia's Aborigines? A perspective from north-east Arnhem Land', *Journal of Religious History*, 20 (1) (June), pp. 53–77.

McIntosh, I. (2009) 'Missing the revolution! Negotiating disclosure on the pre-Macassans (Bayini) in north-east Arnhem Land', in M. Thomas and M. Neale (eds), *Exploring the Legacy of the 1948 Arnhem Land Expedition*, Canberra: ANU E Press.

Macknight, C. C. (1976a) 'Husein Dg. Rangka', *Australian Dictionary of Biography. Volume 6*, Carlton, Vic.: Melbourne University Press.

Macknight, C. C. (1976b) *Voyage to Marege'*: *Macassan trepangers in northern Australia*, Carlton, Vic.: Melbourne University Press.

Macknight, C. C. (2011) 'The view from Marege': Australian knowledge of Makassar and the impact of the trepang industry across two centuries', *Aboriginal History*, 35, pp. 136–57.

Onnudottir, H., A. Possamai and B. S. Turner (2010) 'Islam: a new religious vehicle for Aboriginal self-empowerment in Australia?' *International Journal for the Study of NewReligions*, 1 (1), pp. 49–74.

Russell, D. (2004) 'Aboriginal–Makassan interactions in the eighteenth and nineteenth centuries in northern Australia and contemporary sea rights claims', *Australian Aboriginal Studies*, (1), pp. 3–17.

Spillett, P. (Daeng Makulle) (1987) Gotong Royong: Hubungan Makassar-Marege', Paper presented to the Second International Convention of the Indonesian Educational and Cultural Institute, Ujung Pandang, Indonesia, July.

Tjandrasasmita, U. (1978) 'The introduction of Islam and the growth of Moslem coastal cities in the Indonesian archipelago', in H. Soebadio and C. A. du Marchie (eds), *Dynamics of Indonesian History*, Amsterdam.

Toner, P. (2000) 'Ideology, influence and innovation: the impact of Macassan contact on Yolngu music', *Perfect Beat: The Pacific Journal of Research into Contemporary Music and Popular Culture*, 5 (1), pp. 22, 33–4.

Urry, J. and M. Walsh (1981) 'The lost "Macassar language" of northern Australia', *Aboriginal History*, 5 (2), pp. 91–108.

Walker, A. and R. D. Zorc (1981) 'Austronesian loanwords in Yolngu-Matha of northeast Arnhem Land', *Aboriginal History*, 5 (2), pp. 107–34.

Xiaoping, Z. (2006) *A Dream of Aboriginal Australia* [in Chinese, not translated].

5. Interpreting the Macassans: Language exchange in historical encounters

Paul Thomas

Introduction

The commencement of regular journeys by trepang fishing fleets out of Makassar to the Australian north coast in the second half of the eighteenth century represents the beginning of Asia's regular contact with Australia. The cyclical nature of the visits and the complexity of the engagement meant there was strong motivation for communication to take place, something that went beyond simple hand gestures and a smattering of borrowed words. For the first hundred years of these visits, this produced an exchange across the cultures and languages of Indonesians and Indigenous Australians. Subsequently, after the European discovery of the industry in 1803 and the desire to incorporate it into the colonial trading network, Europeans found they also needed to develop a capacity to freely converse with the trepangers.

This chapter focuses on the lives of three interpreters of Indonesian/Malay heritage who assumed the role of intermediaries between the Europeans and the trepangers during the nineteenth century. It is part of a broader history of communication between Australia and the Indonesian archipelago, which has ebbed and flowed through the decades but retained an inevitable trajectory towards a closer relationship. The fundamental questions of how Europeans initiated the communication, the motivation behind the exchanges, the influence of the languages chosen for the discourse, and the agency of the interpreters are examined within the context of the interpreters' biographies and Australia's relations with the archipelago at the time.

Most research on the industry to date has emphasised the significant cultural exchange between the Indonesians and Indigenous Australians and covers a broad range of topics including: the arts (Palmer 2007; Toner 2000); language (Evans 1997; Harris 1986); and religion (McIntosh 1996). In contrast, research on European Australian contact with the trepangers has been understandably narrower in focus, with an emphasis on the failed attempts at European settlements in northern Australia in the first half of the nineteenth century (see Reid 2007; Spillet 1972; Allen 2008); however, insights into European communication with the trepangers can be evidenced in Macknight's (1976) early pioneering work *The Voyage to Marege'*, biographical reviews of George Windsor Earl, the interpreter at Port Essington settlement (Reece 1992), and writing on Collet Barker, the Commandant at Fort Wellington (Mulvaney and Green 1992; Mulvaney 1994). The overall evolution of this research is further explored in Macknight's chapter in this volume.

For Indigenous Australians, the possibility of cultural exchange was made possible through the ability to communicate at both the mundane and the abstract levels. Trade, an understanding of traditional law and the exchange of labour were crucial elements pressing those involved in the discourse to establish a common language; however, while it was not uncommon in nineteenth-century reports to describe Aborigines in the north as having a facility to speak Malay, the extent to which this was widespread remains unclear. A more likely scenario is that only a few had a substantial knowledge of the language of the visitors. The most likely candidates were individuals who sailed back with the Macassan fleet and resided there for one or more seasons, or the women who had longer-term relationships with the trepangers in Australia. These individuals were potentially the key conduits of cultural and language influence: Australia's first interpreters.

In the case of European contact with the trepangers, the selection of individuals to perform the duty of interpreter is more apparent, albeit an inconsistent process and obscured by the broader context. Interpreters are generally marginal figures within historical narratives, briefly referred to when there is a need to provide evidence that communication across cultures has truly taken place (see Roland 1999). The motivation behind these references commonly relates to the need to legitimise an action, to add credibility to a report or to prove justice has been provided. On those occasions when an individual involved in interpreting is referenced more fully, their role may still be subsumed into their other vocational activities,[1] those acting exclusively as interpreters, even today, being the exception.

In order to provide greater context for the contact events with the trepangers, the three interpreters have been selected to reflect three distinct periods of the history: the European discovery of the industry; efforts to integrate the industry into the colonial economy; and finally, opposition to and eventual rejection of direct Indonesian involvement in the industry in the early twentieth century.

The three interpreters are from diverse backgrounds: Abraham Williams, a Javanese, who was working as a cook onboard Matthew Flinders' *Investigator*

---

1 'Natives', for example, are commonly recorded as guides or trackers, their interpreting role poorly revealed (Karttunen 1994). African slaves, granted the role of headman or teacher, often depended on their ability to act as interpreters to retain their positions (Fayer 2003).

in 1803; Oodeen, of Ambonese/Sri Lankan background, who was appointed Government Interpreter for Fort Wellington between 1826 and 1829; and Tingha de Hans, a Timorese who settled in the Bowen Straits, Northern Territory, in the late nineteenth century. Of the three interpreters only Oodeen identified himself vocationally as an interpreter, the other two being more representative of the majority of interpreters in Australia in the nineteenth century who were part of an ad-hoc process, serving an immediate need.

The significance of viewing these individuals in their roles as interpreters is best appreciated through the manner in which the role elevated them into agents of influence and witnesses of historical events. As active participants in these events, they were involved in both the negotiation of meaning and the flow of ideas. While the ephemeral nature of the interpreting activity may not lend itself to linguistic analysis, the effectiveness of the interpreting, the subjectivity and perspective of the interpreter can be gleaned through their biographies, their interactions with others, and the information that resulted from the interpreting events. In this process, the interpreters themselves become historical figures, humanising further the act of interpreting or translation (see Pym 1998).

As with most Indonesians/Malays in Australia in the nineteenth century, there are few or no personal papers or diaries from the individuals themselves. This study, therefore, relies on a variety of documents in which the interpreters are incidental to the main purpose of the writing. The lack of the direct voice of the interpreter is not uncommon when dealing with interpreting history, but it should not negate investigating them as historical figures (Delisle and Woodsworth 1995, p. 245). Essentially, the influences on the interpreters' lives, their distance from the more authoritative figures at the centre of the events, and the focus on the moment of interpreting have considerable potential to enhance our understanding of the play of communication that takes place.[2]

Flinders and Williams: interpreting first contact with the 'Malays'

When the British established the penal settlement at Port Jackson in New South Wales in 1788, they had no reason to believe there were outsiders other than themselves active on the continent. Neither Dutch nor British explorers had reported any activities beyond those of the Indigenous peoples. Flinders' discovery of Indonesian fishing praus off the north coast of Australia in February 1803 was, therefore, significant both from the perspective of the science of his

---

2 See Rundle (2011, p. 33) for a discussion on the relationship of translation history to historiography.

exploration and for the potential commercial implications, the British East India Company being a major sponsor of the expedition. The discovery, however, could only be fully assessed if Flinders was able to report in detail the nature and scope of the activity. With no knowledge of any the archipelago's languages himself, he was reliant on his cook, Williams, to act as interpreter.

Williams, also referred to as Abraham Williams,[3] has left little of his background to explore. There is no specific record of him joining the voyage, though Flinders' journal[4] accounts for one cook, Joseph Robinott, and two cook's mates being taken aboard in London. His journal[5] also describes Williams as being 'from the island of Java'; however, in his published account, he uses the more general term 'Malay' (Flinders 1814, p. 229). The term Javanese at the time could refer to someone from Batavia (Jakarta) in which case it would not be so much an ethnic identity as a geographical one. The Dutch also commonly referred to Indonesians in Sri Lanka or at the Cape of Good Hope as '*Javaansche*' (Javanese), and Flinders, or Williams, could have been following the more general Dutch use of the word.

The possibility of a connection with South Africa, in particular, needs to be considered as Flinders already had some contact with the Cape through his previous voyages. This was also the period of the first British occupation of the Cape, which started in 1795. If Williams was born or had lived for a time in the Cape, it would strengthen the case for him having a more effective understanding of English and Malay than most Javanese of the period. It would also provide some indication of the variety of Malay he used. In the eighteenth century, Malay had developed as the main medium of instruction at the *madaris* (Islamic schools) of the Cape, and it generally replaced the regional languages amongst the diverse Indonesian diaspora. It was also a lingua franca of some prestige for other Asiatic groups (Stell 2007, p. 92). During the first British occupation, Malay was retained by the community, but there was also a spread of the English language and culture amongst many of the inhabitants to the degree that the Dutch Commissary, De Mist, wrote in 1802 that it would be 'the work of years to transform the citizens of Cape Town once again into *Netherlanders*' (De Mist in McCormick 2002, p. 23).

While it is difficult to piece together Williams' background, his use as an interpreter at the crucial meetings between Flinders and the *nakhoda* (captains of the fishing praus) makes him highly relevant to the event. Between 17 and 18 February 1803, the meetings with the *nakhoda* and Flinders can be defined

---

3 'Abraham' was first used in a publication by Ingleton (1986), but he offers no primary source to verify it.
4 Matthew Flinders, 26 January 1801, *Journal on HMS 'Investigator'*, vol. 1, 1801–1802, Mitchell Library, State Library of New South Wales, Sydney, Australia [hereinafter ML]: MAV/FM3/763.
5 Matthew Flinders, 19 February 1803, *Journal on HMS 'Investigator'*, vol. 2, 1802–1803, ML: MAV/FM3/764.

within four interpreting events. The first occurred shortly after the sightings of the praus when Captain Flinders ordered an armed whaleboat out to meet them, fearing them to be 'piratical Ladrones'.[6] Flinders, however, makes no reference to Williams being aboard the whaleboat, nor does any other journal except for that of seamen Samuel Smith, who states: 'On Opening the Harbour we espied 6 Sail laying at an Anchor, which we supposed to be China Junks, but upon nearer Observation they Proov'd Malay Prows. Sent a Boat on Board of one of them with an Interpreter, & dropt our Anchr close to them' (Smith 1803 in Monteath 2002, p. 61).

This differs from Flinders' account, which suggests he only learnt that they were 'prows from Macassar' after the whaleboat returned. If the craft had been determined to be 'Malay' before the whaleboat had been sent out it is logical that Flinders would have sent Williams to interpret for his lieutenant. It would also explain how Flinders' lieutenant was able to communicate with the praus.

This first contact with the crew of the praus was a tense environment in which to interpret as there was a good deal of suspicion about each other's intent and both parties were armed. Flinders comments: 'Every motion in the whale boat, and in the vessel along-side which she was lying, was closely watched with our glasses' (Flinders 1814, p. 229). The first communication would have been further hampered by negotiations on which form of Malay to use and establishing the status of the speakers.

Having established peaceful relations, six Indonesian *nakhoda* came onboard the *Investigator*. Williams was then asked to interpret, which he did until sunset. The following morning, he was once again asked to interpret, this time accompanying Flinders with the botanist Robert Brown and the artist William Westall to the prau of Pu' Baso'. This was followed by another session onboard the *Investigator* with the six *nakhoda*. In each session, Flinders showed his 'desire to learn everything concerning these people' (Flinders 1814, p. 230), and he admits that his 'numberless questions' had delayed Pu' Baso''s departure by a day (Flinders 1814, p. 232).

For Williams this could only have been an exhausting experience. Hours of interpreting would have taxed an experienced interpreter, whether they were familiar with the variety of language being used or not. In Williams' case, he almost certainly would have needed to constantly adjust his Malay to the variety of Malay used by the *nakhoda*. With possibly no interpreting experience previously, the intensity of the sessions, the discrepancy in different cultural views and the specialist nature of the vocabulary all would have added to the burden.

---

[6] The term 'ladrones' (thieves) in this context was originally applied to rebellious Chinese by the Portuguese in Macao. The ladrones turned to piracy and were at their most menacing at the turn of the nineteenth century.

Another important factor influencing the interpreting events was the level of Malay of the *nakhoda*. Flinders' primary source of information was Pu' Baso' and Malay would not have been his first language. In this period, there were many in Makassar who had only a rudimentary knowledge of Malay, though those closer to the Court, which was a centre for translation from Malay (see Cummings 2009), and those who travelled widely, are much more likely to have a better grasp of the language. The *nakhoda*, particularly Pu' Baso', would have fitted into this latter category.

Remarkably, there is little mention by Flinders of any difficulties arising in the communication. The only critique comes from a short comment by Robert Brown, the expedition's botanist: 'Williams is but an indistinct interpreter' (Brown 1803 in Moore et al. 2001, p. 371). Brown had no knowledge of Malay himself, nor the process of interpreting, and so his critique would have been based mainly on the apparent flow of the conversation and the manner in which Williams conducted himself. This particular comment was related to some confusion over the use of the words '*timur laut*'[7] (northeast/seaward east) and the island of 'Timor', which was west of their position. While this may have kindled Brown's scepticism, it was not a problem of vocabulary. Rather, it suggests Williams was providing little explanation for his interpreting or simply was unaware of the geography involved.

Flinders' lack of critique, either in his log or in his published account, may suggest he was more tolerant of the process, but it also relates to the purpose of referencing Williams in the first place. Williams' position in Flinders' narrative was not as a key participant in the events, but as a tool by which he could validate the information in his report and to indicate that he had taken adequate care in its compilation.

We have no quotes from Williams himself and, therefore, know nothing directly about his response to the interpreting events or his relationship with Flinders, even though he was Flinders' personal cook. There is only the action of Williams, who upon the arrival of the *Investigator* in Timor absconded with 'a youth from Port Jackson' (Flinders 1814, p. 254). Flinders put some effort into tracking the men down and had the town searched, but with no result. Williams' value to the expedition must have risen considerably after the encounter with the trepangers, and his loss was clearly regretted. Perhaps the unreliability of his interpreter was a factor in Flinders himself deciding to learn Malay while under arrest on Mauritius.[8] His intention was to return to the eastern archipelago, but it was a journey he never made.

---

7   The position related to the present Tanimbar group of islands.
8   Matthew Flinders, *Journal*, 2 June 1810, ML: CY 227.

5. Interpreting the Macassans: Language exchange in historical encounters

The extensive information that was derived from Williams' interpreting proved to be substantially correct and formed the basis of European discussion on the topic for more than a century. It also provides a strong contrast with those encounters where there was no interpreter. Phillip Parker King, who followed Flinders in 1818 to further survey the north coast of Australia, knew he was likely to encounter Indonesians on his journey, but instead of taking a Malay interpreter he carried with him two translated letters, one in Malay and the other in Javanese (see Figures 5.1 and 5.2). The letters had been prepared for him to secure safe passage by Sir Thomas Raffles, who had been the lieutenant governor of Java some few years earlier.

Unfortunately, when King did encounter the Indonesian praus near the Bowen Straits, on the north coast in April 1818, they had only symbolic value. The prau's crew could not read the Jawi script in which the Malay letter was written (see Figure 5.1) or the Javanese script (see Figure 5.2) of the accompanying letter. Flinders' meeting with Pu' Baso' had shown that at least some of the fishers/traders were literate when Basso's son made notes during their meeting; however, they used the Bugis or Lontara script, a totally unrelated script.

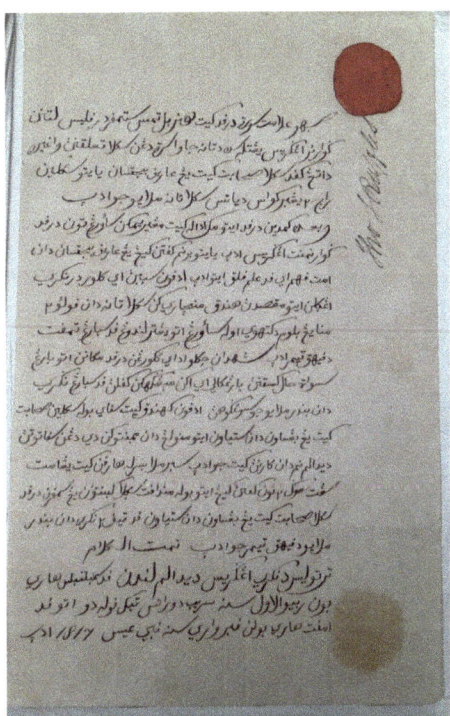

Figure 5.1 Letter of safe conduct written in Malay carried on the voyage of Phillip Parker King

Source: Dixson Library, State Library of New South Wales (DLMSQ 303)

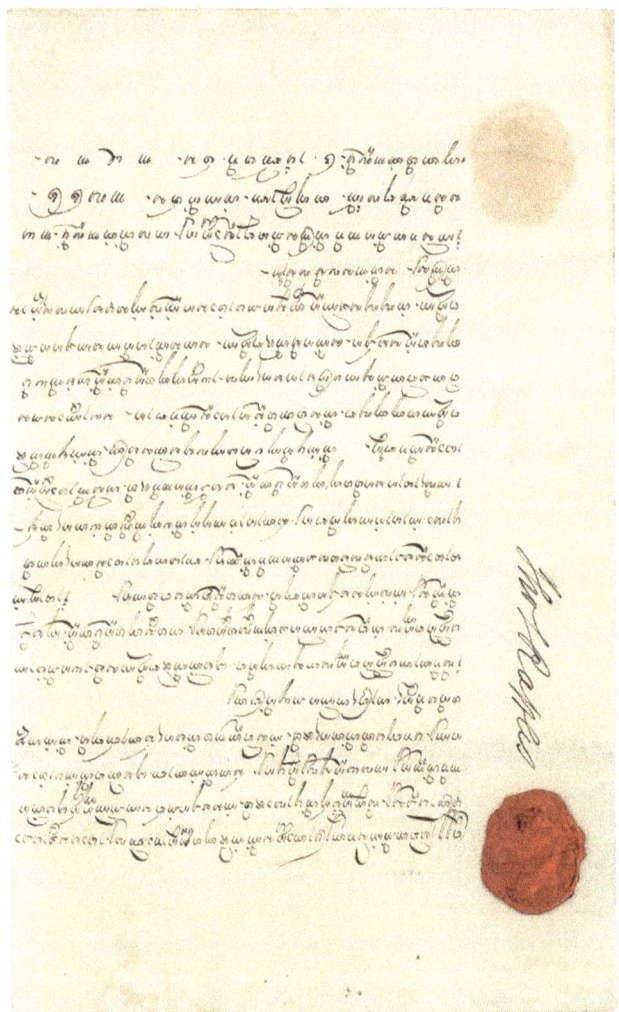

Figure 5.2 A version of the same letter in Javanese, also carried on the voyage

Source: Mitchell Library, State Library of New South Wales (MLMSS 6075)

The lack of knowledge by Europeans of the status of languages in the archipelago would persist throughout the nineteenth century and is emphasised by the comment of the botanist onboard King's ship, Allan Cunningham, who lamented that 'they were too illiterate to read their own language'.[9] Consequently, the additional information gathered by King was mainly through his meeting with the Dutch in Kupang rather than directly from the trepangers.

---

9   Allan Cunningham, *Journal*, 25 April 1818, State Records Office of New South Wales, Australia [hereinafter SRNSW], 6034.

Oodeen: Diplomacy and trade in the north[10]

The significance of the meeting between Flinders and the *nakhoda* became more apparent two decades after Flinders' circumnavigation, when the decision was made to settle northern Australia using the trepang fishing fleet as the catalyst for further trade. While the British signed a treaty with the Dutch in 1824 to delineate their claims on the archipelago, the north coast of Australia provided an opportunity to tap into the resources of the eastern archipelago and stave off any Dutch or French claims. There would be three successive attempts to establish a settlement and each settlement would take a different approach to communicating with the trepangers.

In the establishment of the first settlement at Fort Dundas on Melville Island in 1824 no provision for an interpreter was made; the Governor of New South Wales, Governor Brisbane, simply instructed the men of the garrison to 'learn their language, their customs, their usages, their institutions and pay a respect to them all'.[11] It is possible that there were some amongst the convicts and soldiers at the settlement who knew Malay, but as no trepangers ever called at the fort during its short life the language skills of its inhabitants were never tested.

In the second and third settlements, on the Cobourg Peninsula, an official government interpreter was appointed. At Fort Wellington, Oodeen,[12] a former drum major in the Malay regiment in Sri Lanka, took up his position in 1827. In the third settlement, at Port Essington, George Windsor Earl became Government Interpreter in 1838. Earl had originally migrated to the Swan River Settlement in Western Australia to farm (see Jones 1994), but with no success he eventually sailed to Batavia and en route began learning Malay (Reece 1992, p. 3). He would spend several years in the archipelago gaining knowledge of several Austronesian languages before returning to Australia.

Unlike Earl, Oodeen has received little attention to date, though in recent years he has become a topic of interest for the Malay and Sri Lankan communities as an early Muslim pioneer. Knowledge of Oodeen has spread mainly through the work of a sixth-generation descendent of Oodeen, Glennys Ferguson (2002), and several Sri Lankan newspaper accounts (see Saldin 2003; Jayamanne 2003). These accounts have primarily been concerned with his earlier life in the military in Sri Lanka and in the family's migration to Sydney.

---

10 For an expanded account of Oodeen's biography and interpreting on which this section is based, see Thomas (2012).
11 Gov. Thomas Brisbane, Government House, Parramatta, 14 August 1824, Colonial Secretary's papers, in SRNSW 6013; 4/3512.
12 Variations of Oodeen's name include John and William, as his first name, with Odeen, Odean and O'Dean examples of surname variants. This chapter uses 'Oodeen' based on primary sources from Fort Wellington, the period most relevant to this history, and as a clearer guide to the original pronunciation.

Figure 5.3 Glennys Ferguson of Sydney: sixth-generation descendent of Oodeen

Source: Paul Thomas

Oodeen arrived in Sydney in 1816, having survived frontline service with the Dutch Ambonese regiment, British Malay regiment and Kandyan armies. It was his defection to the Kandyans in 1803 that led to his eventual arrest and trial by the British in 1815 (Hough and Long 1825, p. 326). Oodeen was sentenced to death, but his sentence was commuted to transportation to New South Wales in respect of the wishes of the Sri Lankan Malay regiment whom the British were trying to develop into loyal troops (Thomas 2012, p. 127).

He arrived in Sydney with his wife, Eve, and their three children, a privilege not afforded to all convicts, but an additional concession made after the trial. The *Sydney Gazette* (17 February 1816, p. 1) described him as 'dark complexioned, approaching to a black, and is about 5 feet 10 inches in height' and as a man 'who appears to be intelligent'. It was emphasised that his wife was 'Singhalese, being a true descendant of the aboriginal inhabitants of the island'. In Sydney, Oodeen was given duties as a night watchman on the docks. He was quick to secure the trust of those he worked with to the extent that by 1818 he requested and was granted a ticket-of-leave, allowing him the freedom to apply for other positions.[13] It was at this time that the position of government interpreter at Fort Wellington was offered to him.

Oodeen's suitability for the position was relatively clear, as in addition to speaking Malay: he was literate, though it is unclear to what degree in English; he had experience serving with the British military; he was acclimatised to tropical postings; and he was familiar with other languages, most likely Sinhalese and Tamil, useful for a port that aimed at linking Australia, the Malay/Indonesian Archipelago and India. Another aspect that would have made Oodeen an attractive choice was his religion. Flinders had remarked that the trepangers were 'Mohammadeans' and Oodeen's presence had the potential to demonstrate British tolerance to the Muslim traders from Makassar. In the opening of any interpreting event, it would have also allowed Oodeen to at least greet the *nakhoda* with the universal Islamic greeting, thus providing some initial familiarity before negotiating the form of Malay to use. While his religion is not mentioned by the commandants of Fort Wellington, Oodeen had brought the first recorded Qur'an to the colony of New South Wales and on his return to Sydney would be employed as a court interpreter, swearing in Muslims appearing before the courts.[14]

The decision to employ Oodeen as a government interpreter was motivated by the need for diplomacy and to demonstrate a legitimate desire to develop trade. There was also a desire to promulgate the pre-eminence of the British over the Dutch: 'Let the Indian taste on the shores of New Holland for the first time in his life the sweets of private prosperity.'[15]

Oodeen arrived at Port Raffles in 1827 at the age of fifty-four, which would have made him one of the elders of the settlement. He had been offered a wage of £70 per year, supplies and permission to establish his own house.[16] Ostensibly, this was a substantial improvement from the conditions he was working under

---

13 Petition for mitigation of sentence, 5 December 1818, Colonial Secretary Papers, SRNSW: 3189, 4/1856.
14 *Sydney Gazette and New South Wales Advertiser*, 26 January 1836, p. 3.
15 Governor Brisbane, 14 August 1824, SRNSW, 6013; 4/3512, pp. 240–1.
16 Returns of the Colony, 1828, SRNSW, 4/257, pp. 96–7.

in Sydney and it was a real opportunity for him to settle his family and regain some of his dignity. The rudimentary and fragile nature of the settlement is likely to have been of lesser concern.

Oodeen's interpreting at Fort Wellington was in complete contrast with that of Williams on the *Investigator*. Whereas Williams interpreted intensively over two days with little time to adapt his language, Oodeen acted as interpreter across two trepang fishing seasons: 1828 under Captain Henry Smyth, and 1829 under Captain Collet Barker. This allowed him to derive a considerable amount of experience from the interpreting events he took part in.

Oodeen's first act as an interpreter occurred seven months after his arrival when a prau was sighted at the mouth of the harbour of Palm Bay. Oodeen was dispatched with a letter from Captain Smyth and tasked with enticing the prau to call at the port. Oodeen was successful, leading to the first meeting between Captain Smyth and the *nakhoda* of the prau, Dieng Riolo. Although Smyth had failed in his communication with the Cobourg Peninsula Aborigines, through Oodeen he had the opportunity to develop a more successful relationship with the trepangers. His first impressions of the *nakhoda* Dieng Riolo were clearly positive: 'he is a most polite, graceful Malay and made us several presents.'[17] Smyth in turn presented Dieng Riolo with a 'Hogshead Cast'.[18]

The exchange of gifts was a feature of a number of meetings between the *nakhoda* and the commandants of Fort Wellington. The exchanges were not the commencement of trade, but aspects of cultural etiquette essential to the beginnings of diplomacy and an area in which Oodeen was expected to be of some assistance.

In a meeting between a *nakhoda* and the new Commandant of Fort Wellington, Captain Collet Barker, during the trepang season of 1829, Oodeen was asked to decline a simple gift of rice on behalf of Barker: 'Some of the Captains wanted to make me a present of some rice, which they said was the only thing they had at present, but I declined as civilly as I could, desiring the interpreter to say I did not wish or expect anything from them' (Mulvaney and Green 1992, p. 139).[19] This was, predictably, not possible, and most likely on Oodeen's advice Barker accepted a coconut and some tortoise shell as a substitute.

While Oodeen may not have been fully aware of the nature of Bugis or Makassarese customs, his religious and cultural background would have contributed to his intuitive sense of ritual in these early meetings. Barker in his diary acknowledges

---

17 *Sydney Gazette and New South Wales Advertiser*, 11 July 1828, p. 2.
18 Captain Smyth to Colonial Secretary Macleay, 20 March 1828, Historical Records of Australia [hereinafter HRA], 3.6, p. 789.
19 Mulvaney and Green's (1992) transcription of Collet Barker's diary is used in this chapter for ease of reference. Barker's original papers from Fort Wellington can be sighted in Collet Barker Papers, ML: A2002.

the need to sometimes defer to Oodeen in these circumstances when he recounts an intention to visit only one of several praus that were in port but 'found from the interpreter I should offend the others if I did not also visit them & I went to all, sitting a short time with each in a small cabin thatched above like the roof of a house' (Mulvaney and Green 1992, p. 136).

There were, however, areas in which Oodeen was less likely to be of assistance, such as those related to the terminology of ships or maritime navigation. Oodeen had never served at sea and Williams may well have had an advantage over Oodeen in this area. This lack of knowledge could be further compounded when specific cultural and technical differences emerged during an interpreting event. When Captain Barker, for example, questioned the *nakhoda* Narrein about his navigation of northern waters, Narrein became confused with Barker's use of a chart of some of the nearby bays. He explained he did not understand the charts but Barker became frustrated: 'nor could I through the interpreter explain it' (Mulvaney and Green 1992, p. 135). In this case it is likely that Oodeen was just as confused as Narrein.

Although in the reported interpreting events the trepangers seemed prepared to answer whatever questions they were asked, it cannot be assumed that they were always eager to part with their knowledge. They were not naive to the rivalry between the Dutch and the English and they carried their own suspicions regarding possible taxes or duties that the British might wish to impose. One *nakhoda* was sent by the Dutch to specifically inform them on the state of Fort Wellington (Overweel 2002, p. 9). Essentially, the trepangers would have had occasion to consider their responses carefully and this in turn had the potential to slow or confuse the communication, consequently influencing Oodeen's ability to interpret freely.

Ultimately, the greatest challenge to Oodeen remained the varying Malay dialects and the degree to which the trepangers from Makassar could effectively use them. This may have eroded some of the advantage of the frequent interpreting he was engaged in and may have induced Barker's comment: 'I think the interpreter does not understand their language thoroughly' (Mulvaney and Green 1992, p. 137). This doubt over Oodeen's ability was only recorded once in Barker's diary and it is unclear whether it was specific to an event or a language. Barker, presumably informed by Oodeen, could determine that there was more than one language at play, noting after an interpreting event: 'one of them did not speak Malay, but only the Macassan tongue'[20] (Mulvaney and Green 1992, p. 160).

Despite the possible shortcomings in Oodeen's knowledge of the languages in use, Barker continued to use Oodeen as an interpreter until it was ordered the

---

20 It is likely that Barker was referring to the use of Bugis or Makassarese, which along with Malay were used by the mixed crews from eastern Indonesia.

settlement be abandoned in August 1829. There had been a proposal to replace Oodeen with another Malay speaker of Sri Lankan origins, a convict accountant named Jean Herman Maas;[21] however, this was related to Oodeen's journey back to Sydney to escort his family to the settlement, which occurred before Captain Barker's arrival at Fort Wellington. Causing some confusion, Oodeen's family had departed before he could reach Sydney. On arrival, he was ordered to remain there. Distraught at the separation from his family, he made a personal appeal to the governor, offering to take a reduction in pay, which the Government accepted, and he returned to Fort Wellington.[22]

After the trepang season had finished and the settlement was abandoned, Oodeen was returned to Sydney. There he continued to act as a court interpreter, mainly for *lascars*,[23] late into his life, dying at the age of eighty-seven 'a respected colonist'.[24] If the objective in employing Oodeen at Fort Wellington was to convey a genuine desire to communicate, a willingness to negotiate and an overall intent of goodwill on behalf of the British, it was an objective clearly achieved. Both Barker and Oodeen would have been aware that this goodwill would now be at risk when the trepangers returned the following season, perhaps with a cargo ready to commence trade. The relationship, however, would be rebuilt 10 years later when Port Essington was settled in 1838 and George Windsor Earl arrived to interpret. Once it too was abandoned,[25] however, consideration of the trepangers would move to the margins of northern development and consequently the communication with them becomes more obscure and less direct in the historical record.

Tingha de Hans and the end of the 'Macassans'

Unlike the settlements in the first half of the nineteenth century, with the establishment of Palmerston in 1869, later renamed Darwin, there was no intention of relying on links with the trepang fishers for its commercial development; pearling, cattle and the establishment of a telegraph station were of much greater interest. The trepangers, however, were not ignored and tension began to rise over how the colony of South Australia, which now had authority over northern waters, could manage the fishery. The amount of duties that could be levied and European entry into the industry led to questions on whether

---

21   Captain Warteen, Colonial Secretary Letters sent to Fort Wellington 1827–29, SRNSW 4/3731.
22   William O'Deane to Governor Darling, 14 November 1828, Colonial Secretary's Letters, SRNSW, 4/2000.
23   *Lascar* here refers to seamen from the Indian subcontinent, though the term was also applied to those from the Malay Archipelago.
24   *Sydney Morning Herald*, 24 May 1860, p. 1.
25   The settlement lasted approximately 10 years, abandoned in 1849.

the Makassar-based fleets should have any further part in it at all. Occupying a space that overlapped these two worlds was an Australian-based Timorese trepanger, amongst a number of other occupations, who was both proficient in Malay and English and had ability in the Indigenous dialects of the Cobourg Peninsula.

Tingha de Hans[26] arrived in Darwin from Kupang in West Timor in the first half of the 1870s. He was in his early twenties and started work as a domestic servant. The earliest record of his presence in Darwin relates to a court case in 1874 between a Mrs Catherine Cox and her Malay servant, Mita Ab Doolak, who Mrs Cox accused of deserting her service. In a series of accusations and counteraccusations arising from the case, Tingha appeared as one of several men accused of having slept with Mita. Fortunately for Mita and Tingha, Mrs Cox's accusations were found improbable and both Tingha and Mita had their names cleared. Relevant to Tingha's future role as an intermediary, there is no record of an interpreter being used, suggesting that Tingha already had sufficient English to negotiate his case in the court system.

Described as 'a well educated fellow' (Searcy 1912, p. 160), 'shrewd and intelligent',[27] of 'sturdy build…an exceptionally sober and steady man',[28] Tingha also appears to have been competitive and determined. In 1882, he won a Darwin running race against an overly confident professional runner, Rodney Spencer, who offered him a 7-yard start in a 50-yard race; Tingha pocketed £15 for his effort.[29] In 1898, as a buffalo hunter, he tallied the highest number of hides, well more than 1000, though it was claimed he started earlier than the rest of the hunters.[30] He worked both independently and under the employ of others, building up sufficient funds so that by the 1890s he was able to order an 8 t lugger from Hong Kong.

Crucial to his enterprise and a feature that set him apart from most other pioneers in the Territory was his ability to communicate across a number of cultural and linguistic boundaries. While there are scant accounts where the term 'interpreter' is applied to Tingha, in reports that provide the context of his activities it is often implied or assumed. His interpreting is masked by the task at hand, such as the trading and trepanging, and because he was never paid to interpret. Interpreting was a talent that he offered as part of his general duties or used for his own benefit. Nevertheless, over his lifetime he was probably involved in more ad-hoc interpreting than either Williams or Oodeen.

---

26 Also Tingga and Tènga (Cense 1952), the last being based on pronunciation is likely to be the most accurate.
27 *Northern Territory Times and Gazette*, 31 March 1905, p. 3.
28 ibid., 16 February 1906, p. 3.
29 ibid., 11 March 1882, p. 2.
30 ibid., 4 November 1898, p. 2.

Beyond Tingha's individual context, the preference for pearling and other industries changed the nature of the relationship between the authorities and the trepangers from one that previously required diplomacy, persuasiveness and the building of trust, to one in which the rules of law were dictated. Rather than encouraging Indonesian participation in the industry, new regulations and customs duties contributed to a decrease in the fishing fleet size and constrained the development of further trade. A government interpreter was seen as an unnecessary cost in terms of the day-to-day implementation of this policy, particularly as the consequences of poor communication were mainly borne by trepangers.

Additionally, formal communication from the South Australian authorities bypassed the *nakhoda* all together, instead moving between the colonial authorities in Adelaide and Makassar via the Dutch consul. This reduced further any pressure for official interpreters and translators, as the South Australians simply wrote in English, leaving it to the Dutch to translate into Dutch or Malay. Under these circumstances, the *nakhoda* and the owners of the praus were left to negotiate through the authorities in Makassar (Macknight 1976, p. 108). This created communication that was bureaucratic, aloof and tainted by inter-colonial rivalry.

Even when E. O. Robinson, the first customs official appointed for the Cobourg Peninsula, made a recommendation that the regulations be translated into Malay, it was never acted upon. Admittedly, it would have been difficult in terms of choosing an appropriate written form as not all the *nakhoda* were necessarily literate in either Arabic or the Latin-based scripts.[31] Nevertheless, an official such as Robinson, who eventually learnt some of 'the Makassar language',[32] would have been able to read the translation out aloud, permitting a more confident and consistent message to be transferred.

The usefulness of having an interpreter was appreciated by Alfred Searcy, the Darwin based Sub-Collector of Customs, who visited the trepang fisheries aboard the *Flying Cloud* in 1883. He ensured that the new customs regulations were understood by relying on his Malay *serang* (boatswain) as an interpreter. In a meeting with the *nakhoda* Ban Kassi, he explains: 'Thro' the serang I informed Ban Kassi of the regulations made by the Govt. of South Australia with regard to trepang fishing' (Searcy 1907, p. 69). The *serang* was from Makassar, potentially allowing him to become a very useful interpreter. The crew on the *Flying Cloud*

---

31   Macknight suggests the Makasar language (Makassarese) may have been more useful (1976, p. 105), though once again not all the *nakhoda* or the owners of the praus spoke Makassarese or Bugis and, in any expansion of the trade, Malay would have had greater currency in the archipelago.

32   *Northern Territory Times and Gazette*, 22 November 1917, p. 23. The 'Macassar language' in this context may not be a precise reference to any particular language or dialect but rather to whatever language the trepangers from Makassar were using.

had been recruited from Surabaya, but the *serang*'s Makassar origins must have been seen as an advantage in regards to his ability to communicate with the trepangers.

Unfortunately for Robinson, the *Flying Cloud* was based in Darwin and while Searcy organised a customs officer uniform and a revolver for Robinson, the collector was left to his own devices in regards to the language. It is here that Tingha's move to the new Revenue Station at Bowen Straits in 1884 cannot be considered accidental or purely in the context of buffalo hunting, which he also did for Robinson. Tingha and Robinson developed a longstanding relationship that lasted more than 15 years and there was considerable trust between the men. On occasions, Robinson left Tingha to manage the Revenue Station (Searcy 1907, p. 212), even though he had no official status in regards to customs. Tingha could be trusted to act as a go-between, receiving and passing on information between Robinson and the trepangers. If Robinson was away, the interpreting process would be delayed, the movement from one language to another hidden by the interlude; the information, as one report noted, 'filtered'[33] by Tingha.

At the Bowen Straits Revenue Station, Tingha developed his relationship with the visiting trepangers and no doubt he would have become acquainted with their language as well as the varieties of Malay used on board the praus. This would have led to the incorporation of its vocabulary into their exchanges as his contact with them matured, particularly in informal conversation; however, Malay would have retained its usefulness in more formal or complex communication. Malay was not simply a lingua franca, but it conveyed some prestige and authority to the speaker.

By the turn of the twentieth century, Malay had increasing currency in the eastern archipelago and more of the *nakhoda* would have been familiar with it than had been experienced by either Williams or Oodeen. Additionally, Tingha's Kupang Malay would have been a more familiar variety to those on the fishing fleet than the Malay of Williams or Oodeen. Kupang was settled by Indonesians from Ambon, Timor, Rote, Solor and Sabu in the eighteenth century and this consolidated the role of Malay as a lingua franca on Timor, though localisation of the language still made it distinct (see Grimes and Jacob 2006).

Without a record of Tingha's day-to-day duties at the Revenue Station— neither Robinson nor Tingha has left a diary—the specifics of Tingha's role as an interpreter is largely unknown, though some understanding can be drawn through incidental accounts related to other matters, notably court cases. In a case investigating the killing of five shipwrecked Indonesians near the Bowen Straits in 1892, one of the defendants, Mangerippy, testified: 'at first the Malays

---

33 ibid., 31 March 1905, p. 3.

spoke, but we did not understand and they then said "Tingha" and pointed towards the Bowen Straits.'[34] In fact, the murders were first brought to the attention of the authorities through Tingha, who passed the information on to Robinson, who then relayed it to Searcy.[35] The incident illustrates the role of Tingha as a point of first contact, not only between the visiting trepangers and Robinson, but also in the negotiations between Aboriginal Australians and the Indonesians.

In the 1880s, Tingha had settled with an Aboriginal woman known as Maryanageene. Searcy described her as 'a remarkably handsome native wife, a half caste Malay girl, full of fun and frolic' (1912, p. 160). Maryanageene would have been a key link to the local Aboriginal community for Tingha and influenced greatly his use of the local language, which he was able to speak to some extent. This is most likely to have been Iwaidja, which was used amongst Aboriginal people as a lingua franca in early industries on the Cobourg Peninsula (see Evans 2000). Tingha's good relationship with the Aborigines was admired by some in the Territory: 'Tinggha probably possesses more intimate and thorough knowledge of the native character than any other man in the territory.'[36] There was also a degree of jealousy of his success in being able to employ them: 'and [he] seems to have possessed a happy knack of getting along with the coastal natives, who would work for Tingha when they would work for no one else.'[37] While Robinson was eventually capable of communicating with the trepangers to a limited degree himself, the man who followed him in 1899, Alfred Brown, was much more reliant on Tingha both as an interpreter and as someone who understood the fishery. He had no knowledge of the area[38] but was reassured by the promise of Tingha's assistance (Macknight 1976, p. 119).

The most explicit reference to Tingha's use as an interpreter by Brown comes from what was reported as the killing of another shipwrecked crew in 1902. The murders purportedly occurred in an extremely isolated part of the coast, however, the case was brought to the attention of the Dutch consul and this escalated the incident. The case grew further in complexity as the new Commonwealth of Australia[39] challenged the authority of what was now the State of South Australia over the matter.

Information about the murders relied on a lone survivor, a man called Ahmet, also known as Lau Batoe, who recounted how their vessel struck bad weather and was disabled. It was adrift for 29 days before becoming completely

---

34   ibid., 18 November 1892, p. 3.
35   ibid., 17 February 1893, p. 3.
36   ibid., 31 March 1905, p. 3.
37   ibid., 16 February 1906, p. 3.
38   See Brown's examination in Dashwood (1902).
39   The six Australian colonies had federated into the Commonwealth of Australia only 12 months previously and the Commonwealth's powers were still poorly understood.

wrecked in the English Company's Islands, near Cape Wilberforce. The crew was forced to rescue what they could of their supplies and take refuge on a beach. Marooned, the shipwrecked sailors were approached by two Aborigines requesting rice and who remained with them for two days, the sub-collector of customs' report explaining that the Aborigines were able to use Malay to communicate with them. Three days after the two Aborigines departed, a larger group of Aborigines arrived and Ahmet claimed that it was then that his fellow crewmembers were speared and clubbed.[40]

In Brown's report to the Sub-Collector of Customs in Darwin, William George Stretton, he was explicit about the use of Tingha as an interpreter: 'I have interviewed the survivor and with the assistance of Tinga de Hans as interpreter, have obtained the following particulars.'[41] With such sensitivities related to the legal particulars of the case and the issue of compensation being raised, the need to be able to trace the veracity of the information was critical. It is not surprising, therefore, that statements related to Tingha's interpreting were repeated through many of the relevant documents. Neither the act of interpreting nor the identity of the interpreter was obscured, rather they were formally proclaimed. In doing so, credibility and due process were heralded to the reader.

As the matter proceeded, the verity of Ahmet's statement came under scrutiny, leading to further exchanges between the Dutch, Commonwealth and State governments. The Commonwealth's dissatisfaction with the flow of information would eventually result in the Australian prime minister, through the governor-general, complaining to the British prime minister,[42] 'emphasising the necessity...for referring the constitutional questions involved to the High Court of the Commonwealth as soon as possible after its establishment'.[43]

At the same time that these investigations proceeded, both Tingha and Brown were examined for a Commonwealth report on pearling and trepanging in northern Australia conducted by Justice Dashwood (1902). Tingha was interviewed as a trepanger in his own right, but he was also being questioned on the opinion of the Indonesian trepangers, there being no intention to interview them directly. He is asked why their numbers have dropped, how they get their trepang, and about their difficulty of paying with sovereigns. The interview, as reported, is short but the selection of Tingha is indication of the respect for Tingha's role in the industry and his links with the Indonesian trepangers. Justice Dashwood already had Brown's account of the industry in the Bowen

---

40 Extract of the report by the Sub-Collector of Customs, Port Darwin, National Archives of Australia [hereinafter NAA], 1903/6187.
41 Ibid.
42 The United Kingdom still moderated much of Australia's overseas relations, including its relationship with the Dutch East Indies.
43 Governor-General Chamberlain to the British Prime Minister, Lord Tennyson, 7 August 1903, NAA, A1 1903/6187.

Straits but Tingga acts as an interpreter for the industry in both the narrow and the broader senses of the word; he is seen as a reliable intermediary through which information can pass.

As with both Williams and Oodeen, we know little of what the visiting Indonesians thought of Tingha's role other than that they actively sought him out and that he was remembered long after the annual visits were prohibited. In the 1950s when Daeng Sarro, a former *nakhoda* with the fishing fleets, was interviewed in his home near Makassar by a Dutch scholar, Tingha was one of the few individuals clearly identified (Cense 1952).

Tingha died in the Bowen Straits at the age of fifty-three on 24 January 1906, the same year that the South Australian Government decided to cease issuing licences to the fishers. His lugger and goods were auctioned off by Brown, but it took some time before his family heard the news. His three brothers did not arrive from Kupang until 1910 to settle the estate[44] and it is unclear whether there were any funds left. With the death of Tingha, the last significant contact between European Australians and the independent Indonesian trepangers was cut. Clearly, with the implementation of the new laws there was no real need to look for a replacement.

Conclusion

European Australian contact with the Indonesian trepangers lasted just more than a century. It started with great expectations of trade and cooperation, though in time the relationship withered and was brought to a deliberate end as colonial boundaries became less negotiable, alternative commerce seemed more viable and Australia's cultural view of itself emerged as strictly European. When the Australian colonies were reborn as the Commonwealth of Australia in 1901, the new nation accepted its dependence on British capital and diplomacy and felt no immediate pressure to communicate with its neighbours to the north.

In international negotiations, the new Commonwealth deferred to the British to the extent that contact with the Dutch East Indies was moderated via London and any direct exchange with the 'natives' of the Indonesian archipelago was left to the pearlers and adventurers. From the Government's perspective, it preferred to cocoon itself within an English-speaking dominion, despite the persistence of a diversity of languages in its marginal migrant and Indigenous communities.

---

44   *Northern Territory Times and Gazette*, 2 September 1910, p. 3.

Williams', Oodeen's and Tingha's roles as interpreters provide an alternative history to this isolated perspective. Their lives covered a period of changing responses to Australia's contact with the archipelago. In the first half of the nineteenth century, Williams and Oodeen interpreted in an environment tempered by influences of the Enlightenment and by a technological gap that was not so severe. Macknight (2011, p. 122) makes the point that in this period 'there was much in common between the world of the observers [the British] and that of the trepangers'. They both 'depended upon and were intimately familiar with the operation of sailing vessels, as were the trepangers…Similarly, other aspects of technology, especially guns, and of social and economic organisation were not widely divergent'. In contrast, the Northern Territory of Tingha's time was seeking a far more complex engagement with the world. It was perhaps overly ambitious and under resourced, but its dream of commerce and industry encouraged greater distance from the Indigenous cultures of the north and those of the archipelago.

By revealing the interpreting role of the three men, the voice of the Indonesian fishers and traders is brought into closer proximity with the historical events in which they were participants. It also presents another perspective on the better-known figures the interpreters were associated with: Flinders with Williams, Smyth and Barker with Oodeen, and Robinson and Brown with Tingha. More importantly, the presence of the interpreter is a reminder that what was reported was moderated and filtered by the motivation of those who engaged the interpreters, as well as the constraints and subjectivity of the interpreters.

The biographical references of Williams, Oodeen and Tingha indicate they were independent agents, unlikely to act in an overly subservient way. In the case of Oodeen and Tingha, they were clearly intelligent and determined individuals, characteristics that need to be considered when assessing them as adaptable linguists, capable of going beyond their own language and culture. Further research is still required to pull together the scattered and veiled evidence of these men's roles as interpreters. It would be useful to know more about Williams' origins, Oodeen's religious knowledge and Tingha's role as an arbitrator in conflicts between Aboriginal Australians and the Indonesians. Knowledge of their use of varieties of Malay also remains more deductive, though the remarkable versatility and geographical spread of the language in the nineteenth century are clearly demonstrated.

Deficiencies aside, the interpreters' histories provide a view from the margins and the centre of events, inhabiting both the European culture of their employ and the Indonesian culture of their inheritance. Had they not been present we would be left to ponder their absence as Cunningham, the botanist on Phillip Parker King's voyage, did in 1818: 'Most valuable information might be obtained from these Asiatics as to their seasons of fishing and detention on this coast, the success of their fisheries, the value of their cargoes, their opinion of the natives, could we have conversed with them through the medium of an interpreter.'[45]

Cunningham's wistful comment arises out of his desire for real contact with 'these Asiatics' and ultimately brings to the fore the priority of human interaction in exploration and the potential of the interpreter to engender it.

References

Allen, J. (2008) *Port Essington: The historical archaeology of a north Australian nineteenth-century military outpost*, Sydney: Sydney University Press.

Cense, A. A. (1952) 'Makassaars-Boeginese Prauwvaart op Noord-Australië', *Bijdragen tot de Taal-, Land-en Volkenkunde uitgegeven door het Koninklijk Instituut voor Taa-, Land-en Volkenkunde*, 108, pp. 248–64.

Cummings, W. (2009) 'Garis Luar Penerjemahan di Makassar', in H. Chambert-Loir (ed.), *Sejarah terjemahan di Indonesia dan Malaysia*, Jakarta: Kepustakaan Populer Gramedia, pp. 273–84.

Dashwood, C. J. (1902) 'Report by His Honour Judge Dashwood, government resident, Palmerston on the pearl-shelling industry in Port Darwin and Northern Territory', *Commonwealth Parliamentary Papers—1901–1902*, House of Representatives, Melbourne: Commonwealth of Australia.

Delisle, J. and J. Woodsworth 1995. *Translators through History*. Philadelphia: John Benjamin's Publishing Company.

Earl, G. W. (1846) 'On the Aboriginal tribes of the north coast of Australia', *Journal of the Royal Geographical Society*, 16, pp. 239–51.

Evans, N. (1997) 'Macassan loans and linguistic stratification in western Arnhem Land', in P. McConvell and N. Evans (eds), *Archaeology and Linguistics: Aboriginal Australia in global perspective*, Melbourne: Oxford University Press, pp. 237–60.

Evans, N. (2000) 'Iwaidjan, a very un-Australian language family', *Linguistic Typology*, 4, pp. 91–142.

Fayer, J. (2003) 'African interpreters in the Atlantic slave trade', *Anthropological Linguistics*, 45 (3), pp. 281–95.

---

45   Allan Cunningham, *Journal*, 25 April 1818, SRNSW, 6034/SZ7.

Flinders, M. (1814) *A Voyage to Terra Australis undertaken for the Purpose of Completing Discovery of that Vast Country, and Prosecuted in the Years 1801, 1802, and 1803*, London: G. & W. Nicol.

Ferguson, G. (2002) 'The first Ceylonese family in Australia', *Ceylankan,the Ceylon Society of Australia*, 5 (1), pp. 14–18.

Fox, J. J. (2003) 'Tracing the path, recounting the past: historical perspectives on Timor', in J. J. Fox and D. Soares (eds), *Oceanic Explorations: Lapita and western Pacific settlement*, Canberra: ANU E Press, pp. 1–27.

Grimes, B. and J. Jacob (2006) Developing a role for Kupang Malay: the contemporary politics of an eastern Indonesian creole, Tenth International Conference on Austronesian Linguistics, Linguistic Society of the Philippines and SIL International, <http://www.sil.org/asia/philippines/ical/papers.html> [viewed 3 February 2012].

Harris, J. (1986) *Northern Territory Pidgins and the Origin of Kriol*, Series C, Canberra: Pacific Linguistics.

Hough, C. and G. Long (1825) *The Practice of Courts-martial, also the Legal Exposition and Military Explanation of the Mutiny Act, and Articles of War*, London: Kingsbury, Parbury & Allen.

Ingleton, G. (1986) *Matthew Flinders: Navigator and chartmaker*, Guildford, UK: Genesis Publications in association with Hedley Australia.

Jayamanne, F. S. R. (2003) 'Anecdotal account of the 1st Ceylonese soldier migrant to Australia: pioneer, not convict', *Sunday Observer*, 29 June, <http://www.sundayobserver.lk/2003/06/29/fea14.html> [viewed 12 April 2011].

Jones, R. (1994) 'Out of the shadows: George Windsor Earl in Western Australia', *Indonesia Circle*, pp. 265–78.

Karttunen, F. (1994) *Between Worlds: Interpreters, Guides, and Survivors*, New Brunswick, NJ: Rutgers University Press.

McCormick, K. (2002) *Language in Cape Town's District Six*, Oxford: Oxford University Press.

McIntosh, I. (1996) 'Islam and Australia's Aborigines? A perspective from north-east Arnhem Land', *Journal of Religious History*, 20 (1), pp. 53–77.

Macknight, C. (1976) *The Voyage to Marege': Macassan trepangers in northern Australia*, Carlton, Vic.: Melbourne University Press.

Macknight, C. (2011) 'The view from Marege': Australian knowledge of Makassar and the impact of the trepang industry across two centuries', *Aboriginal History*, 35, pp. 121–43.

Monteath, P. (2002) *Sailing with Flinders: the journal of seaman Samuel Smith*, Nth. Adelaide, S. Aust.: Corkwood Press.

Moore, D. T., T. G. Vallance and E. W. Groves (2001) *Nature's Investigator: The diary of Robert Brown in Australia, 1801–1805*, Canberra: Australian Biological Resources Study.

Mulvaney, J. (1994) *The search for Collet Barker of Raffles Bay*, State Library Occasional Papers No. 44, Darwin: State Library of the Northern Territory.

Mulvaney, J. and N. Green (1992) *Commandant of Solitude: The journals of Captain Collet Barker 1828–1831*, Melbourne: Miegunyah Press.

Mulvaney, J. (1994) *The search for Collet Barker of Raffles Bay*. State Library Occasional Papers No. 44.Darwin: State Library of the Northern Territory.

Overweel, J. (2002) Keep Them Out! Early Nineteenth Century English and Dutch rivalry in eastern Indonesia and Australia, and the founding of Merkus-oord, <http://www.papuaweb.org/dlib/_sejarah.html> [Viewed 15 September 2011].

Palmer, L. (2007) 'Negotiating the ritual and social order through spectacle: the (re)production of Macassan/Yolŋu histories', *Anthropological Forum: A journal of social anthropology and comparative sociology*, 17 (1), pp. 1–20.

Pym, A. (1998) *Method in Translation History*, Manchester: St Jerome.

Reid, B. (2007) 'Convict labour in north Australia's colonial settlements: shifting attitudes', *Journal of Northern Territory History*, 18, pp. 1–10.

Reece, R. (1992) 'The Australasian career of George Windsor Earl', *Journal of Northern Territory History*, 3, pp. 1–23.

Roland, R. A. (1999) *Interpreters as Diplomats: A diplomatic history of the role of interpreters in world politics*, Ottawa: University of Ottawa Press.

Rundle, C. (2011) 'History through a translation perspective', in A. Chalvin, A. Lange and D. Monticelli (eds), *Between Cultures and Texts. Itineraries in translation history/Entre les cultures et les textes. Itinéraires en histoire de la traduction*, Frankfurt Am Main: Peter Lang, pp. 33–43.

Saldin, M. D. (2003) 'Banishment of the first Ceylonese family to Australia', *Sunday Island*, 12 January.

Searcy, A. (1907) *In Australian Tropics*, London & Palung: Kegan Paul & Trubner.

Searcy, A. (1912) *By Flood and Field: Adventures ashore and afloat in north Australia*, London: G. Bell & Sons Ltd.

Spillett, P. (1972) *Forsaken Settlement: An illustrated history of the settlement of Victoria, Port Essington, north Australia, 1838–1849*, Melbourne: Lansdowne.

Stell, G. 2007. From Kitaab-Hollandsch to Kitaab-Afrikaans: The evolution of a non-white literary variety at the Cape (1856-1940). *Stellenbosch Papers in Linguistics* 37: 89-127.

Thomas, P. S. (2012) 'Oodeen, a Malay interpreter on Australia's frontier lands', *Indonesia and the Malay World*, 40 (117), pp. 122–42.

Toner, P. (2000) 'Ideology, influence and innovation: the impact of Macassan contact on Yolngu music', *Perfect Beat: The Pacific Journal of Research into Contemporary Music and Popular Culture*, 5 (1), pp. 22–41.

6. Unbirri's pre-Macassan legacy, or how the Yolngu became black

Ian S. McIntosh

Introduction

From the mid 1980s to the early 1990s, I was most fortunate to make the acquaintance of the Warramiri Aboriginal leader David Burrumarra MBE. A person of great consequence in northeast Arnhem Land, Burrumarra had been a leader in the establishment of Christian missions at Yirrkala and Galiwin'ku in the 1930s and 1940s and an advocate for self-determination in the post-mission period (McIntosh 1994). Burrumarra considered himself and was considered by others to be an intellectual and he was much sought after by politicians, religious leaders and social scientists, both for his astonishing general knowledge and for his influence within the Yolngu realm. His older relative Harry Makarrwola of the Wangurri clan had played a similar mediating role a generation earlier in his work with Methodist missionaries at Milingimbi and also with the pioneering anthropologist Lloyd Warner, author of the 1937 classic *A Black Civilization*.

My lengthy conversations with Burrumarra traversed all aspects of his illustrious career and the highlights were published in a biography in 1994 shortly after his death. Early on in our conversation I was interested in exploring his views on the possibility of pre-Macassan voyaging to Australia, and also the legacy of Macassan trepangers (McIntosh 2008). His homeland in the English Company's Islands included the fabled 'Malay Road' where Matthew Flinders encountered the Bugis Captain Pobassoo in 1803 (Macknight 1976; see also chapters by Thomas, this volume, and Blair and Hall, this volume).

It was evident that the memory of prolonged contact with visitors from Southeast Asia was influencing the ways that Yolngu (Aborigines in northeast Arnhem Land) were then fighting for sea rights, mineral rights and also a treaty with non-Aboriginal Australians, and I was keen to examine that connection. Burrumarra's priorities in those years were in bridging the gap between Christianity and traditional Aboriginal religion and building strong, modern Indigenous communities that integrated the best from both Aboriginal and non-Aboriginal worlds. These two preoccupations, both mine and Burrumarra's, were intimately entwined.

Among Burrumarra's Warramiri clan there is a deeply held conviction that the relationships that were forged between Yolngu and the early seafaring pre-Macassans, also known as the 'Bayini', represented a 'high water mark' in terms of coexistence (McIntosh 2000, 2006a). The two intermarrying moieties (or halves) of Yolngu society, Dhuwa and Yirritja, find harmony in an intricate net of social relations, and such was the case also in the 'golden age' at the dawn of time when Yolngu and pre-Macassans danced together on the beaches of northeast Arnhem Land. Why was there not the same sense of connectedness between black and white Australians, Burrumarra would ask.

This connectedness of Yolngu and others was demonstrated most spectacularly in 1988 with the Northern Territory Museum's recreation of the voyage of Macassan trepangers from Sulawesi to Australia. The *Hati Marege*, a traditional Macassan prau crewed by a group from Makassar and under the direction of historian Peter Spillett, was met at Elcho Island by Yolngu men doing dances associated with the aforementioned pre-Macassans, those early non-trepanging voyagers so closely associated with the Yolngu Dreaming. I was there on the beach and I witnessed the Indonesians being welcomed to Arnhem Land as if they were coming home after a long absence (see Ganter, this volume; Ganter 2006, p. 33).

In this chapter I will share one pre-Macassan story told to me by David Burrumarra. First, I will give an indication of the manner in which the story was told, and second, through his analysis of the content and also mine, I will draw some conclusions on why the story was shared, shining light on what 'coming home' means in terms of contemporary relations between Yolngu and outsiders. The goal is to show how some Yolngu view the history and legacy of trepanging not just through the narrow lens of tamarind trees, pottery shards and the years 1780–1907, but, rather, through an entirely different and sacred lens.

The setting for this story is the period soon after the beginning of the world at a place called Unbirri or Stephen's Island, in northeast Arnhem Land.

The dawn of time

The news would have spread rapidly. Around campfires across Arnhem Land, Yolngu of all ages would have been speaking in hushed tones about developments at Unbirri, a small island north of Galiwin'ku (Elcho Island). A golden-skinned baby girl had made her appearance in the world. She was not an albino, an extreme rarity in Australia, but rather a light-brown colour that did not darken in the days immediately after her birth, as is the norm. Her name was Bayini.

This historical episode, now couched in myth, was described to me as occurring at the 'dawn of time'. It was the cause of much deliberation. The '*Momo*', the baby's paternal grandmother, rubbed the baby's skin with the bark of the gutu tree, which grew along the shoreline at Unbirri. It is black in colour like the people. After all, she believed that you need such a skin colour to be called a Yolngu (or human being). The application of the bark, along with the action of the sun, was understood to be sufficient to transform the baby into a person of appropriate skin colouring. But it wasn't.

Conception beliefs under scrutiny

The study of Yolngu conception beliefs throws some light on how this new arrival may have been perceived at Unbirri and, indeed, beyond. Anthropologists originally thought that Aboriginal people were ignorant of the role of sexual intercourse in reproduction but now we know this view was incorrect. For Yolngu, like most other Indigenous Australians, spiritual explanations of conception exist separately and override more mundane physiological explanations. Yolngu believe that spirit children exist independently in the environment, especially in sacred waterholes associated with a clan's totems. Spirit children go in search of mothers, and mothers in search of them. But according to Merlan (1986), marriage, Australia-wide, was an institution orchestrated and controlled by Aboriginal men, female sexual maturity being attributed to the actions of men and also ritual. When it comes to conception, the father may be visited in a dream by one of these child spirits, which he then directs to the mother, or there might be an unusual occurrence while hunting that he will link to 'finding a child'. The Yolngu word '*Gayi*', a personal name, sums up this male-centred belief. At one level it means 'in the image of the father', but it also represents the 'face of the land', that close bond that exists between people as a whole and totemic spirits.

With a cyclical understanding of the passing of time, Yolngu would envision a world in which there was an eternal balance between the temporal and the non-temporal, the physical and the spiritual, but now that timeless order was thrown into doubt. The arrival of the new child, who was not in the image of the Aboriginal father, signalled to the elders that there was a new order in the universe, a new law in the land, and a new principle guiding human interaction. And they seemed to have little or no control over it.

In search of meaning

Making sense of this occurrence obviously exercised the minds of Yolngu over many generations, long before Burrumarra and I shared our thoughts under the mango trees on the cliffs overlooking the vast Arafura Sea. In the past, Burrumarra said that Yolngu would ask, 'Was Bayini autochthonous, a product or outgrowth of the land? Or had a Dreaming entity deposited Bayini there?' If so, he said, what was its purpose? What was her message? There was much speculation; however, by the 1980s there was an emerging consensus. In conversation with me, Yolngu elders would discuss the significance of Unbirri in the context of the possibility of reconciliation in Australia, as I will explain.

There is no mention of Macassans in the Bayini narrative. No mention either of the trepang trade. Rather, the emphasis in the telling was on the evidence that it provided for the existence of a Dreaming entity, previously undetected, but now made visible in part by the emergence, and look, of this child. This Dreaming entity was understood to hold sway over peoples of all descriptions, black and white, living both in Arnhem Land and elsewhere, and it was the force behind all that was new and entering Yolngu lives (McIntosh 2011).

The place where the Bayini 'arose from the earth' is known as Gutungur, where a gutu tree once grew. In the 1980s a small outstation was built at Unbirri (Stephen's Island) by a Yolngu elder whose Christian name, by no coincidence, was Stephen. Yolngu would travel to Unbirri to consider the legacy of Bayini. People of many clans trace their origins to her, and all Yolngu, without exception, to the Dreaming entity that brought her forth into the world. Regina Ganter, in her book *Mixed Relations: Histories and stories of Asian–Aboriginal contact in north Australia*, quotes the Gumatj-Burarrwanga leader Charlie Mattjuwi, who says that all Yolngu are descended from Macassans (Ganter 2006). What he is actually referring to are not just his own personal connections to a Macassan lineage, but also to the Bayini legacy as a whole.

Bayini's law at Unbirri

Yolngu law at Unbirri was very strict. Bayini was a product of the new world entering Yolngu lives but 'she lived for the black people', Burrumarra said. In what appears to be a contradiction, Burrumarra would say, 'Yolngu for Yolngu and Macassar for Macassar. We do not mix. This Bayini's law.' And Bayini's Yolngu descendants at Unbirri and the neighbouring island of Yirringa (Drysdale Island) jealously guarded their homeland and inheritance.

Across northeast Arnhem Land there are many myths of first encounter in which the question of how Yolngu might react to the presence of the other is discussed. In a majority of narratives, as I detail later, the bricoleur or mythmaker uses the dingo or wild dog as the central character (McIntosh 2006b). In dog myths from Yirringa, for example, the mythical actors use only traditional technology—bark canoes and stone axes—and nothing from the visitors. The message seemed to be that the Yolngu would not be overrun by the new, losing control of their lands and bodies as the influence of newcomers steadily grew. And yet even with this self-imposed regimen of seclusion, the Yolngu landowners of Unbirri and Yirringa, relatives of today's Warramiri clan traditional owners, became extinct in the 1800s in part as a consequence of diseases introduced by Macassans (Burrumarra, Pers. comm., 1988). A 'scratching sickness', most probably smallpox, was experienced along the entire Wessel Island chain and elsewhere in Arnhem Land, leading to the demise of many clans (see Campbell 2002).

In the 1980s, visitors to the region would often avoid the use of non-traditional material culture. Even though Bayini herself represented all things new, her law in this instance meant no metal cooking pots, no axes, knives or any other such items. Baler shells were preferred for carrying water for this was the law of Bayini at Yirringa.

On a hunting trip with Yolngu friends and family to Yirringa in the late 1980s, I witnessed this practice first hand. Our five boats were anchored offshore in a wide semicircle. Some members of the party waded ashore to make fires while others ventured into the swampy hinterland where their hunting dogs were let loose to chase out goanna. It was an extraordinary scene as the dogs, the men and the women, working together, herded dozens of the scurrying lizards onto the beach and into the water, where Yolngu were waiting knee deep in the water with wooden clubs to kill them. After a memorable feast, we left the island, never once using modern technology. I remember how the elders joked as they made fire without matches, to the delight of the children.

Bukulatjpi and cognitive dissonance

What can we deduce from the contradiction at the heart of the Bayini narrative? In Leon Festinger's theory of cognitive dissonance, drawn from his book *When Prophesy Fails* (Festinger et al. 1958), the conflict or tension between established beliefs and new information leads to a disequilibrium, which motivates people to reduce or eliminate the contradictions and justify a new stance through what is called 'adaptive preference formation'. Burrumarra was aware of this term, 'cognitive dissonance'. He had spent many days with world-renowned clinical psychologists and psychiatrists, including Dr John Money, most famous for his work on infant sex assignment in cases where the sexual identity of newborns was not apparent. In relation to the uncertainties and dissonance of those early days of contact, Burrumarra simply said that his ancestor, a Warramiri leader from the early 1800s named Bukulatjpi, dealt with the disequilibrium by 'picking up the swords and doing the dance'.

Burrumarra was referring here to the many ceremonies, some integrating flags and swords, that were understood to be held in common by Yolngu, pre-Macassans and Macassans. 'There were no doubts', Burrumarra said. Bukulatjpi's actions and the thinking behind them, variously interpreted, became the basis of an enduring Yolngu law that emphasised pride in one's Yolngu heritage, and also a pan-Yolngu sense of resistance to unwelcome outside intrusion.

Bukulatjpi's significance to the Yolngu as a whole became evident when, in the 1960s, the lives of Arnhem Landers were becoming increasingly bound by the administrative procedures of the Commonwealth Government of Australia. Yolngu were required to have a surname and the labels Burarrwanga, Yunupingu, Dhamarrandji, Dhurrkay, Marika and so on were adopted by young clan leaders (McIntosh 1994). Each of the aforementioned names has a profound meaning. The Warramiri clan chose the surname of their ancestor, Bukulatjpi, a man who was credited by Burrumarra and others with 'doing the thinking' with regards to the pre-Macassan Bayini.

Bayini narratives drawn from sacred sites across northeast Arnhem Land are centre stage for at least five Yirritja clans—the Warramiri, Wangurri, Birrkili, Dhalwangu and Gumatj—and a number of now extinct groups, such as the Lamamirri and Yalukal (McIntosh 2000). While there is considerable variation in the Bayini narratives, the essential elements are the same and they all derive for the most part from Bukulatjpi, and then through multiple hands and interpretative processes down to the present. Bukulatjpi died at Melville Bay near Nhulunbuy at a sacred place now occupied by the Nabalco aluminium plant (Burrumarra, Pers. comm, 1988). The irony was not lost on Yolngu who look to the Bayini narratives for inspiration in their fight for the recognition of their individual and collective rights in a world in which they had become increasingly marginalised.

Bayini's people

From my discussions with Burrumarra, I gathered that Bukulatjpi had lived at the very end of the heyday of the pre-Macassans in what we might now construe as the first stage of Macassan visitation. Ronald and Catherine Berndt (1954) wrote about distinct periods of foreign contact in northeast Arnhem

Land. In Warramiri oral history, there is a long gap of many generations before the second wave of visitors to his homeland. The Macassan fishermen had avoided the Yolngu, venturing into the Gulf of Carpentaria as far south and east as Mornington Island in Queensland. Burrumarra said that when they returned, they were of a different mind-set. They were now trepangers. Thus we see the differentiation between the two categories of outsiders in the Yolngu world view: 'Bayini' and 'Macassan'. One was considered to be on sacred business and the other profane.

Bayini narratives from other parts of northeast Arnhem Land identify key pre-Macassan leaders, like Luki, Lela and Leku. We know something of their religion, personalities and leadership qualities and also the hierarchical structure of their society (McIntosh 1996, 2004a, 2004b, 2008). Luki, for example, was described to me as a saintly figure who 'lived for the Yolngu'. Members of the Yirritja moiety today are named after these Bayini *bunggawa* (leaders) but they also have personal names drawn from the professions practised by the Bayini on Arnhem Land shores, like boatbuilder, iron-maker, rice-grower and cloth weaver. We also know the names of the Bayini boats, like the *Matjala* with its tripod mast, which was one of the very first, according to Burrumarra. In Yolngu languages, *matjala* means the most precious of things, a great treasure. But it was also the name of this Indonesian sea craft, giving some idea of how these first visitors were viewed by Yolngu. These leaders and their professions, like the memory of the baby at Unbirri, are cherished. As Burrumarra said, 'They are my backbone'.

In that period of hiatus between the departure of the Bayini and the arrival of trepangers, Bukulatjpi—who knew the songs and ceremonies of the early visitors—began to dance for the creational entity that had inspired the partnership of pre-Macassans and Yolngu. He danced with long knives, symbols of that deity, moving his arms and legs in the fashion of these early *bunggawa*, bringing into alignment the world views of both peoples. You will see those same ceremonies performed today, especially at the funerals of Yirritja moiety Yolngu, with all their dazzling references to other worlds: samurai swords, dances with flags and long-barrelled smoking pipes, prayer calls to Allah, and references to Southeast Asian ports like Djakapura (Singapore), Djumaynga (Makassar) and Banda. These songs evoke the rich and diverse world of which Yolngu were now a part (see Berndt and Berndt 1954). Burrumarra stressed that these dances, now performed in public non-ceremonial settings, are not in celebration of Macassans. Rather, they are celebrating the Dreaming entity believed to be shared by pre-Macassans, Macassans and Yolngu.

The colour of affluence and poverty

Cognitive dissonance must have reached profound levels with the arrival of the Bayini child at Unbirri. Before the coming of pre-Macassans and Macassans there was probably no differentiation between people on the basis of skin colour. Black was the colour of humanity. But according to Burrumarra, with the arrival of the Bayini child, colour came to take on a new meaning for Yolngu. They began to think that perhaps in the distant past all people had been the colour of this baby, and that some cataclysm had brought about the change. In the 1980s, this was a foundational belief of all Bayini-inspired clans (see McIntosh 2000). This colour consciousness came hand-in-hand with an awareness that white was the colour of affluence and influence and black was the colour poverty and subservience. As in Stanner's (1966) depiction of the Dreaming and Aboriginal life-worlds as being 'a joyous thing with maggots at the centre', the Yolngu mythmaker Bukulatjpi, his peers and descendants understood that something had gone wrong at the beginning of time, the departure of the Bayini being equated with the withdrawal of this new deity from Yolngu land and lives and the impoverishment of Yolngu. So they would dance for this departed deity. As it was a Yolngu Dreaming, they exercised ritual authority over it, but only in tandem with the other believers could they restore harmony to the universe (McIntosh 2011).

Beginning with the writings of anthropologist Lloyd Warner in the 1930s, we see references to this struggle with myths focusing on the rejection of Macassans and of a concomitant sense of loss right across northeast Arnhem Land. The antisocial and dangerous qualities of the dingo singled it out for use by the bricoleur in many of these myths of encounter, but it is not the only totem that rejects the visitors. Totems of all coastal Yirritja clans reject the Macassans. The honeybee rejects the Macassans in Buckingham Bay on Gupapuyngu land. The scrub fowl rejects them on the Wessel Islands in Golpa territory. Even the trepang itself rejects the visitors at Cape Arnhem in Lamamirri waters. It sends up a torrent of seawater and its own intestines to capsize Macassan fishing canoes. The entire Aboriginal totemic world opposes the presence of Macassans, except at those locations infused with the spirit of the Bayini.

Burrumarra would speak at great length about myths of opposition to the Macassan presence; the dingo's rejection of Macassans at Howard Island was the most famous and the subject of much scholarly reflection (see Berndt and Berndt 1989; McIntosh 2006b; Warner 1937–58). Lloyd Warner, speaking with Harry Makarrwola in the 1920s, for example, wrote of how the dingo was fearful of losing his identity if he accepted the gifts of the Macassans. If the dingo was to take possession of the matches, the rice, the necklace or fishing line on offer, he would become a Macassan, and the Macassan, by this logic, would have to become a Yolngu (Warner 1937–58).

Most notable in these dingo myth variations is the classic tale from the Gupapuyngu and Warramiri territories in which Yolngu, at the beginning of time, are white (just like that Bayini child), but become black as a result of their non-acceptance or violent rejection of Macassans. The Macassan offers everything in the way of material wealth to the dingo but it refuses, believing in the inherent value of Yolngu technology and ways of life (McIntosh 2006b). You will hear similar stories from all the Bayini peoples—the Warramiri, Dhalwangu, Birrkili, Wangurri and Gumatj. They share a common understanding that non-compliance led irreversibly to a new and lesser status for them that was characterised not just by skin colour but also by poverty, powerlessness and immobility in relation to the Macassans and subsequently Japanese and Europeans.

The paradise to come

Now this belief did not mean that the Yolngu wanted to become white once again. Rather, the story of skin colour and identity emerging from Unbirri became the foundation for a struggle to regain what was believed to have been lost at the 'beginning of time', taking back control in a world which was becoming increasingly dominated by others. The Bayini, according to Burrumarra, had a wish for Yolngu.

The continuing sacredness of Unbirri is a reminder to Yolngu of the proper order of the universe—now in disorder, but one day to be remedied. As Bakhtin (1981) reminds us, narratives about a lost paradise are really about a future that is yet to be realised. In the mind of Warramiri leaders like Bukulatjpi and Burrumarra, Bayini speaks to Yolngu about this paradise to come.

So the 'inside' message of the Bayini heritage, then, is one of defiance in the face of outside intrusion by Macassans, Japanese and Europeans. As Yothu Yindi member (and former student of David Burrumarra) Mandawuy Yunupingu sings in his popular 1988 album *Homeland Movement*, the Yolngu might be living in the mainstream, but they should not be fooled by the Balanda (non-Aboriginal) ways. And in classic video clips like 'Djapana' (Sunset Dreaming) and 'Treaty', he dances the traditional movements of the Bayini rituals and calls for justice and reconciliation between Yolngu and Balanda in Australia.

The real legacy of the extended Macassan encounter, which endures today, is embodied not just in tamarind trees and lines of stone that once supported cooking pots, or even in the fascinating rock art associated with visitation. It lies also in the stories of the Bayini at places like Unbirri and elsewhere in northeast Arnhem Land. Many of these are restricted places of contemplation where the identity of Yolngu is affirmed and their authority as landowners is recharged. I believe that this is why Burrumarra shared his story with me. The Bayini narratives are what he described in his Warramiri language as a *'yindi dhawu'* and *'yindi rom'*. Big stories and a big law.

References

Bakhtin, M. M. (1981) 'Forms of time and the chronotype in the novel. Notes towards a historical poetics', in M. Holquist (ed.), *The Dialogic Imagination: Four essays by M. M. Bakhtin*, Austin: University of Texas Press, pp. 84–258.

Berndt, R. M. and C. H. Berndt (1954) *Arnhem Land: Its history and its people*, Melbourne: F. W. Cheshire.

Berndt, R. M. and C. H. Berndt (1989) *The Speaking Land: Myth and story in Aboriginal Australia*, Ringwood, Vic.: Penguin Books.

Campbell, J. (2002) *Invisible Invaders: Smallpox and other diseases in Aboriginal Australia. 1780–1880*, Carlton, Vic.: Melbourne University Press.

Festinger, L., H. Riecken and S. Schachter (1958) *When Prophesy Fails: A social and psychological study of a modern group that predicted the destruction of the world*, Minneapolis: University of Minnesota Press.

Ganter, R. (2006) *Mixed Relations: Histories and stories of Asian/Aboriginal contact in north Australia*, Perth: University of Western Australia Press.

McIntosh, I. S. (1994) *The Whale and the Cross: Conversations with David Burrumarra M.B.E.*, Darwin: Historical Society of the Northern Territory.

McIntosh, I. S. (1996) 'Islam and Australia's Aborigines? A perspective from north-east Arnhem Land', *Journal of Religious History*, 20 (1), pp. 53–77.

McIntosh, I. S. (2000) *Aboriginal Reconciliation and the Dreaming. Warramirri Yolngu and the quest for equality*, Cultural Survival Series on Ethnicity and Change, Boston: Allyn & Bacon.

McIntosh, I. S. (2004a) 'Personal names and the negotiation of change: reconsidering Arnhem Land's Adjustment Movement', *Anthropological Forum*, 14 (2), pp. 141–62.

McIntosh, I. S (2004b) 'The iron furnace of Birrinydji', in A. Rumsey and J. Weiner (eds), *Mining and Indigenous Lifeworlds in Australia and Papua New Guinea*, Wantage, UK: Sean Kingston Publishing, pp. 12–30.

McIntosh, I. S. (2006a) 'A treaty with the Macassans? Burrumarra and the Dholtji ideal', *Asia Pacific Journal of Anthropology*, 7 (2), pp. 153–72.

McIntosh, I. S. (2006b) 'Why Umbulka killed its master: Aboriginal reconciliation and the Australian wild dog', in P. Waldau and K. Patton (eds), *A Communion of Subjects. Animals in religion, science, and ethics*, New York: Columbia University Press, pp. 360–72.

McIntosh, I. S. (2008) 'Pre-Macassans at Dholtji? Exploring one of Arnhem Land's great conundrums', in P. Veth, P. Sutton and M. Neale (eds), *Strangers on the Shore. Early coastal contacts in Australia*, Canberra: National Museum of Australia.

McIntosh, I. S. (2011) 'Missing the Revolution! Negotiating disclosure on the pre-Macasasans (Bayini) in north-east Arnhem Land', in M. Thomas and M. Neale (eds), *Exploring the Legacy of the 1948 Arnhem Land Expedition*, Canberra: ANU E Press, pp. 337–54.

Macknight, C. C. (1976) *The Voyage to Marege': Macassan trepangers in northern Australia*, Carlton, Vic.: Melbourne University Press.

Merlan, F. (1986) 'Australian Aboriginal conception beliefs revisited', *Man*, (NS) 21 (3), pp. 474–93.

Stanner, W. E. H. (1966) *On Aboriginal Religion*, Oceania Monograph 11, Sydney: University of Sydney.

Warner, W. L. (1937–58) *A Black Civilization: A social study of an Australian Tribe*, Chicago: Harper & Roe.

7. 'An Arnhem Land adventure':[1] Representations of Macassan–Indigenous Australian connections in popular geographical magazines

Rebecca Bilous

Introduction

> Long time ago, when the north east wind blew, the Mangatharra would travel from their place up north in Indonesia to Arnhem Land. They came in Macassan boats called prahus. They planted tamarind trees and traded with Aboriginal people. The Aboriginal people, they traded the trepang which is sea cucumber and the Mangatharra traded knives and material. They also introduced smoking, you know with a pipe, and rice, and taught the Yolngu how to make pottery. (Burarrwanga 2008)

Laklak Burarrwanga (Datiwuy and Rirratjingu elder, caretaker for Gumatj and eldest sister) regularly tells visitors to her home at Bawaka in northeast Arnhem Land stories about the Macassans in the same way her fathers and grandfathers told them to her. In 1987 Laklak made her own journey to Sulawesi to find family members (described by Cooke 1987), whom she still remains in contact with, and Indigenous people from all over Arnhem Land have been involved in a number of projects that have, in different ways, celebrated their connections to Makassar (for examples, see Janson 2001; Langton 2011; Palmer 2007; Stephenson 2007).

Details regarding the Macassan visits to northern Australia and the trepang trade have also been the focus of considerable academic attention, much of which is summarised elsewhere in this volume. A lot of it relies heavily on the earlier work of anthropologists Donald Thomson (1949c) and Ronald and Catherine Berndt (1951, 1954) and the archaeological investigations of Campbell Macknight (1976) and D. J. Mulvaney (1989). This research largely focuses on the impact Macassan contact had on Australian Indigenous society, both materially and culturally (see, for example, Baker 1999; Clarke 2000; Evans 1992; McIntosh 2006, 2008; Mitchell 1995; Swain 1991; Urry and Walsh 1981). Macknight has

---

1 This title makes reference to anthropologist Donald Thomson's magazine article 'An Arnhem Land adventure', published in *The National Geographic Magazine* (Thomson 1948a).

107

recently provided a comprehensive review of the literature to date, writing, 'the existence of the trepang industry in northern Australia and some of its effects on Aboriginal societies have long been known, at least to those who cared to look' (2008, p. 139). While this may be the case in academic circles, it is not necessarily the same for the rest of Australia, whose exposure to these stories is arguably quite limited (Bilous 2011; Stephenson 2007).

This chapter therefore aims to examine one of the ways in which Macassan–Indigenous Australian contact stories have been told to a non-academic, popular audience. I look specifically at the ways in which popular geographical magazines, particularly Australia's *Walkabout* magazine, but also the better known *National Geographic* and *Australian Geographic* magazines, have told these connection stories throughout the twentieth and early twenty-first centuries.[2] I identify the discourses that are drawn upon and reinforced in the representations, specifically discourses of *terra nullius*, the 'othering' of Indigenous Australians from Arnhem Land and the presentation of Arnhem Land as a frontier landscape. In order to better understand the context and some of the reasons for the use of such discourses, I draw on a cultural memory framework, a framework that focuses on the ways in which media texts, like popular geographical magazines, contribute to a collective memory of past events.

Cultural memory and entangled discourses

'Cultural memory', 'collective memory' and 'social memory' are all terms used by academics from an increasing range of disciplines to emphasise the notion that a person's memories are not constructed in isolation but as members of a society (see, for example, Ben-Amos and Weissberg 1999; Knapp 1989; Sturken 1997). Sociologist Maurice Halbwachs, a key figure in the study of memory's collective context, wrote, 'It is in society that people normally acquire their memories. It is also in society that they recall, recognize, and localize their memories' (1992, p. 38). While it is in the fields of psychology and sociology that a lot of work on collective memory exists, increasingly cultural memory has been an important area of study for historians and geographers. Many of these studies have to a certain extent focused on how political and social frameworks shape and even control cultural memory, emphasising the influence of various agencies in the construction of identity. For example, cultural geographer

---

2 My definition of 'geographical magazines' is not discipline based, but focuses on those popular magazines that specifically engage with place.

Nuala Johnson argues that '[m]emory as re-collection, re-membering, and re-presentation is crucial in the mapping of significant historical moments and in the articulation of personal identity' (2004, p. 317).

There is also considerable literature that specifically seeks to understand the role of the media in the formation of collective or cultural memories (see, for example, Bonnet 2002; Erll and Rigney 2009). Karen Till, for example, attempts to separate the concepts of 'collective memory' and 'public memory', the latter referring to the cultural space and process through which 'collective memories' are performed: 'Part of that process includes the creation and appropriation of landscapes, cultural objects, narratives (and here I include formal histories) and images by groups to support their social myths of identity' (1999, p. 255). Till aims to disentangle the role of the media in influencing the form and various interpretations of Berlin's *Neue Wache* ('New Guardhouse') memorial. Astrid Erll (2009) also analyses the ways in which different media help shape collective memory. She focuses on the 'Indian Mutiny', the rebellion against British rule in northern and central India in 1857, analysing the contributions made by different media, including the British press, in an ongoing process of remembering and forgetting. One of Erll's arguments is that the British press drew on a set of established images in order to help a largely uninformed public make sense of an event filled with atrocities.

In a similar way, the stories of Macassan and Indigenous Australian connections presented by popular geographical magazines were shaped by authors whose articles arguably reflect a particular set of world views. This chapter examines three well-established and well-entangled discourses—*terra nullius*, frontier landscapes and 'othering' of Indigenous Australians—in order to understand better the role that popular geographical magazines had, and continue to have, in 'constructing, maintaining and transforming' the stories of connection' (Till 1999, p. 263).

Many of these discourses have received attention from geographers. Richie Howitt and Sue Jackson (1998) explored the 'darker aspects' of geography's 'colonial baggage', arguing that geography had an important role in the construction of a particular understanding of the Australian landscape, an understanding that was used to justify European colonisation. The notion of *terra nullius*—a country empty and belonging to no-one—was prevalent in the work and writing of geographical societies in the early twentieth century. These societies, established in the 1880s, aimed to disseminate geographical knowledge and 'helped build a dominant geographical imaginary which saw Australia as empty, unknown, and waiting for (white) settlement' (Howitt 2001, p. 236).

Alongside the creation of a discourse of *terra nullius* is the 'othering' of Indigenous Australians. 'Othering' is an important tool in the formation of identity and many geographers have looked at the ways boundary-drawing practices are used in identity formation, and the ways in which people define themselves in opposition to others (see, for example, Green 2004; Lloyd et al. 2010; Newman 2006). Underlying this is the theme of colonial racism, as 'othering' is also used as a powerful tool to emphasise one group's dominance or superiority over another. Its role in scientifically dehumanising those outside the Euro–American centre and, therefore, legitimising American–European hegemony is challenged by Smadar Lavie and Ted Swedenburg (1996). James Duncan (1993) also discusses the way the discourse of 'other' has been used to socialise or colonise different sites. He argues that the twentieth-century 'other' of cultural anthropology worked to de-historicise people by the 'temporalisation of space', creating a timeless space where past and present were conceived as one and the same. This is certainly the case in the popular geographical magazines analysed for this chapter, where the 'other' is never given a voice.

The third entangled discourse is that of the 'frontier', described by Howitt as an image that 'simultaneously contains the familiar and excludes the alien and incomprehensible Other' (2001, p. 235). The desire to emphasise images of a frontier can be understood in the travel-writing genre. Mary Louise Pratt argues through a series of case studies that this genre has an 'obsessive need to present and re-present its peripheries and its others continually to itself' (1992, p. 5). For Pratt, 'contact zones' or 'social spaces where disparate cultures meet, clash, and grapple with each other' (p. 4) are synonymous with the colonial frontier and there is a need to constantly reproduce them. The use of frontier imagery has an additional role in geographical magazines with the quest to invent and present possible tourist destinations. In specific reference to Queensland's Carnarvon Gorge, Jackie Huggins et al. (1997) describe early depictions seeking to 'reinvent a frontier land, an unoccupied land open to 'discovery'' (p. 240). Tony Bennett (1988) also addresses this in his critical reflections on Australian museum and heritage policy, arguing that the representation of wilderness or heritage is achieved within an organised frame to meet the needs of a particular audience. The same can be seen in geographical magazines where the representation of Arnhem Land is arguably constructed in opposition to life inside Australian cities (the place where the majority of Australians live). *Walkabout*, for example, is quite clear in its aim to present this romantic image.

Walkabout, *National Geographic* and *Australian Geographic*

Walkabout was first published in November 1934 by the Australian National Travel Association, an organisation whose aim was to advertise Australia's tourist attractions internationally. The founder and editor until 1957 was Charles Holmes, who wrote, 25 years later in *Walkabout*, 'I thought Australians, or at any rate the thoughtful few, would welcome a geographical journal telling the story of the vast and comparatively little known Australia which existed beyond the cities' (1959, p. 8). Charles Lloyd Jones, the Deputy Chairman of the Australian National Travel Association when *Walkabout* was launched, introduced the first issue, writing, 'we have embarked on an educational crusade which will enable Australians and the people of other lands to learn more of the romantic Australia that exists beyond the cities, and the enchanted South Sea Islands and New Zealand' (1934, p. 7). From the very first issue, *Walkabout* clearly portrayed an image of Australia as an imagined frontier, in opposition to life in Australian cities. The result was a monthly magazine, published between 1934 and 1972, of illustrated articles written by a range of writers including geographers, anthropologists, missionaries and adventure-seekers.

Much of the academic writing that has focused on *Walkabout* explores the magazine's representation of Indigenous Australians. Max Quanchi (2004), for example, looks at images of the Pacific Islands in *Walkabout*, suggesting that they are full of oppositions and dissonances, presenting stereotypes of both the Pacific Islands and Australian 'Aborigines'. Glen Ross's (1999) focus is on *Walkabout*'s representation of Australia within a masculine, national narrative of progress in which Indigenous Australians were ideologically erased by being presented as a vanishing race.

Jillian Barnes (2007) traces the development of *Walkabout* through the lens of tourism, focusing on the images of Gwoja Tjungurrayi ('One Pound Jimmy'), which were appropriated in order to compare the progress of modern Australia with 'Stone Age' Australian 'Aborigines'. Historian Lynette Russell (1994) also explores the romantic stereotypes of Indigenous people presented by *Walkabout* throughout the 1950s. She argues that '[t]hese visions of Aboriginal Australia were conservative and emphasized a uniform Australia-wide Indigenous Australian culture, which although evidencing a deep genealogy had changed little through time' (p. 4). Russell's work, however, does not acknowledge the numerous articles in *Walkabout* that focus on or make reference to the long and complex histories of contact that exist between the Macassans and Indigenous Australians, stories that problematise this popular Australian discourse.

Walkabout's last issue was published in May 1974 and, in many ways, *Australian Geographic* took up the mantle of promoting Australian tourism. *Australian Geographic* was first published in 1985 by entrepreneur and adventurer Dick Smith, and then sold to Fairfax Media Limited in 1995 and then to ACP (formerly Australian Consolidated Press) magazines in 2006. There is comparatively little academic writing on *Australian Geographic*.

The better known, and internationally focused, *National Geographic* was first published in October 1888. It was produced by the American National Geographic Society, a society whose aim was to organise the diffusion of geographical knowledge. *National Geographic* has been subject to considerable academic scrutiny, much of which examines the interface of media representations and identity (see, for example, Beaudreau 2002; Darling-Wolf and Mendelson 2008; Pauly 1979; Rothenberg 1994). Julie Tuason (1999), for example, looks at *National Geographic* for the ideological undercurrents that drove and legitimatised US Government policies, reminding her readers that the magazine very much reflected and determined the American ideology of expansion. David Jansson's (2003) study of *National Geographic*'s 'internal othering' of the American south in order to assist in the creation of a more positive American national identity is particularly interesting in the context of this chapter.

Before beginning my discussion, it is important to note that in terms of methodology this chapter is based on a survey of articles published in *Walkabout*, *National Geographic* and *Australian Geographic* magazines that make reference to the contact between Macassans and Indigenous Australians. While there are some articles that focus on Indonesia and Arnhem Land in isolation, in this survey I focus only on those that make direct reference to the contact between the Macassans, who in early geographical magazines are predominantly referred to as 'Malays', and Indigenous Australians. There were 31 articles, the majority in *Walkabout* (25), four in *Australian Geographic* and two in *National Geographic* (see Figure 7.1). The articles are analysed in chronological order so as to both acknowledge the entangled nature of the themes and discourses used by the authors and make clearer the ways in which the articles constantly refer to those published previously. In this way, they can be seen to be working together, either intentionally or unintentionally, to reshape the collective memory of Macassan–Indigenous Australian contact, building on or eventually forgetting it.

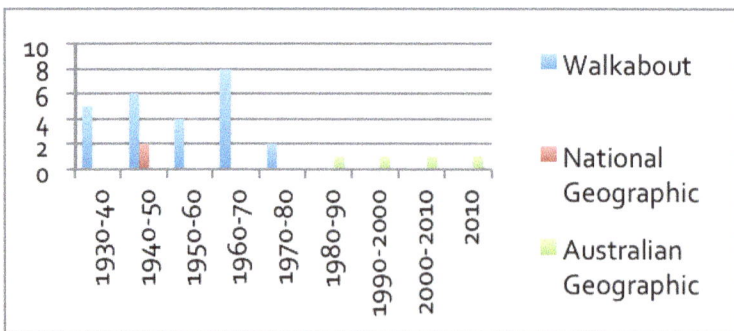

Figure 7.1 Articles in popular geographical magazines *Walkabout*, *National Geographic* and *Australian Geographic* that make reference to connections between the Macassans and Indigenous Australians

Source: Rebecca Bilous

Building and shaping a collective memory of Macassan–Indigenous Australian contact stories

Throughout the 1930s and 1940s, Macassan contact with Arnhem Land is frequently referenced in *Walkabout*, although not always in any detail. The first article that makes any reference was written by Donald MacLean (in January 1935) as the first of a series of five articles focusing on the search for the 'Great South Land'. MacLean acknowledges Malay knowledge of Australia but dismisses the Macassan trade. He compares Malay lack of interest in northern Australia with an initial Dutch lack of interest, writing, 'The Malays were pre-eminently traders, and for the trader Australia held nothing' (1935, p. 39). This is the first of a number of images of *terra nullius*, which were commonly used in the representation of Australia in *Walkabout* magazine during this period.

The following month (February 1935), adventure travel writer and frequent contributor to *Walkabout* Ion L. Idriess invokes a *terra nullius* when he describes Arnhem Land as 'a large vacant space east of Darwin' and as a country represented on maps as 'mostly a series of blanks' (1935, p. 31). Alongside his descriptions of the natural landscape, Idriess describes the Aborigines as 'stone-age' and as 'a relic of long past human history' (p. 33). As well as invoking images of a *terra nullius*, he also uses images of a dangerous frontier landscape, emphasising the people's 'warlike' nature, cataloguing their victories and writing: 'His list of luggers looted and burned at the water's edge makes quite a respectable tally in the annals of canoe piracy' (p. 33). As well as serving to emphasise the author's own heroic qualities, the use of such imagery can arguably be attributed to a desire to represent a frontier landscape, an unoccupied landscape open for exploration and discovery. But how do discourses of a *terra nullius* and frontier landscape account for the centuries of Macassan contact? According to Idriess, the reason Arnhem Landers can be described as 'virile' and 'warlike' is as a result of centuries of contact with the Macassans. This contact had resulted in 'the admixture of Malay blood, for the proas of these sea-raiders have, until recent years, visited our northern shores for centuries past' (p. 33). It is this article, focusing on a genetic difference between Arnhem Land Aborigines and other Indigenous Australians, which sets the tone for other references to the Macassans throughout the 1930s and begins the process of 'othering'.

Three years later, in August 1938, journalist Colin Bednall was commissioned to travel on a patrol boat along the Arnhem Land coast, searching for illegal Japanese luggers. He writes: 'We encountered hundreds of wild natives, some of them cannibals and some very sullen' (1938, p. 14). Bednall says that despite the cannibalistic nature of the people, the presence of Malay blood is a 'valuable addition', and he believes it resulted in better-looking people with improved 'appearance and stature' and women who 'might almost have been termed attractive' with their lighter skin and straighter noses (p. 16). In fact, Bednall took it upon himself to name one of these women after a famous actress he was reminded of. The results of Macassan contact are viewed by Bednall as positive and are used to serve as a contrast with the impact of the Japanese pearlers and trepangers, whom the patrol boat was trying to root out. In the case of Japanese contact, Bednall describes the result as 'tragic', resulting in 'the saddest-looking children' who were 'undersized, and had extraordinary features' (p. 16).

The emphasis again is that people in Arnhem Land are somehow different from Indigenous people in the rest of Australia. While Indigenous people across the rest of Australia are presented by *Walkabout* as being uniformly the same across space and time, Arnhem Land is presented as the exception. Throughout the rest of Australia, Indigenous people were 'othered' by being placed in a timeless space where past and present were one, but those articles that deal with Arnhem Land Aborigines are 'othered' through a focus on Macassan impacts.

In magazine articles that tell contact stories, one might expect to come across a number of 'others', but interestingly, in articles that include both Macassans and Indigenous Australians, the Macassans are not used to represent the 'other' but are only used as a tool in order to emphasise a case for the 'othering' of Arnhem Land Indigenous people. In these cases the authors perceive more similarities between the Macassans and themselves than they do with Indigenous Australians. Not only are Arnhem Landers different from the white Australian authors, the authors argue that they are different from the rest of Indigenous Australia within this European colonial framework. Needless to say, the successful process of 'othering' Arnhem Landers is also a powerful silencing tool seen by the fact that the Indigenous voice is wholly absent from each of the stories presented to readers of *Walkabout*.

One of the possible reasons that Indigenous people of Arnhem Land were considered different to Indigenous people in other parts of Australia at this time was perhaps the result of the negative press they received throughout the 1930s. In particular, the killing of five Japanese crew from two trepang luggers at Caledon Bay, the killing of two white trepangers and the subsequent spearing of Constable Albert Stuart McColl of the Northern Territory Police at Woodah Island in Blue Mud Bay in August 1933—all received extensive newspaper coverage at the time. Articles that describe various aspects of the murders and the indignation relating to the poor handling of the arrests, which were made under false pretences, along with the subsequent trial of Dhaakiyarr and three other Aborigines from Caledon Bay appeared in each of the major Australian newspapers as well as many smaller ones.³ The Indigenous people of Caledon Bay were described in the press as 'treacherous murderers', and a punitive expedition was planned, although never carried out.

These events were what prompted well-known anthropologist Donald Thomson's request to the Commonwealth Government to visit Arnhem Land. Having previously worked in Cape York and publicly protested the treatment of Indigenous people at Aurukun, he was funded by the Commonwealth Government to establish friendly relations with the 'Arnhem Land Aborigines' and to help them to understand the gravity of their actions. In Thomson's own words, published in *Walkabout*, he makes it quite clear that the reason for his visit was 'to make a study of the natives and the causes of fighting and unrest' (1946, p. 5).

Detailed accounts of Thomson's life and expeditions into Arnhem Land have received recent academic attention and his significant contribution both to the discipline of anthropology and to Aboriginal affairs is now recognised (Peterson 2005; Wiseman 1996). Thomson's first account of Arnhem Land was published in *Walkabout* in August 1946 and was entitled '*The* story of Arnhem Land' (*Walkabout*'s italics). Soon after, 'Arnhem Land adventure' was published in March 1948 in *National Geographic* and the much lengthier 'Arnhem Land: explorations among an unknown people' in *The Geographical Journal* for Britain's Royal Geographical Society in three parts between 1948 and 1949 (Thomson 1948b, 1949a, 1949b). The articles in all three magazines focus on the adventurous aspects of the expedition, telling tales of fording crocodile-infested rivers barefooted and starving, rather than providing an anthropological study of Arnhem Landers.⁴

Reflecting Idriess 11 years earlier, Thomson in his opening description in '*The* story of Arnhem Land' describes a frontier into a *terra nullius*—'a vast untamed No Man's Land, unknown and practically unexplored'—and towards the end of the same column: 'Until recent years, this country remained practically unknown' (1946, p. 5). As for the Indigenous Australians of Arnhem Land, Thomson immediately narrates a story of their difference from other Indigenous Australians. In his second paragraph, he writes, 'The aborigines of Arnhem Land are assured of a place in the history of Australia—the only aborigines who have dared to defend their birthright, and who have stood out consistently against the injustice of the white man' (p. 5). While outrageous, this statement reflects

---

3 See, for example, 'Story of Caledon Bay massacre' (*The Advertiser*, Friday, 13 October 1933, p. 21); 'The Caledon Bay natives' (*Sydney Morning Herald*, Thursday, 7 December 1933, p. 1); 'The Caledon Bay killers' (*The Courier-Mail*, Monday, 16 April 1934, p. 1); 'Caledon Bay murder: claim for salvage' (*The Argus*, Thursday, 16 August 1934, p. 7).
4 Peterson (2005) writes that in the *National Geographic* version, '[i]t is clear that editors played fast and loose with Thomson's text…[it] contains typographical errors…misleading captions, obvious rewrites and interpellations from the editors' (p. 44).

that of Matthew Flinders, whose description of the Aborigines of Caledon Bay in 1803 as not 'showing that timidity so usual with the Australians', is quoted by Thomson (1946, p. 5). Both Flinders and Thompson claim this lack of timidity to be a result of their contact with the Macassans, and while Thomson dismisses outright any evidence of the genetic impact emphasised by previous contributors to *Walkabout*, he does continue to narrate a story of Arnhem Land Aborigines' difference or 'otherness' as a result of this contact.

Thomson's was one of several anthropological expeditions made into Arnhem Land during the late 1930s and 1940s that also included Ronald and Catherine Berndt (in the mid 1940s) and the *National Geographic* sponsored 1948 American–Australian Scientific Expedition to Arnhem Land. This expedition was also well publicised in Australian and US newspapers and then in the *National Geographic* in December 1949. Australian ethnologist Charles P. Mountford again invokes an isolated, unknown *terra nullius*, but unlike Thomson, almost dismisses the Macassan presence in Australia, writing that after Dutch discovery in the 1600s, '[s]ave for natives, of course, and occasional Malay fishing fleets, the coast was virtually deserted for the next century and a half' (1949, p. 746). He traces the history of Arnhem Land's 'discovery', including the exploratory journey of Flinders, followed by the sentence, 'Since that master map maker's departure, the world has heard little about Arnhem Land' (p. 746). Again, Mountford draws on a frontier myth that emphasises Arnhem Land's obscurity.

While serving perhaps to glorify Mountford's own explorations, Arnhem Land's obscurity is a myth that is not backed up in Australian newspapers at the time due to the reporting of violence in the 1930s and the numerous expeditions in the 1940s. In fact, V. C. Hall, in *Walkabout* in May 1948, completely debunks the idea of Arnhem Land as the last unexplored frontier when he writes, 'Arnhem Land is no longer untrodden and unknown…Much of the colour, the romance and dangers of this region belong to the past, awaiting the pen of an inspired writer to cause the fascinating stories of the days before the coming of the European to live again—in Australian literature' (1948, p. 35).

While perhaps not the 'literature' Hall was referring to, Thomson's next published articles for *Walkabout* in 1957 contribute to this idea. He focuses first on the '*lippa-lippa*' or dugout canoe introduced from Makassar (in June 1957) and then in the following month (July 1957b) explores other cultural impacts Macassan visitors had on the people of Arnhem Land. In particular, Thomson explains the pattern of behaviour or conduct that Indigenous people established with the Macassan visitors, whereby there was mutual respect and a good working relationship. Thomson argues that it was because this code of conduct was ignored by the 'white man', who 'assumed that they were like all the other "aborigines" he had encountered and had attempted to walk rough-shot over them' (1957b, p. 30), that subsequently led to the violent clashes described in the 1930s. While Thomson comes out in support of the Indigenous people of Arnhem Land, working to provide his readers with explanations for the problems facing them, he still continues to emphasise their difference from other Indigenous Australians. While on the surface a person whose understanding goes beyond the assumption that Indigenous Australians are the same across the country seems positive, it is clear that Thomson attributes this difference solely to their previous contact with the Macassans. At this point Thomson is also focusing on interactions that he believes belong to the past and are well over. In fact, in his earlier articles Thomson's concern is that 'the aborigines of Arnhem Land are a little farther down the road to extinction' (1946, p. 22).

Through the 1950s and 1960s the focus of articles in *Walkabout* regarding Indigenous Australians and Macassans seems to change again. The majority of articles about Arnhem Land Aborigines are written by anthropologists and Macassan contact is just one part of that narrative. They provide only general information regarding the contact and resultant impact on Indigenous Australians. For example, well-known anthropologist Fred McCarthy, who was present on the 1948 American–Australian Scientific Expedition to Arnhem Land led by Mountford, writes two articles, one on utensils used by Indigenous Australians and another on rock art (McCarthy 1957, 1964).

In several articles published by *Walkabout* in September 1952, April 1963 and December 1965, however, the Macassan–Indigenous Australian contact period is invoked in articles that aim to highlight the positive work being done by missionaries. In September 1953, Trevor Tuckfield reminds readers of a period of hostility when '[t]he Arnhem Land natives were perhaps the most savage and ferocious of all the Australian aborigines' (p. 14), and reflects on the success of the missionaries. This success, Tuckfield suggests, was because Arnhem Landers were, of all Australian Aborigines, 'the easiest to teach'. He continues: 'To us they were the most intelligent and finest physical examples of all that we had so far come in contact with. This, no doubt, was due to an infusion of Malay and Macassan blood' (p. 14). Ignoring the research and articles published by Thomson that dismissed a genetic impact, Tuckfield instead chooses to reflect on the images of Aborigines that were created much earlier, in the 1930s.

Cecil Holmes in 1963 again invokes the dark, violent time of the 1930s and makes reference to the eminent and fondly remembered Thomson, using this to contrast with the current situation at the Yirrkala mission. The new picture invoked is peaceful and purposeful. He writes: 'Along the beach at Yirkalla, in the shade of the great Tamarin trees, the artists sit in the sand painting with slow care and patience. There are up to a hundred of them, perhaps one of the strangest concentrations of creative endeavour anywhere' (p. 12). In a similar way, an unattributed photographic essay in *Walkabout* in December 1964 focuses on the fame of the Yirrkala paintings. The author is unsurprised regarding the artists' adept painting style on the basis that these are Aboriginal people who also used steel for 200 years as a result of Macassan visits (Anonymous 1964, p. 42). In a similar way, in 1965, Keith Willey, when describing Bathurst Island in *Walkabout*, compares the current 'happy, smiling people' of the mission with men who 'were savage warriors, blood drinkers, reputed cannibals and polygamists who treated their women as chattels' and massacred the Macassans (p. 51). Again, the reader is reminded that the Malay and Melanesian facial characteristics of these Aborigines meant that they were far more advanced in comparison with those on the mainland and were, therefore, able to learn quickly from the missionaries. While the discourse is no longer one of a violent or empty frontier, the 'othering' of Arnhem Land Indigenous people is still being emphasised by yet again focusing on the ways in which they were different from their contemporaries in the rest of Australia. It is at this time that *Walkabout* was also publishing articles that focused on the removal of Indigenous people from their homelands (see, for example, Carter and Carter 1965; Ford 1968; Smith 1967).

By the 1970s the number of articles that make reference to the Macassans decreases sharply. There are only two, both making only brief reference to the Macassans in terms of the discovery of Australia, questioning who discovered it first. The first article, in January 1973, is part of a special focus issue on the 'Top End'. Given the focus of this magazine it is surprising that the only reference to the Macassans is by author, Joan Cobb, who focuses on Groote Eylandt's 'discovery' by the Macassans. Similarly, in April 1973, the last reference to Macassan contact in *Walkabout* is very similar to the first (by MacLean in 1935) and relates in a similar way to the early 'discovery' of Australia by the 'Malays' (Rooke 1973). Just more than 12 months later, with no more references to the Macassans, publication of *Walkabout* ceases and it is another 11 years before *Australian Geographic*'s launch.

In *Australian Geographic* the references to Macassans in Arnhem Land are sporadic and very brief: four articles in 26 years make the briefest of references. Two of these articles make reference to rock paintings that include the depiction of praus (Curl 1990; Eastwood 2010). In addition to these, adventure traveller Rory McGuinness (1989) narrates his visit to Sulawesi and is surprised to learn of the local fishermen and sailors' knowledge of northern Australia, stories of their ancestors' regular visits and the 'amicable' relationships formed with the Indigenous people they met there. McGuinness is perhaps surprised because by the late 1980s, despite the fact that Macassan–Indigenous Australian contact histories are still being celebrated in Arnhem Land itself, the stories are no longer being told in the popular media. They are no longer considered significant and, as Erll and Rigney argue, media shapes memory, the 'ongoing process of remembrance and forgetting in which individuals and groups continue to refigure their relationship to the past and hence reposition themselves in relation to established and emergent memory sites' (2009, p. 2).

The next reference to the Macassans is in 2006, in an article written by Amanda Burdon, who, just like many contributors to *Walkabout*, invokes the same entangled discourses in her description of Arnhem Land. The article is entitled 'Still Arnhem Land' and she writes: 'What makes the Yolngu of Arnhem Land unique among the Aboriginal peoples of Australia is that they were never completely displaced and have occupied their country since the time of the Dreaming' (p. 72). Burdon succeeds in 'othering' the Indigenous people of Arnhem Land and, yet again, Arnhem Land is placed at the frontier, described as a land that was 'left undisturbed for centuries by all but Macassan seasonal fishermen', despite this single reference to the Macassans. She provides no information about these 'seasonal fishermen' and they are dismissed as something belonging to the past. In this particular case, Indigenous culture serves as a promotional tool, essential to the creation of an Australian frontier.

Silencing Indigenous Australians on the Arnhem Land 'frontier'

A number of discourses are at work in the popular geographical magazines of the twentieth and early twenty-first centuries, discourses that represent Indigenous Australians as unchanged across time and place. The representation of Macassan and Indigenous Australian contact stories—in which Indigenous Australians were an integral part of an informal international trading network—would presumably disrupt some of these. Instead, these contact stories are told in a way that strengthens and reinforces the stereotypes and geographical marginalisation of Arnhem Land and the people who live there.

One of the ways in which this was done was through the construction of Arnhem Land as an unknown, empty frontier. Part of this frontier discourse was the idealising of Arnhem Land as an untouched and exotic land. In articles published in the 1930s, it was an area of Australia represented as largely 'undiscovered'. Later on, during the 1940s, a period that saw numerous anthropological expeditions, Arnhem Land was no longer referred to as empty but instead the dangers present in an exotic landscape were emphasised: the crocodiles, the mosquitoes and the humidity.

The creation of a frontier that emphasised the violence and danger present in Arnhem Land, not only in the landscape but also as a result of the Indigenous people themselves, enabled the 'othering' of Arnhem Landers. They were considered dangerous as a result of a series of violent incidents that were well reported in the media in the 1930s and this was blamed on the influence of 'outside' Macassan blood and culture. The dangerous and violent Arnhem Land 'Aborigine' was imagery that continued through the 1930s until the 1970s and was arguably used to justify both missionary and state intervention in Arnhem Land.

In many ways, and again attributed to the influence of Macassan culture, Indigenous people from Arnhem Land were also considered superior to other Indigenous people; their technology and culture were considered more advanced and in several places there is respect shown to their resistance of European intrusion into Arnhem Land. Even as late as 2006 Burdon in *Australian Geographic* emphasises an exotic 'other world'; not a country that has been connected to Southeast Asia for many centuries as a result of the important relationships Arnhem Landers formed with Macassan traders.

These representations and myths are all written by non-Indigenous authors. Indigenous voices, let alone authorities, are completely absent from these magazines. The violence, advanced culture and technology are all considered to be the result of centuries of Macassan contact—contact that was placed quite conveniently in the past; contact that is outside academic circles and Arnhem Land itself, where it is celebrated daily, is now rarely referred to in popular media. This analysis shows how rather than engaging with the often fraught connections forged between Macassan traders and Arnhem Landers through the centuries, popular geography drew on these connections to reinforce myths of *terra nullius* and to create a mythical northern frontier that was used to differentiate and silence the Indigenous people who lived there.

References

Anonymous (1964) 'Arnhem Land', *Walkabout*, (December), pp. 42–3.

Baker, R. (1999) *Land is Life: From bush to town: The story of the Yanyuwa people*, Sydney: Allen & Unwin.

Barnes, J. E. (2007) 'Resisting the captured image: how Gwoja Tjungurrayi, "One Pound Jimmy", escaped the "Stone Age"', *Transgressions: Critical Australian Indigenous Histories*, 16, pp. 83–133.

Beaudreau, S. (2002) 'The changing faces of Canada: images of Canada in National Geographic', *The American Review of Canadian Studies*, (Winter), pp. 517–46.

Bednall, C. (1938) 'Arnhem Land coast patrol', *Walkabout*, (August), pp. 13–19.

Ben-Amos, D. and L. Weissberg (eds) (1999) *Cultural Memory and the Construction of Identity*, Detroit: Wayne State University Press.

Bennett, A. (1988) *Out of Which Past? Critical reflections on Australian museum and heritage policy*, Nathan, Qld: Griffith University.

Berndt, R. M. (1951) 'Ceremonial exchange in western Arnhem Land', *Southwestern Journal of Anthropology*, 7 (2), pp. 156–76.

Berndt, R. M. and C. H. Berndt (1954) *Arnhem Land: Its history and its people*, Melbourne: F. W. Cheshire.

Bilous, R. (2011) 'Macassan–Indigenous Australian "sites of memory" in the National Museum of Australia and Australian National Maritime Museum', *Australian Geographer*, 42 (4), pp. 371–86.

Bonnett, A. (2002) 'Geography as the world discipline: connecting popular and academic geographical imaginations', *Area*, 35 (1), pp. 55–63.

Burarrwanga, L., D. Maymuru, R. Ganambarr, B. Ganambarr, S. Wright, S. Suchet-Pearson and K. Lloyd (2008) *Weaving Lives Together at Bawaka: North east Arnhem Land*, Callaghan, NSW: Centre for Urban and Regional Studies, University of Newcastle.

Burdon, A. (2006) 'Still Arnhem Land', *Australian Geographic*, 84, pp. 70–4.

Carter, J. and M. Carter (1965) 'Beswick leads the way', *Walkabout*, (February), pp. 11–16.

Clarke, A. (2000) 'The "Moorman's trowsers": Macassan and Aboriginal interactions and the changing fabric of Indigenous social life', in S. O'Connor and P. Veth (eds), *East of Wallace's Line: Studies of past and present maritime cultures of the Indo-Pacific region*, Rotterdam: A. A. Balkema, pp. 315–35.

Cobb, J. (1973) 'The two faces of Groote Eylandt', *Walkabout*, (January), pp. 48–51.

Cooke, M. (1987) *Makassar and Northeast Arnhem Land: Missing links and living bridges*, Batchelor, NT: Educational Media Unit, Batchelor College.

Curl, D. (1990) 'The changing moods of Kakadu', *Australian Geographic*, 19, pp. 44–71.

Darling-Wolf, F. and A. L. Mendelson (2008) 'Seeing themselves through the lens of the other: an analysis of the cross-cultural production and negotiation of *National Geographic*'s "The Samurai Way" story', *Association for Education in Journalism and Mass Communication*, 10, pp. 285–322.

Duncan, J. (1993) 'Sites of representation: place, time and the discourse of the Other', in J. Duncan and D. Ley (eds), *place / culture / representation*, London: Routledge.

Eastwood, K. (2010) 'Where in the desert is Ludwig Leichardt?', *Australian Geographic*, 98, pp. 106–12.

Erll, A. (2009) 'Remembering across time, space, and cultures: premediation, remediation and the "Indian Mutiny"', in A. Erll and A. Rigney (eds), *Mediation, Remediation, and the Dynamics of Cultural Memory*, Berlin: Walter de gruyter GmbH & Co.

Erll, A. and A. Rigney (2009), *Mediation, Remediation, and the Dynamics of Cultural Memory*, Berlin: Walter de gruyter GmbH & Co.

Evans, N. (1992) 'Macassan loanwords in Top End languages', *Australian Journal of Linguistics*, 12, pp. 45–91.

Ford, M. (1968) 'Citizen Aborigines—their problem', *Walkabout*, (June), pp. 20–2.

Green, L. (2004) 'Bordering on the inconceivable: the Pacific solution, the migration zone, and "Australia's 9/11"', *Australian Journal of Communication*, 31 (1), pp. 19–36.

Halbwachs, M.aurice (1992), *On Collective Memory*, ed. (Donald N. Levine, ed., trans. Lewis A. Coser trans.), (The Heritage of Sociology,; Chicago: University of Chicago Press).

Hall, V. C. (1948) 'Arnhem Land Aboriginal Reserve', *Walkabout*, (May), pp. 33–5.

Holmes, C. (1963) 'Some people of Arnhem Land', *Walkabout*, (April), pp. 10–13.

Holmes, C. H. (1959) 'How "Walkabout" began', *Walkabout*, (November), p. 8.

Howitt, R. (2001) 'Frontiers, borders, edges: liminal challenges to the hegemony of exclusion', *Australian Geographical Studies*, 39 (2), pp. 233–45.

Howitt, R. and S. Jackson (1998) 'Some things do change: Indigenous rights, geographers and geography in Australia', *Australian Geographer*, 29, pp. 233–45.

Huggins, J., R. Huggins and J. M. Jacobs (1997) 'Kooramindanjie: place and the postcolonial', in R. White and P. Russell (eds), *Memories and Dreams: Reflections on twentieth-century Australia*, St Leonards, NSW: Allen & Unwin.

Idriess, I. L. (1935) 'Arnhem Land', *Walkabout*, (Feburary), pp. 31–3.

Janson, J. (2001) *The Eyes of Marege*, Hobart: The Australian Script Centre.

Jansson, D. R. (2003) 'American national identity and the progress of the new south in National Geographic magazine', *Geographical Review*, 93 (3), pp. 350–69.

Johnson, N. C. (2004) 'Public memory', in J. S. Duncan, N. C. Johnson and R. H. Schein (eds), *A Companion to Cultural Geography*, Blackwell Companions to Geography, Malden, Mass.: Blackwell.

Jones, C. L. (1934) *Walkabout*, (November), p. 7.

Knapp, S. (1989) 'Collective memory and the actual past', *Representations*, 26, pp. 123–49.

Langton, M. (2011) *Trepang: China and the story of Macassan–Aboriginal trade*, Melbourne: Centre for Cultural Material Conservation,

Lavie, S. and T. Swedenburg (1996) 'Between and among the boundaries of culture: bridging text and lived experience in the third timespace', *Cultural Studies*, 10 (1), pp. 154–79.

Lloyd, K., S. Suchet-Pearson, S. Wright and L. Burrarwanga (2010) 'Stories of crossings and connections from Bawaka, north east Arnhem Land, Australia', *Social and Cultural Geography*, 11 (7), pp. 701–17.

McCarthy, F. D. (1957) 'Utensils of the Australian Aborigines', *Walkabout*, (August), pp. 36–7.

McCarthy, F. D. (1964) 'Island art galleries', *Walkabout*, (February), pp. 38–40.

McGuinness, R. (1989) 'Berkeley River: a Kimberley voyage in a traditional Indonesian sailing craft', *Australian Geographic*, 14, pp. 104–17.

McIntosh, I. (2006) 'A treaty with the Macassans? Burrumarra and the Dholtji ideal', *The Asia Pacific Journal of Anthropology*, 7 (2), pp. 153–72.

McIntosh, I. (2008) 'Pre-Macassans at Dholtji?: exploring one of north-east Arnhem Land's great conundrums', in P. Veth, P. Sutton and M. Neale (eds), *Strangers on the Shore: Early coastal contacts in Australia*, Canberra: National Museum of Australia.

Macknight, C. (2008) 'Harvesting the memory: open beaches in Makassar and Arnhem Land', in P. Veth, P. Sutton and M. Neale (eds), *Strangers on the Shore: Early coastal contacts in Australia*, Canberra: National Museum of Australia.

Macknight, C. C. (1976) *The Voyage to Marege': Macassan trepangers in northern Australia*, Melbourne: Melbourne University Press.

MacLean, D. (1935) 'The search for the great south land', *Walkabout*, (January), pp. 38–41.

Mitchell, S. (1995) 'Foreign contact and Indigenous exchange networks on the Cobourg Peninsula, north-western Arnhem Land', *Australian Aboriginal Studies*, (2), pp. 44–8.

Mountford, C. P. (1949) 'Exploring Stone Age Arnhem Land', *The National Geographic Magazine*, (December), pp. 745–82.

Mulvaney, D. J. (1989) *Encounters in Place: Outsiders and Aboriginal Australians 1606–1985*, St Lucia, Qld: University of Queensland Press.

Newman, D. (2006) 'The lines that continue to separate us: borders in our "borderless" world', *Progress in Human Geography*, 30 (2), pp. 143–61.

Palmer, L. (2007) 'Negotiating the ritual and social order through spectacle: the (re)production of Macassan/Yolngu histories', *Anthropological Forum: A journal of social anthropology and comparative sociology*, 17 (1), pp. 1–20.

Pauly, P. J. (1979) 'The world and all that is in it: the National Geographic Society, 1888–1918', *American Quarterly*, 31 (4), pp. 517–32.

Peterson, N. (2005) 'Thomson's place in Australian anthropology', in B. Rigsby and N. Peterson (eds), *Donald Thomson: The man and scholar*, Canberra: The Academy of the Social Sciences in Australia.

Pratt, M. L. (1992) *Imperial Eyes: Travel writing and transculturation*, London & New York: Routledge.

Quanchi, M. (2004) 'Contrary images: photographing the new Pacific in Walkabout magazine', *Journal of Australian Studies*, 79, pp. 73–88.

Rooke, S. (1973) 'They came in hope', *Walkabout*, (April), pp. 10–15.

Ross, G. (1999) 'The fantastic face of the continent: the Australian geographical Walkabout magazine', *Southern Review*, 32 (1), pp. 27–41.

Rothenberg, T. Y. (1994) 'Voyeurs of imperialism: the National Geographic magazine before World War II', in A. Godlewska and N. Smith (eds), *Geography and Empire*, The Institute of British Geographers Special Publications Series, Oxford: Blackwell.

Russell, L. (1994) 'Going walkabout in the 1950s: images of "traditional" Aboriginal Australia', *The Olive Pink Society Bulletin*, 6 (1), pp. 4–8.

Smith, P. A. (1967) 'Winds of change in the Territory', *Walkabout*, (August), pp. 35–7.

Stephenson, P. (2007) *The Outsides Within: Telling Australia's Indigenous–Asia story*, Sydney: UNSW Press.

Sturken, M. (1997) *Tangled Memories: The Vietnam War, the AIDS epidemic, and the politics of remembering*, Berkeley: University of California Press.

Swain, A. (1991) 'The earth mother from northern waters', *History of Religions*, 30 (3), pp. 223–60.

Thomson, D. F. (1946) '*The* story of Arnhem Land', *Walkabout*, (August), pp. 5–22.

Thomson, D. F. (1948a) 'An Arnhem Land adventure', *The National Geographic Magazine*, 93 (March), pp. 403–30.

Thomson, D. F. (1948b) 'Arnhem Land: explorations among an unknown people Part I. The journey to Bennet Bay', *The Geographical Journal*, 112 (October–December), pp. 146–64.

Thomson, D. F. (1949a) 'Arnhem Land: explorations among an unknown people Part II. The people of Blue Mud Bay', *The Geographical Journal*, 113 (January–June), pp. 1–8.

Thomson, D. F. (1949b) 'Arnhem Land: explorations among an unknown people Part III. On foot across Arnhem Land', *The Geographical Journal*, 114 (July–September), pp. 53–67.

Thomson, D. F. (1949c) *Economic Structure and the Ceremonial Exchange Cycle in Arnhem Land*, Melbourne: Macmillan & Co.

Thomson, D. F. (1957a) 'Some watercraft of the Australian Aborigines', *Walkabout*, (June), pp. 19–20.

Thomson, D. F. (1957b) 'Early Macassar visitors to Arnhem Land', *Walkabout*, (July), pp. 29–31.

Till, K. E. (1999) 'Staging the past: landscape designs, cultural identity and Erinnerungspolitik at Berlin's Neue Wache', *Ecumene*, 6 (3), pp. 251–83.

Tuason, J. A. (1999) 'The ideology of empire in National Geographic magazine's coverage of the Philippines, 1898–1908', *Geographical Review*, 89 (1), pp. 34–53.

Tuckfield, T. (1953) 'Along the coast of Arnhem Land', *Walkabout*, (September), pp. 14–18.

Urry, J. and M. Walsh (1981) 'The lost "Macassar language" of northern Australia', *Aboriginal History*, 5, pp. 91–108.

Willey, K. (1965) 'Mission to the islands', *Walkabout*, (December), pp. 51–3.

Wiseman, J. P. (1996) *Thomson Time: Arnhem Land in the 1930s: A photographic essay*, Melbourne: Museum Victoria.

8. Rock art evidence for Macassan–Aboriginal contact in northwestern Arnhem Land[1]

Paul S. C. Taçon and Sally K. May

Introduction

Some of the most important evidence for the activities of Southeast Asian or 'Macassan'[2] visitors to Australia prior to the European settlement of this continent can be found in the rock art of northern Australia—from the Kimberley to the Top End of the Northern Territory to parts of northern Queensland (for example, see Chaloupka 1993, pp. 191–2; 1996; Clarke and Frederick 2006; Roberts 2004). Rock art is widely acknowledged as encoding social, economic and cultural information about the artists and their cultural groups and it can reflect changes in these societies as well as the wider landscape. This is the case for the early encounters and ongoing regular interaction between Australian Aboriginal people and Macassans. Rock art illustrates some of this complex, sustained and diverse story.

As discussed in Clark and May (this volume), the commonly accepted date for the earliest Macassan visits is contested, as is the theory of pre-Macassan contact (see, for example, Berndt and Berndt 1954; Evans 1992, p. 66; McIntosh 2004). European accounts, such as those of Matthew Flinders in 1801 (Flinders 1814), have led researchers to suggest that these visits began between 1650 and 1750 (for example, Macknight 1976; Crawford 1969); Macknight later revised this to 1780 (Macknight 2011). The interpretations of early radiocarbon dates continue to be debated (Clarke 2000); however, recent accelerator mass spectrometry (AMS) dating of a beeswax snake design overlaying a prau (*perahu*/ship) painting

---

1   We thank Ronald Lamilami and his family for supporting this research, as well as for their generosity and hospitality in the field. 'Picturing Change' is funded by Australian Research Council (ARC) Discovery Grant DP0877463, and we would like to acknowledge Dr June Ross and Associate Professor Alistair Paterson as fellow Chief Investigators on this project. Thanks also to the following people for their assistance in the field: Meg Travers, Janet and Phil Davill, Wayne Brennan, Ines Domingo Sanz, Melissa Marshall, Kirsten Brett, Michelle Langley and Megan Berry. Thanks to Injalak Arts and Crafts, the Northern Land Council and Kakadu National Park (Natural Cultural Programs Unit), as well as Griffith University and The Australian National University for their ongoing support of rock art research.
2   Following convention, we use the term 'Macassan' to refer to those people from Southeast Asia visiting northern Australia as part of the trepang industry. As Macknight (2011, pp. 128–9) notes, it appears anthropologists Ronald and Catherine Berndt replaced 'Malay', prevalent in historical documents, with 'Macassan' to describe Southeast Asian visitors.

at the Maung site of Djulirri suggests praus were present prior to at least 1664, and possibly much earlier (Taçon et al. 2010; see also May et al. 2010). This is supported by recent archaeological excavations and dating of human skeletal remains (of Southeast Asian origin) buried near Anuru Bay. Theden-Ringl et al. (2011, p. 45) argue that one individual was buried before AD 1730 while another could predate the 1700s. We mention these dates as they directly relate to northwestern Arnhem Land, the area of focus of this chapter (Figure 8.1).

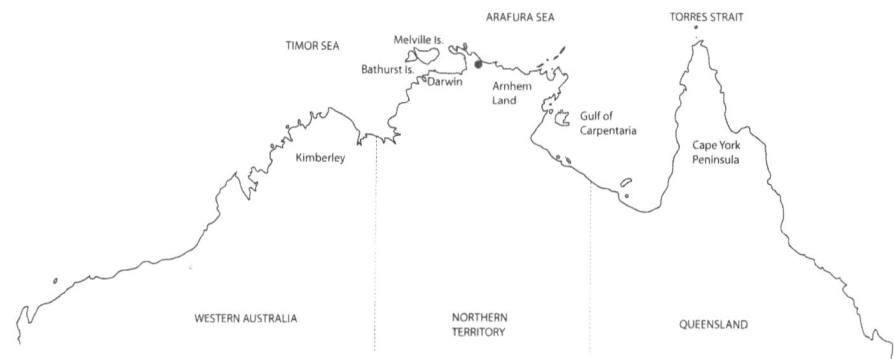

Map of Northern Australia

Figure 8.1 Map of Australia showing the study area in northwestern Arnhem Land

Source: Meg Travers and the Picturing Change Project Team

Macassan praus were home to diverse crews, with sailors from Sulawesi, Madura, Java, Borneo, Flores, Timor, Rote and even New Guinea (see, for example, Earle 1846, p. 240). While the main motivation for coming to Australia may have been to obtain trepang for trade with China, they were also part of wider regional trade patterns which, after AD 1500, included Arab, Chinese and the newly arrived Portuguese and Spanish. Southeast Asian visits were largely over by the early twentieth century, with the Dutch and then British dominating these trade networks from the seventeenth century (Macknight 1976).

In this chapter we focus on the Aboriginal–Macassan story as illustrated by rock art in northwest Arnhem Land and, specifically, at a site complex known as Malarrak, as it is beyond the scope of this chapter to undertake a continent-wide survey. The Malarrak complex is located within the Wellington Range, the northernmost outlier of the Arnhem Land Plateau. The Wellington Range is home to extensive and diverse rock art, including many examples of paintings that reflect contact between local Aboriginal people and international visitors (May et al. 2010; Taçon et al. 2010; May et al. in press). This range covers a large geographical area and is associated with various Aboriginal language groups. The Malarrak sites are located within the traditional country of Maung speakers, where Ronald Lamilami is a Manganowal senior traditional owner.

Macknight (see, for example, 1976, 2011) and Theden-Ringl et al. (2011) have demonstrated aspects of the extensive Macassan occupation of this region. It is no surprise then that evidence for this relationship also appears in rock art at Malarrak, a complex of multiple rock shelters. All of the paintings depicted at the four main shelters within Malarrak were comprehensively documented between 2008 and 2010 as part of the Australian Research Council project 'Picturing Change' (Taçon et al. 2012). This rich record reveals many examples of contact rock art including European watercraft, smoking pipes, a building, guns, horned animals and even a drinking mug. While we have discussed aspects of the contact rock art corpus at Malarrak elsewhere (see, for example, May et al. 2010, in press; Taçon et al. 2010), in this chapter our aim is to analyse the depictions argued to relate to Macassans within their wider rock art context.

For most Australians the story of Macassan–Aboriginal relations is unknown— it is a forgotten history. Some may even argue that this pre-European contact with Australia has been deliberately erased from our history books and left out of our school classrooms. Yet this history is painted across northern Australia. The following is just a snapshot of a much wider and more complex Macassan-related rock art heritage.

Rock art recording in the Wellington Range

During the dry season of 2008, the Malarrak complex was recorded using rock art recording procedures developed by the authors over many years. This included compiling a detailed inventory of the art and noting the layering of different styles and subject matter. The main shelter (Figure 8.2) comprises one large art panel that measures 31 m long by 4.8 m deep. Despite poor preservation conditions, this shelter contains a minimum of 232 paintings and eight stencils. The remaining three rock shelters contain at least: 1) 33 paintings; 2) 62 paintings and two beeswax figures; and 3) 33 paintings and six stencils (May et al. 2010, pp. 61–2). A total of 34 paintings that clearly depict introduced subject matter (contact art) was recorded at Malarrak and includes 17 European sailing vessels and much smaller numbers of horned introduced animals, guns and smoking paraphernalia. Importantly, a number of these paintings are argued to relate to Macassan contact and will now be explored in more detail.

Figure 8.2 Main shelter, Malarrak

Source: Paul S.C. Taçon

The prau

A single white Macassan prau is depicted at Malarrak, with yellow ochre added to the image at a later date. The painting (Figure 8.3) measures approximately 102 cm in width and 99 cm in height and is depicted with its bow oriented to the right, sails furled and with no visible crew. It has an overall shape, mast and decking typical of Southeast Asian praus (see Chaloupka 1996, p. 137).

Figure 8.3 Macassan prau painted at Malarrak

Source: Sally K. May

The knife

A Macassan-style knife was also painted in the main Malarrak shelter, using the 'x-ray technique' so that features of the blade can be seen within its sheath (Figure 8.4). It has a solid white background and red-purple outline. Measuring 33 mm by 119 mm, it has typical features of an Indonesian small sword-like object known as a *'badik'* (see Chaloupka 1996, p. 136). The *badik* is a dagger with a hilt (handle) set at an angle in the plane of the blade (Gardner 1992, pp. 8, 41). Most notably, the *badik* has a 'small, straight, usually single-edged blade, with a straight or concave edge' (Gardner 1992, p. 41), as shown in the Malarrak depiction (compare Figure 8.4 with 8.5).

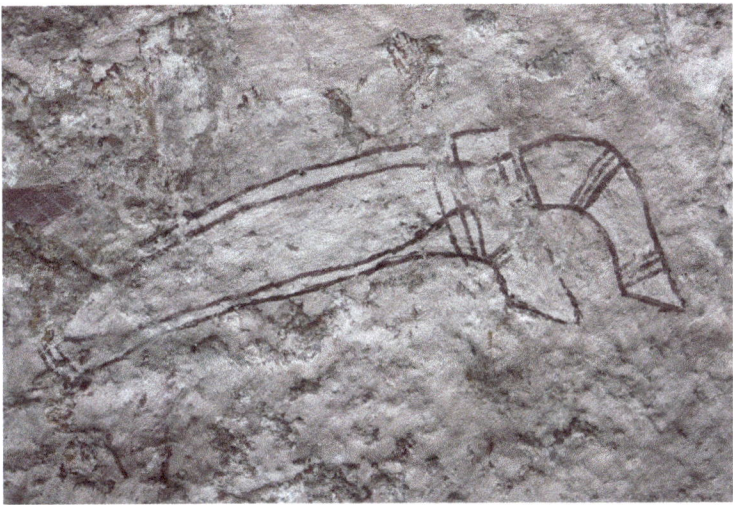

Figure 8.4 Knife painted at Malarrak

Source: Sally K. May

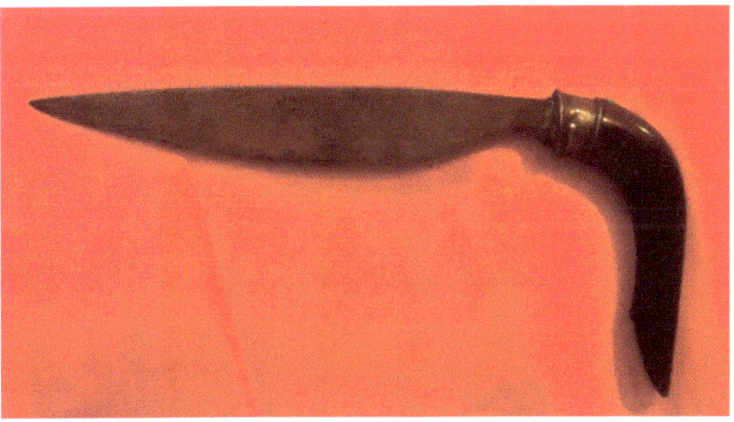

Figure 8.5 A typical *badik* on display at Museum Balla Lopa, Gowa, Sulawesi, in 2012

Source: Paul S.C. Taçon

A monkey?

The third painting that is argued by others to relate to Macassan contact is highly contentious (Figure 8.6). Chaloupka (1996, p. 136) argues this scene 'represents two monkeys in a tree and is, in all probability, the work of one of the many men from this western region who travelled with the Makassans to Sulawesi'. While the figure on a lower branch does resemble a macaque in many regards, it is clearly a human-like figure on the higher branch holding what appears to be a curved object that has both a boomerang-like and a *kris*-like shape.

Figure 8.6 Rock painting possibly depicting a monkey in a tree, Malarrak

Source: Paul S.C. Taçon

Although the lower figure is macaque-like in form and many people visiting the site interpret it this way, it is possible that the artist depicted some other animal. For instance, when shown a photograph of this painting, Aboriginal elder the late Jimmy Galareya Namarnyilk immediately identified it as '*djabbo*', the northern spotted quoll (*Dasyurus hallucatus*). He interpreted the composition as a hunting scene with a *Bininj* (Aboriginal person) in the tree above. The painted image does have a quoll-like bushy tail but the rounded head/face looks macaque-like. Given that quolls are nocturnal, whether someone would climb a tree at night to catch such a fast-moving animal is questionable. Of course, Jimmy was primarily thinking about Australian fauna from his region when looking at the photograph and this influenced his interpretation just as a pro-Macassan bias may have influenced the monkey interpretation of many researchers. Thus, we conclude there is not enough information to confirm or deny this is a Macassan-related piece of art and only further research will clarify this issue.

A smokehouse?

Another painting subject to varying interpretation is the rare depiction of a building, in this case with a peaked roof (Figure 8.7). Internal elements suggest vertical supports and possibly a second storey, also with decorative elements. It has been argued that this painting represents a Southeast Asian building or, more specifically, a Macassan smokehouse (Chaloupka 1993, 1996). Chaloupka (1996, p. 136) states that:

> Reports from European observers, and an outfitter's contract located by Macknight (1976:20) in South Sulawesi record that Makassans brought with them bamboo and prefabricated wall panels, in a form of kajang and ataps, mats of woven cane and palm leaf from which they constructed their living quarters and smokehouses for curing trepang.

The rock painting also resembles some Macassan structures shown in an 1845 sketch from Victoria, Port Essington, by H. S. Melville (see Macknight 1976, Figure 11).

Figure 8.7 Painting of a building, possibly a smokehouse, Malarrak

Source: Sally K. May

Certainly, the building painted does not appear to be consistent with any British structures at Port Essington (described in Allen 2008); however, it may represent a structure at later settlements such as the Oenpelli or Goulburn Island missions. Indeed, it is just as likely to represent a house or church made from sheets of bark or corrugated iron at such settlements. This argument is strengthened by its proximity and similarity in colour and style to two non-Macassan ships—one immediately to the right and one below the house painting. Thus, we are inclined to interpret the building painting as being more European influenced than Macassan, but also are open to the interpretation that the painted structure may exhibit features of both Macassan and European types of buildings and may have been produced during the period of overlap between Macassan visitors and European settlement in the north.

Discussion and conclusion

Rock art imagery, such as the examples explored in this chapter, provides us with Indigenous accounts of contact encounters and relationships that developed between local communities and visitors from Southeast Asia. These images are historical records—a visual narrative of contact experience—and are part of a much wider and important body of rock art that informs us of past cross-cultural contact from an informed, Indigenous perspective (for example, see Taçon et al. 2012). In this sense they are a form of historical documentation that is visually based rather than text based. They also are accounts produced from the perspective of the encountered rather than those doing the encountering, as is usually the case. Therefore, they need to be better considered when researching contact history within Australia, especially as they provide unique insights into past Indigenous experience of encounter rather than that of people of Asian or European descent—the so-called 'reverse gaze' (Ouzman 2003, p. 253).

An analysis of historical documents has revealed that from at least the mid seventeenth century until 1906 Macassans made seasonal visits to the region to harvest trepang and to trade with Aboriginal groups for goods such as turtle shell, ironwood, pearls and pearl shell. In return, they provided Aboriginal people with food, tobacco, alcohol, cloth, axes and knives (Earle 1846; Clarke 2000; Macknight 1976). These visits also provided artists with new subjects to paint, with praus a particularly popular topic (Chaloupka 1993, pp. 191–2; 1996; Clarke and Frederick 2006; Macknight 1976, p. 84; May et al. 2009; Roberts 2004). Importantly, the detail of the prau painting at Malarrak, like those at the nearby site of Djulirri (see Taçon et al. 2010), shows intimate familiarity with Macassan fleets. It is depicted with key features shown, such as a characteristic tripod mast and deck structures. It is also shown with a flat bottom, likely the artist's understanding and illustration of the waterline.

The artist's intimate knowledge of praus, and the way in which they sailed, is suggestive of direct experiences with the Macassan fleets along the coast, several kilometres to the north. There, Aboriginal people not only observed praus in their waters but also sometimes ventured onboard. Occasionally they would travel to other parts of northern Australia and even all the way back to Makassar, where they visited before returning during the next monsoon season or settled into a new way of life, never to return to Australia (Earle 1846, pp. 239–40; Lamilami 1974, p. 70; Macknight 1976, p. 85). It is also interesting to note that when other details were added in yellow to the original white prau depiction, a European ship (possibly a cutter) was painted next to it, reflecting changing times and the arrival of new (European) ships. Consequently, these sorts of contact rock art images should be considered as historical accounts of activities that have local, regional and international dimensions, especially as Southeast Asian trade articulated with global trade and communication networks (for example, see Sukkham et al. 2011).

The painting of the *badik* in its sheath is likely evidence of its importance in trading relationships between Aboriginal people and Southeast Asian visitors but also later between different Aboriginal groups. Metal knives were a highly sought-after trade item during cross-cultural encounters across Australia (for example, see Layton 1992). As Mitchell (2000, p. 182) notes, 'one of the most visible consequences of culture contact with outsiders…was the adoption of foreign material culture as trade goods within indigenous societies'. Importantly, and as mentioned earlier, the *badik* painted in the main Malarrak shelter is illustrated using the traditional x-ray manner of depiction, with the blade shown in its sheath. The use of this technique indicates the continuation of artistic conventions that may demonstrate something of what Frederick (1999, p. 134) argues are 'the measures Indigenous Australians took towards securing their own cultural survival in a transforming world'. Of course, from a practical point of view, it also allows the artist to depict all the key features of the object, with the blade inside being most important.

The presence of both the prau and the *badik* paintings at the main Malarrak shelter, along with other depictions of praus at nearby sites, clearly indicates that the Macassans had a profound influence not only on the art but also on the material culture of the Arnhem Land region. Yet, the majority of introduced subject matter at Malarrak relates to contact with Europeans across the nineteenth and twentieth centuries.

This overall lack of Macassan-related rock art in an area known to have been visited by Macassans for hundreds of years prior to (and overlapping with) European settlement is intriguing. One of the key issues is whether a more detailed rock art record of Macassans once existed and has naturally deteriorated over time. Accurate interpretation of contact rock art is another consideration:

are some of the paintings we attribute to the European or pre-contact period actually depicting Macassan contact? For example, many human figures painted throughout northwest Arnhem Land are difficult to interpret and only more detailed analysis will allow us to accurately identify their subject matter.

On the other hand, we could argue that preservation and identification are not key factors in this problem and that there was, in fact, a lesser visual record of Macassan life in northwest Arnhem Land compared with European life. In order to start to explore this issue it is important to begin by understanding something of pre-contact rock art. It is not enough to view contact-period rock art as a collection that stands alone and that can be analysed separately. Is there a tradition of non-literal depictions in northwest Arnhem Land that might explain the lack of Macassan-related rock art? If so, why is this rule broken for European-related rock art? We must question the overall system of representations in rock art by Aboriginal artists in this region and how these systems are affected by first Macassan and later European contact (May et al. 2010). In the Wellington Range we are asking these questions of the rock art based on thousands of individual paintings, stencils and beeswax figures and we are comparing these findings with other detailed research that has taken place in Arnhem Land for decades.

The study of Macassan-related rock art in Australia is only at its beginning but because of a lack of detailed previous research, and indications that there are hundreds of rock art sites yet to be documented across the Wellington Range, new, important insights into the nature of cross-cultural contact during the past few hundred years are likely to emerge. A related issue to explore is whether older rock art will reveal much earlier contact with people from across Asia. For instance, the curious introduction of the dingo into Australia at least 3500 years ago is linked to earlier contact or colonisation events (Gollan 1984; Oskarsson et al. 2011), and recent DNA studies suggest people travelled from as far away as India about 4200 years ago (see Pugach et al. 2013). Indeed, there is evidence in the form of ancient stencilled objects in various parts of Arnhem Land, including the Wellington Range, that are unlike any forms of material culture known from Australian Indigenous ethnographic records. Once they are better dated and interpreted, and further genetic research highlights other forms of ancient cross-cultural encounter, a whole new picture of Aboriginal Australian contact with Asia will finally refute the long-held theory that Aboriginal Australians were isolated from the rest of the world until just a few hundred years ago.

References

Allen, J. (2008) *Port Essington: The historical archaeology of a north Australian nineteenth century military outpost*, Sydney: Sydney University Press in association with the Australasian Society for Historical Archaeology.

Berndt, R. M. and C. H. Berndt (1954) *Arnhem Land: Its history and its people*, Melbourne: F. W. Cheshire.

Chaloupka, G. (1993) *Journey in Time: The 50,000 year story of the Australian Aboriginal rock art of Arnhem Land*, Chatswood, NSW: Reed Books.

Chaloupka, G. (1996) 'Praus in Marege: Makassan subjects in Aboriginal rock art in east Arnhem Land, Northern Territory, Australia', *Anthropologie*, 34, pp. 131–42.

Clarke, A. (2000) 'The "Moorman's trowsers": Macassan and Aboriginal interactions and the changing fabric of indigenous social life', in S. O'Connor and P. Veth (eds), *East of Wallace's Line: Studies of past and present maritime societies in the Indo-Pacific region*, Modern Quaternary Research in Southeast Asia 16, Rotterdam: A. A. Balkema, pp. 315–35.

Clarke, A. and U. Frederick (2006) 'Closing the distance: interpreting cross-cultural engagements through indigenous rock art', in I. Lilley (ed.), *Archaeology of Oceania: Australia and the Pacific islands*, Oxford: Blackwell, pp. 116–33.

Crawford, I. C. (1969) Late prehistoric changes in Aboriginal culture in Kimberley, Western Australia, Unpublished PhD thesis, University of London, London.

Earle, G. W. (1846) 'On the Aboriginal tribes of the northern coast of Australia', *Journal of the Royal Geographical Society of London*, 16, pp. 239–51.

Evans, N. (1992) 'Macassan loanwords in Top End languages', *Australian Journal of Linguistics*, 12 (1), pp. 45–91.

Flinders, M. (1814) *A Voyage to Terra Australis…in the Years 1801, 1802 and 1803, in Two Volumes with an Atlas*, London: G. & W. Nicol.

Frederick, U. (1999) 'At the centre of it all: constructing contact through the rock art of Watarrka National Park, central Australia', *Archaeology in Oceania*, 34 (3), pp. 132–43.

Gardner, G. B. (1992) *Keris and other Malay Weapons*, Singapore: Progressive Publishing Company.

Gollan, K. (1984) 'The Australian dingo: in the shadow of man', in M. Archer and G. Clayton (eds), *Vertebrate Zoogeography and Evolution in Australasia*, Carlisle, WA: Hesperian Press, pp. 921–7.

Lamilami, L. (1974) *Lamilami Speaks, the Cry Went Up: A story of people of Goulburn Islands, north Australia*, Sydney: Ure Smith.

Layton, R. (1992) *Australian Rock Art: A new synthesis*, Cambridge: Cambridge University Press.

McIntosh, I. (2004) 'Personal names and the negotiation of change: reconsidering Arnhem Land's adjustment movement', *Anthropological Forum*, 14 (2), pp. 141–62.

Macknight, C. (2011) 'The view from Marege': Australian knowledge of Makassar and the impact of the trepang industry across two centuries', *Aboriginal History*, 35, pp. 121–43.

Macknight, C. C. (1976) *The voyage to Marege': Macassan trepangers in northern Australia*, Carlton, Vic.: Melbourne University Press.

May, S.K., J. McKinnon and J. Raupp (2009) 'Boats on Bark: an Analysis of Groote Eylandt Aboriginal Bark-Paintings featuring Macassan Praus from the 1948 Arnhem Land Expedition, Northern Territory, Australia', International Journal of Nautical Archaeology 38/2: 369-385.

May, S.K., P. S. C. Taçon, M. Travers and D. Guse (2010) 'Painting history: Indigenous observations and depictions of the "other" in far north Australia', *Australian Archaeology*, 71, pp. 57–65.

May, S. K., P. S. C. Taçon, A. Paterson and M. Travers (in press, 2013) 'The world from Malarrak: depictions of Southeast Asian and European subjects in rock art from the Wellington Range, Australia', *Australian Aboriginal Studies* [accepted December 2012].

Mitchell, S. (2000) 'Guns or barter? Indigenous exchange networks and the mediation of conflict in post-contact western Arnhem Land', in R. Torrence and A. Clarke (eds), *The Archaeology of Difference: Negotiating cross-cultural engagement in Oceania*, London: Routledge, pp. 182–214.

Oskarsson, M. V. R., C. F. C. Klütsch, U. Boonyaprakob, A. Wilton, Y. Tanabe and P. Savolainen (2011) 'Mitochondrial DNA data indicate an introduction through mainland Southeast Asia for Australian dingoes and Polynesian domestic dogs', *Proceedings of the Royal Society B*, pp. 1–8, <doi:10.1098/rspb.2011.1395>

Ouzman, S. (2003) 'Indigenous images of a colonial exotic: imaginings from Bushmen in southern Africa', *Before Farming*, 2003/1 (6), pp. 239–56.

Pugach, I., F. Delfin, E. Gunnarsdóttir, M. Kayser and M. Stoneking (2013) 'Genome-wide data substantiate Holocene gene flow from India to Australia', *Proceedings of the National Academy of Sciences*, <doi:10.1073/pnas.1211927110>

Roberts, D. A. (2004) 'Nautical themes in the Aboriginal rock paintings of Mount Borradaile, western Arnhem Land', *The Great Circle*, 26 (1), pp. 19–50.

Sukkham, A., P. S. C. Taçon and N. H. Tan (2011) 'Rock art of Phrayanaga (Viking) Cave, southern Thailand: the illustration of ancient vessels', The Museum of Underwater Archaeology, <http://www.themua.org/collections/items/show/1214>

Taçon, P. S. C., S. K. May, S. J. Fallon, M. Travers, D. Guse and R. Lamilami (2010) 'A minimum age for early depictions of Macassan praus in the rock art of Arnhem Land, Northern Territory', *Australian Archaeology*, 71, pp. 1–10.

Taçon, P. S. C., A. Paterson, J. Ross and S. K. May (2012) 'Picturing change and changing pictures: contact period rock art of Australia', in J. McDonald and P. Veth (eds), *A Companion to Rock Art*, Chichester, UK: Blackwell, pp. 420–36.

Theden-Ringl, F., J. Fenner, D. Wesley and R. Lamilami (2011) 'Buried on foreign shores: isotope analysis of the origin of human remains recovered from a Macassan site in Arnhem Land', *Australian Archaeology*, 73, pp. 41–8.

9. Drug substances introduced by the Macassans: The mystery of the tobacco pipe

Maggie Brady

The *real* first fleet

It has become conventional wisdom to assert that the arrival of Captain Arthur Phillip's First Fleet in 1788 was the means by which both alcohol and tobacco were first introduced to Australia's Indigenous people. This was not the case, of course, for it was Australia's other 'first fleet', of Macassan praus, already established as an annual event well before Phillip's arrival (Burningham 1994), which brought these drug substances to a virgin population in the north. Until the first British attempts at settlement on that northern coast,[1] the Macassans were the only regular source of alcohol and tobacco for the Aboriginal people who became users of these substances.

Aboriginal people formed regular and orderly trading relationships with these foreigners, who were no threat to their primary ownership of the land and sea, and who took a resource—trepang—for which Aborigines had no use. These relationships made it possible for significant numbers of Aboriginal men to travel to and live in Makassar, where they experienced the daily life of people from another society. Contact with the Macassans in Makassar itself and in Australia introduced Aboriginal people along the northern coastline to people of another religion, to a foreign language that many learned and spoke, and it exposed them to the customs, artefacts, food and drugs of another culture. The Yolngu of northeast Arnhem Land refer to these people as the '*batharripa*'. The term derives from the Makassarese and Bugis word '*pataripang*', meaning 'trepang fisherman' (Zorc 1986, p. 20).

Drug substances (alcohol, tobacco, betel nut and possibly opium) were brought on the voyages, perhaps initially for the use of the captains and crew. Once two drug items—alcohol and tobacco—were found to be particularly welcome, more supplies would have been brought as items of trade. There has long been debate about how influential the Macassans were and about how much alcohol

---

[1] Fort Dundas on Melville Island (1824–28) was a disastrous failure, followed by two more failed settlements on the Cobourg Peninsula: Fort Wellington at Raffles Bay (1827–29) and Victoria at Port Essington (1838–49).

and tobacco they might have brought. W. L. Warner, for example, famously downplayed their influence and Macknight (1976, p. 84) suggested there was no sign that vast quantities of food or other goods were made available to Aborigines, partly because of space restrictions on praus. Irrespective of the quantities involved, it was the prestige attached to these items that was important. For Aboriginal people these two drug substances were significant enough to be commemorated in song, ceremony and cosmology, in art and artefacts, and in handed-down stories and memories. Aboriginal people experimented with these substances, learned to smoke and drink, experienced inebriation, had fun, incorporated the material culture associated with them into their ceremonial and trading networks and borrowed words from another language to describe them (Brady 2008). '*Nganitji*' (alcohol) and '*ngarali*' (tobacco)—the Yolngu/Makassarese language terms—are firmly part of the intercultural experience of the region today.

Figure 9.1 Numbulwar dancers perform the Macassan 'red flag' dance at Barunga Festival, 1988

Photo: M. Brady

Arrack

The alcoholic drinks brought by the Macassans appear to have been predominantly arrack; some brandy and Dutch 'square-face' gin bottles have been found in excavations of Macassan campsites, although what the bottles might have actually contained is not known. Gin is mentioned by some observers, but it is unclear whether these are references to the drink we know by that name or whether they use 'gin' as a convenient generalisation for a clear, distilled spirit that was, in fact, arrack.

Arrack is a spirit that can be made from the fermented sugars and sugary sap of a large number of plants and trees, including dates, sugar cane, rice and several types of palm. Nearly every variety of palm produces a saccharine juice in various quantities (Brady and McGrath 2010). In the Indonesian archipelago, palms used for making these drinks include the lontar palm in Rote, Timor and Makassar (*Borassus sundaicus* Becc.), the fan or 'toddy' palm on Savu (*Borassus flabillifer*), and the nypa palm (*Nypa fruticans*) in a number of locations. Wallace noted large numbers of sugar-palms (*Arenga saccharifera*) growing around Makassar (Wallace 1989, p. 239; cf. Beaglehole 1963, p. 162; Earl 1882, p. 152; Fox 1977). The juice can be drunk fresh from the tree, having been collected as it drips from cuts made in the buds that are to produce flowers. At this stage it is non-alcoholic, or it can be consumed after a day or two when it becomes fizzy; a few more days and it becomes sour and fermented—this is what is now commonly known as 'toddy' or 'sour toddy', and contains alcohol. The Macassans called this drink '*sagueir*', according to Alfred Wallace, who said that it took the place of beer. An 1885 drawing of a Macassan bamboo container for collecting palm juice reiterates the use of this term (Atlas 1885, plate 10, figs 34, 35; Wallace 1989, p. 224).[2] Distillation of this fermented liquid produces arrack.

Figure 9.2 Sugar palm (*Arenga saccharifera*)

Source: Wallace (1989, p. 238)

---

2 The term '*ballo*' is also used in Makassar for palm wine.

In Batavia in 1770, arrack was cheaper than claret wine and had a high alcohol content (Wallace described it as being as strong as West Indian rum—that is, anything between 40 per cent and 70 per cent alcohol by volume). Sometimes referred to as 'Java rum', arrack was consumed widely and with great abandon across the archipelago. The locally distilled version was available for sale legally and illegally in Makassar (Knaap and Sutherland 2004, p. 93) and high-quality arrack was imported from Batavia to Makassar. The terms *'arrack'*, *'rak'* and *'raki'* derive from the Arabic *'araq'* ('sweat', presumably a reference to the droplets of clear fluid made during distillation), and the drink has a long history in the Middle East as well as in northern parts of Africa, in India and Southeast Asia. Unlike the fermented toddies (often known as 'palm wine') also made in Southeast Asia and the Pacific (which became unpalatable over time), distilled arrack travelled well. Because of this it was frequently carried by maritime explorers, including James Cook on the *Endeavour* and the French expeditions led by Nicolas Baudin and Dumont d'Urville. Arrack was given to Aboriginal people in exchange for tortoise and pearl shell (Gillen 1968, p. 317), to pay for their labour and, according to Ronald and Catherine Berndt (1954, p. 47), for women.

Betel nut

Betel nut—probably the oldest indigenous psychoactive substance in Southeast Asia—was chewed by Macassans and was (and still is) commonly used throughout the archipelago (Rooney 1993). Strictly speaking, it is not the betel nut at all, but the nut or seed of the areca palm (*Areca catechu*) that is chewed, together with the leaf of the betel pepper (*Piper betle*) and lime; tobacco was added as flavouring. Tobacco could also be held in the mouth after the initial salivation produced by the betel chew, producing copious red, blood-like saliva (Reid 1985, p. 537). French and English observers in the nineteenth century such as Nicolas Baudin and P. P. King frequently expressed disgust at the practice, which was probably a response to the discolouration and blackening of users' teeth and the regular spitting out of red saliva (Hordern 2002, p. 117). Because of this, some early European visitors believed that many Asians had tuberculosis—they were thought to be spitting blood (Rooney 1993, p. 1).

Apart from the observations of betel-nut use in Southeast Asia made by contemporary travellers and maritime explorers (including Wallace, whose local assistant, Baderoon, was a chewer of betel),[3] we know that the Macassan men who came to Australia were users of betel. In the 1890s, for example, Searcy noticed that boxes containing the 'necessary ingredients, etc., for making their

---

3   Baderoon had made several visits to northern Australia with the trepang fleets (Wallace 1989, p. 412).

"quids" were lying around everywhere' (Searcy 1984, p. 26; cf. Mulvaney and Green 1992, p. 135). The archaeological record provides further evidence. An excavation at Anuru Bay (on the coast adjacent to South Goulburn Island) of the burial site of two Macassan men showed signs of betel use on their teeth (Macknight and Thorne 1968).

Despite the apparent pleasures and benefits of chewing betel nut, it seems that, like Europeans, Aboriginal people must have found the practice distasteful. They chose not to take up this drug use. According to Macknight (1976, p. 30), there is only one report of an Aboriginal person using betel, no available evidence of its adoption and no oral histories record its use. The areca palm occurs in north Queensland but there seems to be no record of Aboriginal people chewing the nuts there either (MacPherson 1921, p. 121). It is inconceivable that the Macassans would not have offered betel nut to their Aboriginal hosts, for in Southeast Asia betel functions as an avenue of communication that produces relaxed social interactions and as a marker of hospitality; its use is not restricted by the usual barriers of age, sex or class that are often invoked for other drug uses. It was also common practice to offer betel nut when greeting or farewelling visitors. Chewing betel nut is, however, an acquired taste and not immediately pleasurable: the first taste of betel is acrid and unpleasant. This may partly explain why Aboriginal people did not take to it. Nevertheless, an initial aversion to a drug is not the whole story (Courtwright 2001, p. 54); smoking tobacco is also usually thought disagreeable at first and yet the evidence shows that Aboriginal people rapidly took to this new way of ingesting nicotine.

Tobacco

The English, Dutch and Portuguese were responsible for the rapid spread of tobacco, which had arrived in Java around 1600 (Burkhill 1966, p. 1579). In the eighteenth century tobacco was a major import item into Makassar from China and Java (Knaap and Sutherland 2004, p. 94). In the 1850s Wallace saw tobacco growing on the lower slopes of the hills in Maros, 50 km from Makassar, and noted it was in high demand in Dobbo on Aru, along with other items carried on the large trading praus from Makassar, Ceram, Goram and Ke (Wallace 1989, pp. 239, 485).

Tobacco was one of the most popular items that Aboriginal people obtained from the Macassans (Macknight 1976, p. 30). Ronald and Catherine Berndt heard it called '*ji*' (in its loose flake form), or '*batariba*' (also the term used by the Yolngu for the Macassans themselves) (Berndt and Berndt 1954, p. 44). Others list '*dhambaku*' (Mkr: *tambáko*) (Cooke 1987, p. 57; Zorc 1986). Thomson (1939, p. 90) notes that before the presence of Europeans, Arnhem Landers were entirely dependent for tobacco upon the Malay visitors, who brought with them 'large supplies' of coarse tobacco in twist form.[4] This reliance manifests itself in a segment of the Macassan song cycle still performed today in northeast Arnhem Land: in the 'Tobacco Song', the dancers 'beg' and 'ask' (the Macassans) for tobacco.[5]

The 'Macassan' pipe

The Macassans apparently also introduced the use and the manufacture of a distinctive, usually long, straight wooden pipe that has since been used for the smoking of tobacco by coastal Aboriginal people of Arnhem Land and the western Gulf of Carpentaria. Warner stated:

> The Malays introduced both the use and manufacture of the tobacco pipe during the period in which they traded with the aborigines. Although the aborigines know that they acquired the pipe from the Malays, they believe they practiced smoking before this time…but nearly all the evidence seems to point to the introduction of smoking into Australia from a Malay source. (Warner 1958, p. 458)

Donald Thomson (1939, p. 87) wrote that 'the wooden pipes of Arnhem Land are…definitely of Indonesian origin and were probably introduced into Arnhem Land, with tobacco, by the early Macassar voyagers, or their predecessors'.

Figure 9.3 Decorated tobacco pipe, Arnhem Land

Source: South Australian Museum, A47642

---

4   Macknight (1976, p. 116) provides cargo manifests for two *praus*, noting 1 picul of tobacco in 1883–84 and 0.75 piculs in 1902–02; 1 picul = 60 kg.
5   Dr Franca Tamisari, Personal communication. Loosely translated, the *ngarali* (tobacco) song includes the following: 'They saw them smoking *ngarali*. Smoking that *ngarali*. *Djigirit* [cigarette]. [The smoke goes] inside the head. They like it very much. They bin bought many tobacco in the city. Still smoking *dhambaku*. Smoke goes up and up, round and round, and turns into the sunset' (Eunice Djerrkngu Marika, Personal communication, 26 May 2005; cf. Cooke 1987, p. 17).

Thomson (1949) documents pipes among other *gerri* ('goods') that were traded by coastal people with partners further south as part of the ceremonial exchange cycle, and he wrote the definitive ethnography of the pipe, describing Arnhem Land versions that ranged from about 20 cm to 90 cm in length (Thomson 1939). He detailed the quirky adaptations made by Aboriginal people to create the lining or bowl into which the tobacco goes: scrap tin, metal matchboxes, iron bands and hoops from driftwood; thimbles with their tops removed. The long wooden 'Macassan' pipes adopted by Aboriginal people were often decorated by their owners, not only as artistry but also as a way of claiming personal ownership of the pipe—and presumably the precious hoard of tobacco that went with it. Some pipes were incised or painted with totemic designs, transforming them into sacred items, the use of which could be restricted to initiated men, as Thomson perceptively noted. In a society in which generosity and sharing were pre-eminent values, this strategy enabled a man to conserve his tobacco and the means of smoking it, while being able to avoid any accusations of meanness (Thomson 1939, p. 89). Even today, the oral histories provided by Yolngu refer to the hoarding and protection of tobacco supplies during the Macassans' time:

> They'd smash up the tobacco, squash it, and put it to keep in a bottle, a *nganitji* [alcohol] bottle; you could sleep with it: tobacco in bottle to keep it safe [mimes someone sleeping with their head resting on such a bottle]. Because *ngarali*, once they get the taste, they were addicted to that *ngarali*. You can't live without it.[6]

These pipes continued to be used in coastal Arnhem Land by Aboriginal men and women for smoking tobacco until the 1990s, although in recent years this has become less common. As has been the case elsewhere, cigarette smoking has taken over. 'Macassan-style tobacco pipes' are also sold as tourist art objects; museum curators and anthropologists interested in Macassan heritage and material culture are particularly drawn to some modern versions of these pipes, in which their makers have cleverly adapted soda siphon bulbs and empty shell casings to serve as the tobacco container.

Confounding issues

So the Macassans are the ones who have been universally credited with introducing the smoking of tobacco to Aboriginal people of the northern coastline, using these long pipes. The assumption has been that Aboriginal people observed the Macassans smoking the long pipes and replicated the pipes

---

6 Interview with Banampi Wunungmurra at Yirrkala, NT, 16 August 2005.

and the behaviour. Nevertheless, this apparently straightforward example of the diffusion of drug use and drug paraphernalia from one people to another has some puzzling inconsistencies in this instance.

The first problem with this proposition is it appears that the people of Sulawesi, including the people we refer to as the Macassans, did not commonly smoke tobacco in pipes—in fact, they hardly smoked at all. Several commentators note that in Sulawesi and in the Indonesian archipelago as a whole, using pipes to smoke tobacco was the exception, rather than the rule. Smoking itself was not that common because the people of the region were betel-chewers, and betel-chewers tend not to *smoke* tobacco, they use it in another way. Reid (1985, p. 537) states unequivocally: 'By the time of the British interregnum in the Indies (1811–1816), the primary use of tobacco in the [Indonesian] Archipelago was undoubtedly as a wad to cram between lip and gum after the initial salivation produced by the betel chew.'

Others agree that by the end of the eighteenth century the most popular way of consuming tobacco among ordinary Indonesians was to chew it with or without betel nut (Achadi et al. 2005; MacPherson 1921, p. 113; Goodman 1993, p. 89; Wallace 1989, p. 485).[7] Earlier in the eighteenth century people did smoke to some extent: the elite in Java used fashionable, long European-style pipes, and even before this, in the mid seventeenth century, an indigenous form of cigarette appeared, wrapped in dried maize or banana leaf (Knaap and Sutherland 2004, p. 94; Reid 1985, p. 536).[8] But according to Reid (1985, pp. 536–7), the practice of tobacco smoking had been generally discontinued among the islanders of the Indonesian archipelago by 1820. It was only in the twentieth century, after the Macassan trepang voyages had ended, that tobacco smoking—using cigarettes, not pipes—became widespread, as younger, 'modern' people from Sulawesi abandoned the chewing of betel (Strickland 2002, p. 86).

The second puzzling element to consider is the scant documentary or visual evidence of Macassans themselves smoking tobacco using these pipes. In rock art depictions of Macassans and praus, I know of only one showing a Macassan smoking what appears to be a long pipe.[9] Most rock art, bark paintings and works on paper seem to portray the use of clay (European) pipes. Several of

---

7   Musing in 1921 on how Torres Strait Islanders learned how to smoke, MacPherson (a physician) believed it could not have been from the Malay nations 'since these people, even if they had ever reached thus far, rarely or never smoked tobacco, but only chewed it with their betel' (MacPherson 1921, p. 113).
8   This hand-rolled cigarette was introduced to coastal Aboriginal people either by the Macassans or by the 'Bayini', who were said to precede them. In the 1890s, Searcy (1984, p. 27) observed Aboriginal people 'lolling about' smoking cigarettes of Malay tobacco, rolled up in pandanus palm leaf. Warner's informants asserted they previously smoked native tobacco rolled in paperbark (Warner 1958, p. 461). The term for cigarette in several non-Yolngu languages derives from the Bugis and Makassarese '*galuru*' ('to roll up') (Evans 1992, p. 74; Walker and Zorc 1981, p. 120), strongly suggesting a Macassan origin.
9   Thanks to Paul Taçon for this information. He photographed the site in the Mann River region (his ref. A1001).

the Aboriginal crayon drawings collected in 1947 by Ronald Berndt at Yirrkala show goods brought by the Macassans (cf. Berndt and Berndt 1954). Two in particular[10] are detailed illustrations showing trepang pots, stirrers, axes, glass bottles, knives, '*keris*' (ceremonial daggers), rifles, frying pans, fireworks, coloured plates, tobacco (or betel) boxes and rice pots among other items. But there are no long 'Macassan' pipes among this trove of objects, nor are there drawings of Macassans with the long pipes.

Figure 9.4 Goods introduced by the Macassans (crayon drawing on brown paper by Mawulan, 1947)

Source: Berndt Museum of Anthropology, WU7246

Clay pipes were undoubtedly more numerous. When maritime visitors and others encountered Aboriginal people during the Macassan years, they often found them using old clay pipes, and were besieged by requests for more of them. People such as Alfred Searcy were happy to oblige. The urgency of these demands implies that there were no other pipes available.[11] Macknight (1976, p. 82) noted that fragments of clay pipes have been found in Macassan contexts and that clay pipes were 'probably' brought on the praus; however, they seem to date from the nineteenth century and, as Aborigines were given vast numbers of clay pipes, it is impossible to be certain they are imports from Makassar.

Finally, there is strong evidence that the long pipes used by Aboriginal people to ingest tobacco were originally opium pipes (Cawte 1985; Macknight 1976). The only difference between the opium pipes used in Makassar and elsewhere, and the pipes made by Aboriginal people for tobacco, is that the Aboriginal version of the pipe has a hole near the distal end lined with tin, or some other

---

10 Drawings numbering WU7246 and WU7163, Berndt Museum of Anthropology, Perth.
11 In the 1860s Webling (1995, pp. 67–8) reported seeing a Dutch-made pipe at an Aboriginal campsite near Croker Island.

material, making an open cylindrical container into which the tobacco can be tamped. An opium pipe has a covered, round metal bowl at this spot in which the ball of opium is heated.

Figure 9.5 Opium pipe and bowl made in China. Collected by Police Inspector Waters, Darwin, 1890

Source: South Australian Museum, A19124

Opium was widely used in Makassar and the surrounding region during the eighteenth and nineteenth centuries (Wallace 1989, p. 381). It was said to help digestion, to strengthen the stomach and, perhaps something of an understatement, to produce charming dreams. A contemporary account of the habits of the people of the kingdom of Macassar held that opium was the 'most admired' of all their 'simples' (Gervaise 1971).[12] When Dumont D'Urville and the *Astrolabe* visited Makassar in May 1839, the French observed that the local population were reckless gamblers and addicted to opium smoking; this did not, however, prevent some of the *Astrolabe*'s officers from trying it (Rosenman 1992, p. 181). In 1885 the opium pipe was thought common enough to warrant its inclusion alongside depictions of everyday Macassan household objects and artefacts (Atlas 1885, plate 10). Gervaise (1971) commented on the apparent contradiction inherent in such drug-taking among a people who had converted to Islam, suggesting that using opium had a strategic advantage: it gratified users with the pleasures of intoxication, while adhering to the prohibition on drinking wine (cf. Courtwright 2001 p. 33). In a similar vein, during the *Endeavour*'s 1770 visit to the region, Joseph Banks opined that Islamic restrictions on the use of strong liquors had driven the Indonesians from liquid to solid intoxicators such as opium and tobacco (Beaglehole 1963, p. 214).[13]

---

12 'Simples' is probably used here in the sense of a medicine or medicament with only one constituent, such as a herb or plant (*Oxford Shorter English Dictionary*).
13 Wallace (1989, p. 224) observed that the Macassans were 'nominal Mohammedans' and lax in their religious observances.

There is strong linguistic evidence from Aboriginal Australia to support the proposition that the Macassan pipe was originally an opium pipe. In their studies of Makasar or Makassarese loan words, linguists have documented numerous terms that associated the pipes with opium. In the Yolngu language a widespread term for pipe, '*bamutuka*', derives from the Makassarese '*pammudukan*', meaning 'bamboo opium pipe'. Other loan words used in the region include '*ma:ta*' (long wooden pipe), which derives from the Bugis or Makassarese '*mada*' for 'prepared opium' (Zorc 1986). Yet another word used for pipe, '*jandu*', is borrowed from the Bugis, Makassarese, Javanese and/or Malay '*candu*', meaning 'prepared opium, softened with water before use' (Walker and Zorc 1981, pp. 118, 126; cf. Evans 1992). In order for these introduced words to become embedded in Aboriginal languages, they, and the objects they describe, must have been in frequent use by the Macassans.

So, should we assume that the pipes and/or the opium itself travelled to Australia with the trepang fishers? And do we therefore assume that there were opium-smokers among the crews? We know that opium entered Makassar, was available and was commonly in use there. We also know that Macassan captains in Australian waters were interested in opium. When praus arrived at the British settlement of Raffles Bay for the trepang season of 1829, for example, some captains approached the British wanting items to take back with them such as scissors, razors, saws and muskets, and they were particularly interested in whether the British had any opium (Mulvaney and Green 1992, p. 139). Macknight thought it unlikely that much, if any, opium ever came on the praus (1976, p. 118). The Berndts thought it 'possible' (Berndt and Berndt 1954, p. 44), and provided a term for it used by Aboriginal people: '*ji*' (the same term for tobacco). It would surely have been problematic to have had opium addicts among the trepang crews: they were expected to engage in hard labour in a relatively limited time in order to maximise the profits from trepang sales. It would also have been virtually impossible to smoke opium in the time-honoured way in the crowded and unstable conditions onboard. Opium is most efficiently smoked in a reclining position, so that with concentration and a steady hand, the opium ball in its metal container can be 'cooked' over a heat source, usually an open flame (Zheng 2003). An open flame itself would be a fire risk onboard any sailing ship.[14] Nevertheless, if the trepang crews did include opium users then these men would have brought with them their opium-smoking 'layout' including the pipes. This would explain the arrival of the pipes in Australia, but not their use for tobacco.

It is likely that Aboriginal people witnessed opium smoking in Makassar itself. Hundreds of Aboriginal men undertook what Searcy referred to as 'the grand

---

14 Smoking onboard Portuguese and Dutch ships was forbidden because of the risk of fire (Reid 1985, p. 537).

tour' to Makassar with the praus, lived there and returning the following year (Searcy 1984, p. 86). In 1828–29, around 100 Aboriginal men were said to be in Makassar (Mulvaney and Green 1992, p. 140; Mulvaney 1988). MacGillivray at Port Essington wrote in 1845 that Aborigines 'frequently' accompanied the Macassans (Cameron 1999, p. 147). Yolngu informants said some Yolngu people had lived in Makassar for many years, married and had children there (Djalatjirri in Cooke 1987, p. 46). Not only could Aboriginal men have observed opium smoking, they also would have had the opportunity to obtain opium pipes themselves. But perhaps of greater significance for this discussion about the transformation of the opium pipe into a tobacco pipe is an observation made in Makassar early in the eighteenth century. In an account published in 1701, the French naturalist and explorer Nicolas Gervaise provided a description from Makassar of people smoking tobacco with opium, with the tobacco as a flavouring or enhancer of the drug:

> Tis dangerous therefore to contract a habit of smoaking tobacco thus sprinkl'd with this tincture of Ophyon; for in a short time it will become so necessary, that there will be no living without it. Seeing that they who leave it off, presently grow lean, languish, and soon after die of a consumption. But it is much more dangerous to use it to excess: for if the strongest man in the country take it above four or five times in twentyfour hours, he is sure to fall into a lethargy...that sleep, as sweet as it seems to be, carries him insensibly to his grave. (Gervaise 1971, p. 23; cf. Hodgson 1999, p. 32)

Gervaise was describing what was known as *'madak'*, a mixture of shredded tobacco and semi-refined opium with which the Chinese (in China) were experimenting (Zheng 2003, pp. 10–11, 14). It had evidently found its way to Makassar.[15] Chinese opium smoking developed as an offshoot of tobacco smoking; *madak* was an interim development until around 1760, when it was discovered how to prepare opium for smoking without tobacco. This brought about the development of the distinctive metal bowl at the distal end of an opium pipe: the opium in fact vaporises (it does not burn) when heated (Courtright 2001 p. 33). Is it possible that the practice of mixing tobacco and opium and smoking *madak* was witnessed and tried by Aboriginal people, in Makassar perhaps, and that this triggered the idea of using the pipes for tobacco alone?

In other, mostly inland regions of the Northern Territory, the long pipe was adopted directly from Chinese opium users and modified for use as a tobacco pipe. Thousands of Chinese labourers were brought into the Northern Territory from the 1870s to work in mining enterprises in the Top End, which they soon

---

15 In the late eighteenth century, the natives of Batavia were also said to be 'very fond' of opium, which they smoked 'together with their tobacco' (Zheng 2003, p. 10).

came to dominate. By 1888 the Chinese population peaked in the Territory at more than 6000, outnumbering Europeans (Ganter 2003). Aboriginal people from the Alligator rivers region, Adelaide River, Roper and Daly rivers regions made wet season migrations into the many small mining settlements where they mixed with Chinese workers and, by the early twentieth century, the extent of fraternisation between Aboriginal people and the Chinese had precipitated sensational press reports of Aboriginal opium smoking. The South Australian newspaper *The Observer* reported on 20 August 1904 that 60 per cent of the Chinese were opium smokers, and that

> [i]n spite of every precaution and vigilance on the part of the police, the blacks succeed in getting it from the Chinese, and frequently rough-made opium pipes, manufactured from reeds and glass bottles and bamboos, which blacks have used, are found. Formerly the blacks smoked in Chinese quarters and used Chinese pipes, but the visits of police have led them to construct their own pipes and to take opium into the bush, where they smoke it.

Frank Gillen saw Aboriginal people using what he referred to as 'Chinese' pipes for tobacco. During his 1901–02 expedition across the centre to the Gulf of Carpentaria with Baldwin Spencer, Gillen noted in his journal the adaptations Aboriginal people were making to their material culture using introduced objects. Heading east from Powell's Creek, Spencer and Gillen encountered two men holding crocodile spears they had adapted by adding prongs made from iron nails and the blade of a butcher's knife. 'Another of their adaptations', Gillen wrote,

> is the Chinese pipe which is modelled on the pipe used for smoking opium by the Chinese. We saw these pipes first at Powells Creek [past Renner Springs, well inland] and since then there has been one or more in every camp visited. In some cases the stem of the pipe is of bamboo in which case it must have been traded through from the coast but in most cases it is of hollow wood one end being stuffed up and a piece of tin inserted an inch or two back to hold the tobacco…The idea of smoking tobacco in this way must have originated with the coastal blacks who have come in contact with the Chinese and the custom is gradually spreading inland. (Gillen 1968, p. 298)

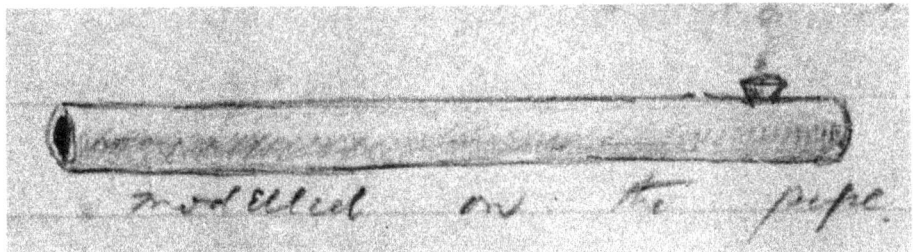

Figure 9.6 '...the Chinese pipe which is modelled on the pipe used for smoking opium...'

Source: Drawing in Gillen's diary (1968, p. 298)

In November at Borroloola, Gillen noted that many Aborigines had pipes fashioned 'like the Chinese opium pipes and made out of bamboo' (Gillen 1968, p. 316). He mentions that at Borroloola there was both a Chinese gardener and a Chinese garden; but it is peculiar that Gillen does not associate the pipe with the Macassans: he was well aware of the 'Malay traders' and commented that some Borroloola men 'talk Malay' (Gillen 1968, p. 317).

Conclusion

The style and uses of the long smoking pipe have undergone numerous historical, cultural and social transformations, with the Chinese originally smoking tobacco alone in long-stemmed pipes, then adding tobacco to opium—a practice that spread to Southeast Asia. The invention of the closed-bowl opium pipe later allowed raw opium alone to be 'cooked' or vaporised. This was the pipe that, with a minor alteration to the bowl, reappeared as the 'Macassan' pipe in Australia, adapted by coastal Aboriginal people to the smoking of tobacco. Gillen confidently assumed that Aborigines had adapted the pipe directly from the Chinese. It is notable that Macknight, Warner and Thomson all chose their words carefully when discussing the origins of this pipe. Macknight, for example, said that it was 'possibly' borrowed from the Macassans and that it derived from a type of pipe used mainly for smoking opium (Macknight 1976, p. 91). I believe it was wise to be so cautious: after all, while there is no doubt that Aboriginal people tasted and enjoyed Macassan arrack, there remains considerable doubt about the process whereby the opium pipe metamorphosed into an Aboriginal tobacco pipe. Mysteriously, the Macassans who supposedly introduced pipe smoking were a people who did not usually smoke, but instead were chewers of betel and tobacco—methods of ingestion that northern Aborigines never adopted.

References

Achadi, A., S. Widyastuti and S. Barber (2005) 'The relevance and prospects of advancing tobacco control in Indonesia', *Health Policy*, 72, pp. 333–49.

Atlas (1885) *Ethnographische atlas, bevattende afbeeldingen van voorwerpen uit het leven en de huishouding der Makassaren*, 's Gravenhage: Nijhoff.

Beaglehole, J. C. (ed.) (1963) *The Endeavour Journal of Joseph Banks, 1768–1771. Volume II*, Sydney: Trustees of the Public Library of New South Wales & Angus & Robertson.

Berndt, R. M. and C. H. Berndt (1954) *Arnhem Land: Its history and its people*, Melbourne: F. W. Cheshire.

Brady, M. (2008) *First Taste. How Indigenous Australians learned about grog*, Canberra: Alcohol Education and Rehabilitation Foundation.

Brady, M. and V. McGrath (2010) 'Making *Tuba* in the Torres Strait Islands: the cultural diffusion and geographic mobility of an alcoholic drink', *Journal of Pacific History*, 45 (3), pp. 108–22.

Burkhill, I. H. (1966) *A Dictionary of the Economic Products of the Malay Peninsula*, Kuala Lumpur: Ministry of Agriculture and Co-operatives.

Burningham, N. (1994) 'Aboriginal nautical art: a record of the Macassans and the pearling industry in northern Australia', *The Great Circle: Journal of the Australian Association for Maritime History*, 16 (2), pp. 139–51.

Cameron, J. M. R. (ed.) (1999) *Letters from Port Essington, 1838–1845*, Darwin: Historical Society of the Northern Territory.

Cawte, J. (1985) 'Psychoactive substances of the South Seas: betel, kava and pituri', *Australian and New Zealand Journal of Psychiatry*, 19, pp. 83–7.

Cooke, M. (1987) *Makassar and Northeast Arnhem Land: Missing links and living bridges*, Batchelor, NT: Educational Media Unit, Batchelor College.

Courtwright, D. T. (2001) *Forces of Habit: Drugs and the making of the modern world*, Cambridge, Mass.: Harvard University Press.

Earl, G. W. (1882) *Handbook for Colonists in Tropical Australia*, London: George Rivers.

Evans, N. (1992) 'Macassan loanwords in Top End languages', *Australian Journal of Linguistics*, 12, pp. 45–91.

Evans, N. (1997) 'Macassan loans and linguistic stratification in western Arnhem Land', in P. McConvell and N. Evans (eds), *Archaeology and Linguistics: Aboriginal Australia in global perspective*, Melbourne: Oxford University Press, pp. 237–60.

Fox, J. J. (1977) *Harvest of the Palm: Ecological change in eastern Indonesia*, Cambridge, Mass.: Harvard University Press.

Ganter, R. (2003) 'Mixed relations', in P. Edwards and S. Yuanfang (eds), *Lost in the Whitewash: Aboriginal–Asian encounters in Australia 1901–2001*, Canberra: Humanities Research Centre, The Australian National University, pp. 69–83.

Gervaise, N. (1971 [1701]) *An Historical Description of the Kingdom of Macassar in the East-Indies*, Farnborough, UK: Gregg International Publishers [Originally printed in London by Tho. Leigh & D. Midwinter].

Gillen, F. J. (1968) *Gillen's Diary. The camp jottings of F. J. Gillen on the Spencer and Gillen expedition across Australia 1901–1902*, Adelaide: Libraries Board of South Australia.

Goodman, J. (1993) *Tobacco in History: The cultures of dependence*, London & New York: Routledge.

Hodgson, B. (1999) *Opium. A portrait of the heavenly demon*, San Francisco: Chronicle Books.

Hordern, M. (2002) *King of the Australian Coast: The work of Phillip Parker King in the* Mermaid *and the* Bathurst *1817–1822*, Melbourne: Melbourne University Press.

Knaap, G. and H. Sutherland (2004) *Monsoon Traders: Ships, skippers and commodities in eighteenth century Makassar*, Leiden: KITLV Press.

Macknight, C. C. (1976) *The Voyage to Marege': Macassan trepangers in northern Australia*, Carlton, Vic.: Melbourne University Press.

Macknight, C. C. and A. G. Thorne (1968) 'Two Macassan burials in Arnhem Land', *Archaeology & Physical Anthropology in Oceania*, III (3), pp. 216–22.

MacPherson, J. (1921) 'The use of narcotics and intoxicants by the native tribes of Australia, New Guinea, and the Pacific', *Sydney University Medical Journal*, (May), pp. 108–22.

Mulvaney, J. (1988) 'Aboriginal Australians abroad 1606–1875', *Aboriginal History*, 12 (1), pp. 41–7.

Mulvaney, J. and N. Green (1992) *Commandant of Solitude: The journals of Captain Collet Barker 1828–1831*, Melbourne: Miegunyah Press.

Reid, A. (1985) 'From betel-chewing to tobacco-smoking in Indonesia', *The Journal of Asian Studies*, 44 (3), pp. 529–47.

Rooney, D. F. (1993) *Betel Chewing Traditions in South-East Asia*, Kuala Lumpur: Oxford University Press.

Rosenman, H. (ed.) (1992) *Two Voyages to the South Seas. Capt. Jules S. C. Dumont D'Urville*, Melbourne: Melbourne University Press.

Searcy, A. (1984 [1909]) *In Australian Tropics*, (Facsimile edn), Perth: Hesperian Press.

Strickland, S. S. (2002) 'Anthropological perspectives on use of the areca nut', *Addiction Biology*, 7, pp. 85–97.

Thomson, D. F. (1939) 'Notes on the smoking-pipes of north Queensland and the Northern Territory of Australia', *Man*, 39 (June), pp. 81–91.

Thomson, D. F. (1949) *Economic Structure and the Ceremonial Exchange Cycle in Arnhem Land*, Melbourne: Macmillan & Co.

Walker, A. and R. D. Zorc (1981) 'Austronesian loanwords in Yolngu-Matha of northeast Arnhem Land', *Aboriginal History*, 5 (2), pp. 109–34.

Wallace, A. R. (1989 [1869]) *The Malay Archipelago*, Oxford: Oxford University Press.

Warner, W. L. (1958) *A Black Civilization: A social study of an Australian tribe*, (Revised edn), New York: Harper & Brothers.

Webling, A. C. (1995) *The Journals of Alfred Charles Webling*, Western Creek, ACT: Genie Publishing.

Zheng, Y. (2003) 'The social life of opium in China, 1483–1999', *Modern Asian Studies*, 37 (1), pp. 1–39.

Zorc, R. D. (1986) *Yolngu-Matha Dictionary*, Batchelor, NT: School of Australian Linguistics.

10. Tangible heritage of the Macassan–Aboriginal encounter in contemporary South Sulawesi

Marshall Clark

Introduction

There are several under-explored areas in the scholarship on the so-called 'Macassans', the trepang fishers of diverse ethnicity originating from the Sulawesi port of Makassar who voyaged to the coastline of northern Australia to fish for trepang, also known as sea cucumber, from at least 1720 to the 1906/7 season. The most noticeable gap in the field is in respect to China, the final destination of the processed trepang in the Macassan era.[1] The other relatively under-explored area is Makassar itself, the major disembarkation point for the Macassan trepang fishing fleets. This chapter will partly redress this scholarly lacuna by highlighting Makassar's Macassan heritage, with an emphasis on tangible heritage. The body of this chapter will discuss what could be understood as Macassan tangible cultural heritage: authentic monuments and historical sites with distinctive connections to the Bugis and Makassarese fishers and entrepreneurs of centuries past. But it will soon become evident that in the contemporary era there is very little in the way of tangible Macassan heritage, either in Makassar itself or in South Sulawesi in general.

This sorry state of affairs might not have needed to be the case. As a point of comparison, the penultimate section of this chapter will discuss the seafaring and fisheries galleries in the Terengganu State Museum in the port city of Kuala Terengganu on the eastern coastline of peninsular Malaysia. Such a comparison is apt because in many respects Terengganu and Makassar can be considered as cultural counterparts, most obviously in the sense that they have long been ports of significance in archipelagic Southeast Asia. This comparative discussion is not meant to be exhaustive, but rather an illustration of how a tangible Macassan or seafaring cultural heritage might have been—or still yet could be—embodied or interpreted.

Of course, it should be noted from the outset that using a Malaysian heritage case study as a point of comparison with Makassar has its flaws. As Karim Raslan

---

1 A notable exception is Sutherland (2000).

observed in the mid 1990s, Malaysia is a middle-class nation with middle-class preoccupations (Raslan 1996, p. 128). Today this is even more so the case. One of these preoccupations is the preservation and promotion of history and heritage. In Malaysia, the promotion of museums, traditional craft fairs and cultural theme parks, with the associated 'museumising' of the material culture of both the modern and the past, is closely related to government initiatives to instil national pride among Malaysian citizens (Hoffstaedter 2008). The Malaysian Government has a proclaimed aim of Malaysia becoming a fully industrialised country by 2020, and modern elements of this project, such as Kuala Lumpur's Petronas Twin Towers, the tallest 'twin towers' in the world, are given equal weighting to 'traditional' elements of the nation's narrative, such as the sultan's palace with its wood-crafted dwellings and the many material cultural artefacts found in museums and theme parks (Hoffstaedter 2008). The post-colonial state's reification, which Nor (2011, p. 53) calls 'heritagization', of traditional Malay court and folk dances, is another expression of this pattern. Kuala Lumpur's Handcraft Museum, with its 'colony' of artists and artisans employed for the purposes of daily performances of *batik*-making, jewellery-making, dancing, and so on, is a similar expression of this museumising impulse.[2]

In contrast with Malaysia, Indonesia is a vastly different kettle of fish.[3] In terms of economic progress and democratic consolidation, developing Indonesia is still very much a work in progress. In terms of print literacy, despite rising educational levels and a sharp decline in the level of illiteracy, Indonesia's oral cultural and literary traditions still predominate (see Derks 1996, 2002). This means that libraries and other cultural institutions such as museums are in an important sense anachronistic, marginal phenomena harking back to the colonial era. Museums are also poorly patronised, as besides the colonial overtones described above, state museums have long been seen as sites of New Order indoctrination. Fortunately, it can be argued that in Makassar, as in Indonesia in general, 'living history', as opposed to the anachronism of 'museumified' history, is far more relevant. This chapter will argue, therefore, that any serious

---

2 Given its undeniable lack of authenticity, not to mention its blatant exploitation of rural artisans, India's national handicrafts museum in New Delhi has been harshly criticised (see Greenough 1993; Bharucha 2000). Similar criticisms can be levelled at the Kuala Lumpur Handcraft Museum.
3 In fairness, it should be noted that, despite the obvious economic differences, Indonesia has not been completely left behind by its wealthier neighbours. For instance, there is a modest amount of museumising in Indonesia, such as the well-established Taman Mini Indah Indonesia theme park in Jakarta and the Sultan of Yogyakarta's Palace in Central Java, which has a number of ceremonial and historical artefacts. Moreover, there appears to be modest growth in the establishment of new museums and cultural heritage tours and trails, particularly in regional cities and towns such as Magelang, Jepara, Banten and Demak. With rising incomes, the regions appear to be seeking to claim and highlight their specific and unique heritage and culture. But on the whole these efforts are still poorly funded, ad hoc in nature and poorly patronised. The government-funded Makassar City Museum, for example, is unkempt and dusty, with depressingly inadequate lighting and labelling. The museum is free of charge and is manned by student volunteers with little understanding of the historical significance of any of the museum artefacts, which are seldom rotated or enhanced by new acquisitions.

examination of the Macassan history and heritage of contemporary Indonesia must move beyond a negative comparison with a Malaysian cognate form. Instead, it should be premised on the understanding that the contemporary Macassan or maritime culture of South Sulawesi is an ongoing cultural process, an intangible 'living history', rather than an objective cultural product. The final section of this chapter will delineate this argument in more detail.

Contemporary Makassar and the question of World Heritage listing

If perchance a historian were to put on a stout pair of boots and search for evidence of tangible Macassan heritage in present-day Sulawesi, the phrase 'blink and you'll miss it' is apt. But this should not mean that there is no Macassan heritage in Indonesia—far from it. This is especially the case if the Macassan heritage of Sulawesi is defined not simply in terms of a selection of tangible cultural products but rather as an ongoing cultural process with associated intangible values. To do this, however, Macassan heritage needs to be understood as an element of a continuous and dynamic process by which a variety of identities is formed. Part of this process is to understand the ongoing 'boom-town' nature of contemporary Makassar itself.

Makassar is now one of the largest cities in Indonesia and, after Jakarta and Surabaya, the third-largest port city. The city, which was known in the New Order period as Ujung Pandang, is the capital city of the province of South Sulawesi. Makassar is also southern Sulawesi's primary port and has many domestic and international shipping connections, which means that it is the major maritime trading centre of the eastern part of the Indonesian archipelago. Makassar has a modest international airport, with direct and regular flights to and from Singapore, Jakarta, Denpasar, and many other domestic destinations, including all the major centres in Sulawesi. Makassar has been described, somewhat romantically, in the following way:

> Bugis schooners, the ancient walls of the city and the minarets and domes of mosques impart a medieval look to South Sulawesi's bustling port and capital, Ujung Pandang. Indeed, the city still exhibits many vestiges of the 16th century when it was known the world over as Macassar, maritime center of the Dutch East Indies. (Behr 1990, p. 204)

Two decades later, much of this description holds true. In Makassar's Paotere Harbour, among many other types of vessels, there certainly are the odd *pinisi* (Bugis schooner) or two, distinguished by their spectacular masts and spinnakers. The minarets and domes of Makassar's mosques are still in abundance.

The imposing walls of Fort Rotterdam are a stark reminder of Makassar's Indies past. During the early mornings and evenings, when the *adzan*, or Muslim call for prayers, over numerous loudspeaker systems seems particularly pronounced, Makassar's Muslim heritage is obvious. These days, however, the Makassar skyline is dominated by a string of five-star luxury hotels along the Losari beachfront thoroughfare, not to mention the many large container cranes at Makassar's main wharf. As the region's major trading hub, Makassar is the self-proclaimed gateway to the many provinces and islands of eastern Indonesia and to the idyllic heritage tourism area of Tanah Toraja in the highlands of South Sulawesi. Much has been written about the rich Torajan cultural heritage, with an emphasis on the role of heritage tourism and its impact on traditional Torajan society and culture (see, for example, Adams 2006; Waterson 2011). There have also been ongoing calls for the Toraja region to be proposed as a site for the UNESCO World Heritage List (Adams 2010).

Despite the push for Tanah Toraja to be listed by UNESCO as a World Heritage site, there has so far been little interest in listing tangible or intangible evidence of South Sulawesi's major role in the Macassan trepang industry, which is a significant feature of the history of the region. As Macknight (1976) and many others have observed, the regular arrival of the Macassan fleets along the coastline of northern Australia resulted in frequent social, cultural and economic interactions between the trepangers and the peoples of the Australian coastline, which included the movement of Australian Aboriginal people to live, work and die in Makassar. The Macassan heritage is therefore imbued with cultural and historical significance for the Indigenous people of northern Australia and for the people of South Sulawesi, which, most neutral observers agree, needs to be rediscovered, preserved and conserved. As Indonesia's vibrant democratic consolidation begins to attract more international investment and tourists, and allows for the growth of a truly globalised middle class, it may now be timely for Macassan heritage sites to be nominated for UNESCO listing as world heritage, perhaps in a joint proposal by Australia and Indonesia. More precisely, the Makassar–Marege' maritime trade route might be appropriate for nomination in the category of cultural routes, introduced by UNESCO's World Heritage Committee in the mid 1990s. There is also the possibility of documenting and assessing Australian components of the Macassan trepangers' heritage for inclusion on Australia's National Heritage List in recognition of their relevance in Australian history. At present, although none of the Macassan sites along the northern coastline has been inscribed on Australia's National Heritage List, they are protected as archaeological sites under the Northern Territory's *Heritage Act 2012*.

The case of Unusu Daeng Remba's house in Jalan Maipa

The best-known Macassan heritage site, a house (see Figure 10.1), is in fact one that would fall short of UNESCO's requirements for World Heritage listing. The house is described by Macknight (1976, Plate 18) as 'the building said to have been Unusu Daeng Remba's house in Kampong Basi, Macassar'. Unusu Daeng Remba was captain of the *Lakarinlong* on its voyages to Arnhem Land between 1882–83 and 1889–90 and of the *Kampong Basi* in 1897–98, and he also sailed on several other boats, including the *Mannongkoki*. One of the most prominent captains as the trepang industry declined, he was known to have hosted Aboriginal people in his house in Makassar (Macknight 1976, p. 86). According to Ibu Saribinong Nganne (b. 1904), the daughter of another well-known captain in the last years of the Macassan trepang industry, Using Daeng Rangka, at least two of the Aborigines were men who lived and worked in Remba's house and died there in the 1930s (Stephenson 2007, p. 31). Cooke (1987, p. 45) gives their names as Lahurru and Lakkoy, while Stephenson (2007, p. 31) names them Lahurruk and Lido. They were 'responsible for guarding the *empang* or fishponds at the back of the house, cleaning the *mushollah* [small Muslim prayer house]...and pump[ing] water up bamboo ducts to the house and *mushollah*' (Ganter 2006, p. 36). The Kampung Basi locale is around Jalan Maipa, a street that is now in central Makassar, walking distance from Makassar's palm-fringed Losari Beach and several of Makassar's best-known luxury hotels. The main roof beams, posts and structural foundations of the house are said to have been constructed of ironwood brought back from Arnhem Land more than 100 years ago.

At this point it should be noted that Unusu Daeng Remba's house no longer exists. The house, which in its final form consisted of an impressive two-storey house and a row of boarding rooms and classrooms, set in a courtyard extending 50 m to the south, was demolished on 3 November 2011. This fact alone will ensure that it will never meet UNESCO's protection and management criteria. It was demolished so that the nearby upmarket Kenari Towers Hotel could construct a new wing. A sign in the front yard of the house, prominent on the day of the demolition and in the following weeks, read: '*Mohon Doa Restu: Lokasi Ini Akan Dibangun Kenari Tower Hotel Unit 2* [Please Offer Your Prayers of Blessing: This Location will be used to Build Unit 2 of the Kenari Tower Hotel].' The house was reportedly sold for Rp10 billion (US$1 million), which by Indonesian standards is a fortune. There is little doubt that the neighbourhood around Jalan Maipa, which runs from the picture-postcard beach into an area of schools and luxury hotels, holds some of Makassar's most sought-after real estate.

The previous owner of the property, K. H. Darwis Zakaria, was well aware of the heritage value of the house's timber. Before its demolition, in conversation with us, the visibly upset Darwis, who grew up in the house, claimed that it would be carefully collected and used in the construction of a new house on the rural outskirts of Makassar. Nevertheless, much of this historically precious timber was destroyed in the demolition and large chunks of it lay strewn amongst the ruins (see Figure 10.2). When we asked a neighbour why the leftover timber was not being collected—or indeed stolen, considering the very high cost of ironwood—the response was prescient: 'No-one would be brave enough to steal that wood, as it is sacred [keramat].' Carbon testing would probably confirm that the wood was well more than 100 years old and, therefore, would be considered, as the neighbours suggested, far too *lapuk* (dilapidated) for further use.

Figure 10.1 Unusu Daeng Remba's house in Jalan Maipa, Makassar, shortly before its demolition on 3 November 2011

Source: Marshall Clark

Figure 10.2 The remains of the Daeng Remba house, mid November 2011

Source: Marshall Clark

It was widely understood in the Jalan Maipa neighbourhood that the timber used in constructing Unusu Daeng Remba's house was transported from Arnhem Land in a boat captained by Daeng Remba more than 100 years ago. Some believed, perhaps mistakenly, that the house was built by a team of Aboriginal people. As noted earlier, Aboriginal Australians were known to have lived in the house, perhaps as slaves, from time to time. It is possible that an Aboriginal woman may also have lived at the Jalan Maipu house. Aboriginal people in Arnhem Land knew of an Aboriginal woman, Garngarr, who lived out her life in Makassar. Garngarr was taken as a teenage girl from Arnhem Bay, northeast Arnhem Land, to live in Makassar, where she married a Macassan man and had a number of children. At the age of ninety-nine, Garngarr was reunited in 1986 with a number of her family from northern Australia, including Yolngu elder Laklak Burarrwanga, who may be her great-great-granddaughter.

Although the Garngarr story is shrouded in uncertainty, it is fascinating. According to Mattjuwi's account in Ganter (2006, p. 36), an Aboriginal woman from Elcho Island, not far from Arnhem Bay, named Garnggar, was abducted by someone known as Captain Maliwa. Cooke (1987, p. 45) suggests that this person may be Daeng Mallewa, a trepanger from the Spermonde island of Barrang Lompo. Ganter observes that Garnggar had a daughter, Gunano, who was born in Makassar. There are differing versions of Gunano's story, however, with varying accounts of how long she may have lived in Makassar, if at all. For instance, Macknight (1976, p. 87) reports that Using Daeng Rangka is said to have fathered about 10 children by three mothers in eastern Arnhem Land and one of his daughters there, Kunanu, later visited Makassar, but it is unlikely that she spent the rest of her life there. According to Mangngellai Daeng Maro, the son of Unusu Daeng Remba, 'a woman named "Kunano" went to Makassar and was later returned home before the end of the trepang industry with all the other Aborigines who were in Makassar at the time' (Cooke 1987, p. 43). Putting aside the question of how long Gunano/Kunano lived in Makassar, we can discount the notion that Gunano/Kunano is the same person as Garngarr/Garnggar, as their names have not been linked by any sources. It remains difficult to determine precisely how Laklak is related to Garngarr/Garnggar and it is likely to remain difficult to do so. As noted by Cooke (1987, p. 39), 'most Aboriginal kinship terms simply do not have an English equivalent, and must be expressed in a roundabout way and with plenty of explanation'. Laklak's account of the reunion in Makassar in 1986 reads: 'When we got there she jumped from the chair and walked towards us saying this is the family from Arnhem Land. She was still thinking of when she left many years before. So we grieved. She was crying for me and we were crying for her' (Lloyd et al. 2010, p. 710).

After the initial reunion, stories were shared:

> So we talked about what happened to her. She told stories. She was really old—about 99—but she was very strong. She told the story for the great grandsons. So we stayed there, made her company. Her husband had now died. We stayed for one night with her, me and my cousin Djalinda. The next day we went back and she called us up so that we should go to the museum where her nephew worked. His name was Hussein and we went to see. When she was young she was beautiful. We saw all the things she wore and her husband. We could see the sword. He was a prince, her husband. We see clothes. Everything was kept in the museum. (Burarrwanga 2012)

Garngarr has now passed away and, according to residents of Jalan Maipa, is purportedly buried with her husband somewhere in West Sumatra. Unusu Daeng Remba's great-great-grandchildren and other Jalan Maipa residents vividly recall a large group of Aborigines (presumably Laklak's group of six) touring the house several decades ago (in 1986, to be precise). Laklak has also recounted a few other Makassar-related stories, most notably that Garngarr worked at a church where she used to sweep and mop the wooden floor, which was apparently made of ironwood from northeast Arnhem Land. There is a Catholic school in the Kampung Basi locale, so perhaps this is an avenue for future investigation.

One further point about the Jalan Maipa house is that neighbours were certain that it was haunted. Haunted houses are not a phenomenon unique to Makassar, of course, as belief in ghosts and other supernatural activity is widespread and deeply rooted throughout maritime Southeast Asia. The stories of ghosts inhabiting the Jalan Maipa house may explain the general reluctance to tamper with the abandoned timber. One middle-aged man told us of how he had slept overnight in the house a few times when he was a boy. He distinctly remembers being disturbed in the early hours of the morning by dark-skinned *'hantu Marege"* (Aboriginal ghosts). Although the ghosts were not threatening, the experience was unsettling and not easily forgotten. It might be useful to establish whether the new house on the outskirts of Makassar, which will purportedly utilise the remaining Arnhem Land ironwood, is haunted as well. Given that intangible heritage such as ghosts and other paranormal activity are often associated with objects of tangible heritage, particularly in relation to objects of historical or spiritual significance to Aborigines, it would be not be surprising if there were reports of the new house being haunted.

Museums, tombs and graveyards

Makassar's other Macassan heritage sites can be summarised in a few paragraphs. The Makassar City Museum occasionally mounts a display on the Macassan trepang industry, such as that referred to by Macknight (2008, p. 141). At present, the City Museum holds mounted photographs relating to the Macassan voyages to Arnhem Land, as well as of joint theatre productions between Australian and Makassar-based performing arts groups. One of the mounted images is an intriguing map of the indigenous state of Gowa, which was a dominant local power around the city of Makassar by the end of the sixteenth century. According to this map, which has been observed in other locations in present-day Makassar (Cooke 1987, p. 45), Gowa's authority is shown to have stretched throughout eastern Indonesia and to the Northern Territory in the first half of the seventeenth century. According to Macknight (2008, p. 141), who has seen two editions of the map, 'the Top End of the Northern Territory is included with a date of $\pm$ 1640 in the first edition of the work in 1967, and $\pm$ is removed in the second edition of 1983'. Although most scholars would suggest that a map such as this one is unreliable (see Macknight 2008, p. 141), it is generally understood that Gowa's influence was felt on the east coast of Kalimantan, in Lombok and eastwards to the Aru-Kei island group (Ricklefs et al. 2010, pp. 160–1). Gowa's role as the main spice-trading state of eastern Indonesia attracted Asian and European communities, including the Dutch East India Company, whose attentions resulted in hostilities with Gowa in 1615. In the wake of this warfare, the peace treaty of Bungaya eventually brought Gowa's dominance of trade to an end. This information is not documented in the Makassar City Museum and the mounted photographs referred to above are currently locked in a dusty cabinet in one of the museum's ground-floor galleries.

Similarly difficult to locate is the tombstone of Puddu Daeng Tompo, who died about 1912. The tombstone is in a laneway off Jalan Somba Opu, behind Mesjid Ansar, the main mosque of Kampung Maloku, central Makassar (see Figure 10.3). Daeng Tompo was the main financier or entrepreneur (*punggawa*) of the Macassan trepang industry in its final stages. According to Macknight (1976, Plate 16), he probably devoted some of his profits to building the mosque, which might explain why his tombstone has remained reasonably well maintained to this day. Several prominent figures in the neighbourhood, including the Kampung Maloku district head and direct descendants of Daeng Tompo, informed us that Daeng Tompo owned much of the property in the area around the mosque, at the southern end of what is now Makassar's modest Chinatown.

Figure 10.3 The tombstone of Puddu Daeng Tompo in Kampung Maloku, Makassar

Source: Marshall Clark

The final location of Macassan heritage that is worth highlighting is quite possibly in fact a series of sites. On the larger islands in the Spermonde Archipelago out from the Makassar coastline are a number of cemeteries said to contain the graves of fishers who voyaged to Arnhem Land. It is extremely difficult to ascertain simply by looking at the graves which are those of trepangers from the time of the Macassan trepang industry, and local people are unable to identify them either. The oldest graves are very dilapidated and many of them are unmarked, but it is very likely some of those buried beneath them were islanders involved in trepang fishing. According to Meereboer (1998, p. 257), 'some sea cucumber species were named after one of the islands, that is Kodingaring (Lompo), the southern-most island in this archipelago'. In 1823, at the height of the Macassan trepang industry, the *kodingaring* trepang, named after the Spermonde island, Kodingareng Lompo, were the most valuable and the *pasir kodingaring*, also named after Kodingareng, were the most expensive of them all (Sutherland 2000, p. 88). As noted earlier, it was a trepanger from one of the Spermonde islands who was said to have kidnapped an Aboriginal woman. There is a strong possibility, therefore, that the Spermonde cemeteries contain the graves of trepangers from the Macassan era, thus making them potentially sites of Macassan historical significance.

One of the largest of the Spermonde cemeteries can be found on Kodingareng Lompo, which is most probably the island Laklak Burarrrwanga referred to in her account of her trip to Sulawesi:

> Then the next day we crossed in a Makassan boat to an island called Gunyaŋgarri, a small island about 1000 people staying there and it was also very difficult. There was an outside shower with the water hole. We saw the grave for the people who had been there, to Arnhem Land. It held people from Sulawesi who had been to Arnhem Land. They take them to that island to get away from the city when they got old and they died there. All the poles and flags were there. It's similar to here. One man took us to the wishing stone where they used to wish for the NE wind. It's a rock there (Burarrwanga 2012).

The island of Kodingareng Lompo, popularly known as Kodingareng, is indeed heavily populated and life there could well be described as 'very difficult' because of such inconveniences as outdoor showers located near wells. The 'wishing stone' mentioned in Laklak's account is not immediately identifiable in Kodingareng, but there are a number of very large boulders near the cemetery. There are also a number of Chinese tombstones that might be of marginal relevance. The calligraphy on the headstones of these imposing tombstones identifies them as marking the graves of Chinese entrepreneurs (see Figure 10.4). From my conversations with local residents, I learned that many of the Chinese who lived and died in the Spermonde islands were traders and trepang collectors. On Barrang Lompo, in particular, there are several very prominent Chinese tombstones, as well as the tombs of prominent Muslim traders or aristocrats, one of which is at the base of a 15 m high banyan tree—the roots of the tree literally grow in and around the tombstone, which is now part of the tree itself. Of course, none of this tangible Macassan history and heritage is documented or advertised and only mosque officials and the very oldest people in the community are able to give any account of the significance of these sites. In present-day Makassar and its environs there is little tangible evidence of a distinct Macassan cultural heritage. So, if there were to be such a thing as a Macassan heritage, what form would we like it to take? More precisely, in order to fulfil UNESCO's criteria for World Heritage listing, what shape or form might an appropriately managed Macassan heritage site or interpretative facility take? We can look to Malaysia for some answers.

Figure 10.4 Chinese tombstone, Kodingareng Lompo Island

Source: Marshall Clark

Terengganu State Museum

A good example of what could have been labelled a seemingly ideal Macassan interpretative facility is the Fisheries Gallery at Kuala Terengganu's Terengganu State Museum, Malaysia. In one sense, using a Malaysian example to support an argument for the identification of heritage sights in Indonesia is a little unfair as it is, after all, Malaysian, rather than Indonesian. Yet, as anyone who has stepped inside a museum in Indonesia, Malaysia or Singapore can attest, the archipelagic and peninsular Malay worlds share a great deal, especially in terms of history and heritage. Indeed, museums in each nation—above the protestations of Indonesian football fans and online commentators—magnanimously showcase many of the same cultural traditions, such as *batik*, *wayang*, *gamelan* and *keris*. The origins of many of these heritage items, be they the Bugis of southwestern Sulawesi, the Minangkabau of western Sumatra or the Javanese of central and eastern Java, are also publicly acknowledged. This theme of cultural affinity is a common thread uniting the Indonesian/Malay archipelago. Moreover, Kuala Terengganu, like Makassar, is a port city with a long and proud history as a coastal hub, connecting the trading vessels of the eastern Malay Peninsula with the Bugis traders of Sulawesi and vessels from China, Thailand, Vietnam and elsewhere in the Malay world. So, in an important sense, Makassar and Kuala Terengganu have more similarities than differences.

In terms of physical structure, the Terengganu State Museum is the largest museum in Malaysia. Several displays in the museum highlight the close historical links between Terengganu and Sulawesi, in the fashion gallery, where the *batik* styles of Terengganu are placed alongside the silk *batik* styles of the ethnic Bugis. To this day, the Bugis 'boxed', or quadrate, silk *batik* motif is very popular in Terengganu, if not all of Malaysia, and can be seen in many items, including sarongs, blinds, tablecloths and seat furnishings.

Outside the Terengganu Museum building, two schooners are housed in the museum grounds: a *Perahu Besar* (big boat) and a *Pinis Dogol* (Dogol schooner). The semantic link between the Malay *pinis* and the Bugis *pinisi* is evident in the two words and supports claims that for many centuries there were strong trade links between the coastal kingdoms of peninsular Malaysia and the seafaring Bugis, who were distinguished by the majestic *pinisi* schooners they sailed (Ricklefs et al. 2010). The value of each of the *pinisi* vessels at the Terengganu Museum is such that security guards are camped nearby and the boats appear to be closed for onboard tours while renovations occur. Although there may be conservation and preservation concerns with the present set-up, the location of both boats—barely 20 m from the banks of the Terengganu River, which is often swollen by heavy rains, especially during the monsoon season—is in one sense perfect. Each boat has appropriate interpretative signs, in English, Malay and Chinese, giving full and helpful details of its style, provenance and sailing history, and of historical links with the Bugis *pinisi*.

The Bugis, like the Indians and Chinese, have had an important and widely influential role in the history of the Malay Peninsula. After the rise of a Bugis dynasty in Aceh in 1727, Bugis power was established in the Kingdom of Johor in 1728. According to various accounts, a branch of the Bugis royal family was transferred to the Johor line after a particularly brutal regicide. The Bugis domiciled in Riau and Johor took pains to demonstrate their support of the Malays and their traditional institutions (Andaya 2010, p. 139). Intermarriage with Malay royalty and nobility enabled the Bugis to identity with and become increasingly 'Malay', and their influence spread throughout the peninsula. In 1766, for instance, Raja Lumu, son of the powerful Bugis Raja Muda of Johor, was installed as the first Sultan of Selangor (Andaya 2010, pp. 228–9). Although the Bugis are relatively recent settlers and, therefore, associated with a home area outside Malaysia (Andaya 2010, p. 13), in the post-colonial era the links between the Bugis and the Malays have proven to be a cause of great pride for both peoples. For example, Makassar has a street named Jalan Tun Abdul Razak, which recognises the much-publicised fact that both Malaysia's first prime minister and the prime minister at the time of writing this chapter can trace their lineage back directly to the sixteenth-century Bugis royal line of the Bugis–Makassarese Kingdom of Gowa. The present-day royal family of Johor is equally proud to share these ties with Bugis royalty. Occasionally Malaysian Government delegations tour Makassar, where they are met with great fanfare.[4]

Returning to our discussion of the Terengganu State Museum, not far from the large *pinisi* schooners is another area where several full-sized fishing and trading prau are displayed. These vessels are included in the museum because they are used in the Terengganu area, both up its rivers and in the open seas. Each replica has an accompanying interpretative sign in English and Malay, discretely located to respect the great care taken both in the preservation of the boats and in the landscape of the site. Indeed, in the prau exhibition precinct one is likely to encounter half-a-dozen gardeners, such is the care being taken to maintain a site that is beautified with ornamental flowers and trees and with water features around each display island, on which the boats are raised above the ground. Visitors can take any number of routes through the display islands to the Fisheries Gallery, which in many ways is exactly what Makassar needs to display its fishing heritage.

Inside the Fisheries Gallery, Terengganu's maritime history is revealed, with an emphasis on local history, through the use of dioramas. Displays focus on such

---

4   My thanks to Raimy Ché-Ross for this observation.

things as the types of vessels used in the Terengganu region, traditional nets and fish traps together with modern trawler nets, hooks, sinkers and fishing lines of all shapes and sizes, the clothing of traditional Malay fishers, and decorated prau prows, some of which represent characters from the traditional *wayang kulit* shadow theatre. About 90 m from this gallery, along the riverbank, a small footbridge passes halfway across the Terengganu River to a small island, Pulau Sekati. Inhabitants of this island, ethnic Malays, collect coconuts from the island's many coconut trees to sell to the museum's cafeteria. Although Pulau Sekati is not officially part of the museum, the detour certainly enhances the maritime ambience of the seafaring and fishing section of the museum.

What if there were to be a similar museum, in similar marine environs, in Makassar? After all, Makassar's maritime heritage is no less impressive than that of Terengganu.[5] But, it is unrealistic to assume that the experience of setting up a museum in Malaysia has any relevance to preserving maritime heritage in Indonesia. Compare, for instance, the Terengganu museum's army of security guards and gardeners with the army of highly skilled boatbuilders and trepang fishers one encounters anywhere along the southern Sulawesi coastline. It is no secret that foreign workers, including many Indonesian fishing crews, are the mainstay of Malaysia's fishing industry, not to mention its very limited boatbuilding industry. In a more general sense, it could be argued that the comparison neatly highlights the difference between middle-class Malaysia's thoroughly museumised cultural heritage and developing Indonesia's living history continuum. In Indonesia, especially in South Sulawesi, trepang fisheries and trade and traditional prau building are still big business.

South Sulawesi's living maritime heritage

If we expand our understanding of Macassan history and heritage to include post-Macassan trepang fisheries and trade, it soon becomes evident that Makassar's Macassan heritage is alive and well. It is convincingly demonstrated in a number of locations and contexts: Makassar's proud maritime culture; Makassar's Paotere Harbour, where many traditional prau wooden sailing vessels come and go; the traditional wooden boatbuilding industry of Bulukumba in southern Sulawesi; and the contemporary trepang fishery, in which Bugis and Makassarese trepangers from the Spermonde islands and from Makassar participate.

---

5   In Makassar, the maritime display in the La Galigo Museum in Fort Rotterdam is the closest one can get to Terengganu's impressive maritime and fisheries display. It must be said that it is not in any sense a very good display, in which the boats are miniature models rather than life-size replicas.

Makassar's much-vaunted maritime culture, based on centuries of demonstrated seafaring prowess by the Bugis and the Makassarese, is acknowledged still in many ways, most obviously in the many statues and images displaying traditional Bugis *pinisi*. The masthead of the Makassar edition of the *Tempo* newspaper is distinguished by an image of a *pinisi*, and the architectural facade on the top storey of the building housing the local newspaper, *Fajar*, replicates the style of a billowing *pinisi* sail. Makassar's inexpensive seafood cuisine is well known throughout the region and one of Indonesian President Susilo Bambang Yudhoyono's favourite restaurants is said to be a seafood grill not far from Makassar's Paotere boat harbour. At Paotere, echoes of the Macassan trepang industry can be seen every day, as trepang specimens are sometimes sold at the open-air fish market. Many wooden sailing vessels line the harbour (see Figure 10.5). They are still known as praus (*perahu*), as they were in the Macassan industry era (Macknight 1976). The praus moored at Paotere are intraregional fishing boats, inter-island goods transportation boats and local ferries, many of which connect the populations of the nearby Spermonde islands with the major businesses and educational institutions of the region in Makassar. Indeed, schoolchildren travel from the many Spermonde islands each morning to attend school in Makassar. Apart from motors, these praus have very little in the way of modern fishery and maritime technological accoutrements, such as sonar, radar, GPS and satellite beacons. As in the Macassan era, many of the contemporary fishers and traders making their way to and from Makassar rely on traditional navigation methods, such as the position of the stars and a deep and intimate knowledge of all the islands, ports, reefs, straits and other major landmarks passed down through generations.

Figure 10.5 Moored prau at the Paotere boat harbour, Makassar

Source: Marshall Clark

As noted above, most of the many sailing vessels frequenting Makassar's harbours and ports are prau, made almost entirely of wood. Although some boats are built in the offshore islands of the Spermonde Archipelago, the region of Bulukumba, on the southernmost shores of South Sulawesi's peninsula about three-and-a-half hours southeast of Makassar, remains Indonesia's best-known hub for wooden boatbuilding. Here, the sandy shores are lined with stalls devoted to the construction of prau of all shapes and sizes (see Figure 10.6). After I had spoken to many boatbuilders along the shores of Bulukumba's heritage town of Tanah Beru in particular, it became evident to me that many of the completed prau, particularly *perahu padewakang* (trading prau), end up in the Spermonde islands, where fishers continue to fish for trepang (see Figure 10.7). In many ways, these present-day trepangers, mostly of Bugis or Makassarese ethnicity (or a combination of both), are the contemporary embodiments of the Macassans of centuries past. Although the supply of trepang in the Makassar area, and indeed throughout the Indonesian archipelago, is greatly diminished (Choo 2008), large quantities continue to be collected and processed in Makassar and its environs for export to China, Singapore, South Korea and Malaysia. The consistently high prices that the trepangers get for their trepang are what drive the industry, which, according to members of the fishing community of South Sulawesi, is still centred in Makassar, with the Javanese port of Surabaya also playing a significant role.

It should be emphasised that most of the present-day Bugis-Makassarese trepangers are based offshore in the Spermonde islands, where the trepang (see Figure 10.8) are initially processed and cured by *'pengumpul teripang lokal'* (local trepang collectors) (see Figure 10.9). As is the case elsewhere in the Indonesian archipelago (see Adhuri, this volume), Spermonde trepangers focus on more profitable species, such as *tripang susu* or *koro susu* (white teatfish, *Holothuria fuscogilva*) and *tripang nanas* (prickly redfish, *Thelenota ananas*). Many other species, however, are caught and processed for sale, including *cerak hitam* (lollyfish, *Holothuria atra*), *teripang ballang ulu* (surf redfish, *Actinopyga mauritiana*), and *tripang hitam* (black teatfish, *Holothuria whitmaei*). After initial processing on the praus, or on jetties or dry land in the Spermonde islands, the trepang are then delivered to Makassar-based trepang collectors, known as *'pengumpul teripang'*. These *pengumpul teripang* procure and then process the trepang to meet the particular requests and demands of the overseas markets. Thus, as in the heyday of the Macassan trepang industry in the mid 1800s (Meereboer 1998; Sutherland 2000), today Makassar remains a vital hub for the fishing, processing and exporting of trepang. Makassar-based middlemen continue to play just as an important role in the industry as the trepang fishers do. Makassar is, however, not the only centre of the trepang trade, and diasporic communities of Bugis-Makassarese trepang fishers are to be found throughout the Indonesian archipelago. Many of these trepangers, by the way, report that they have fished Australian waters on numerous occasions, despite the harsh punishments.

Figure 10.6 Boatbuilding at Tanah Beru, South Sulawesi

Source: Marshall Clark

Figure 10.7 *Perahu padewakang*, used for trepang fishing, in the Spermonde Archipelago, South Sulawesi

Source: Marshall Clark

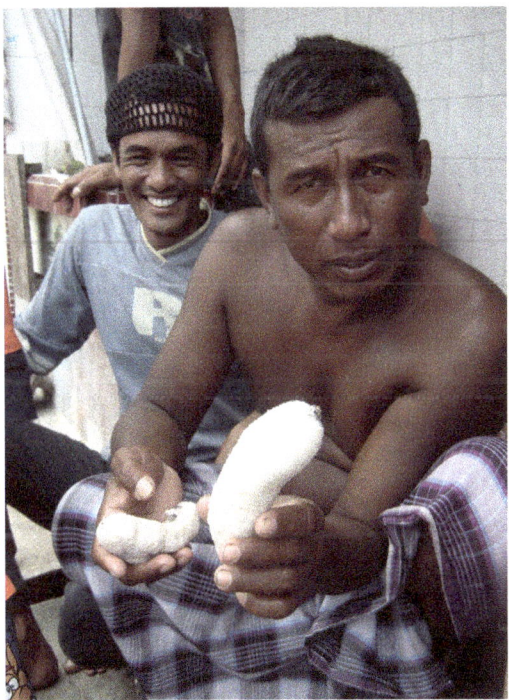

Figure 10.8 A trepanger with cured *tripang susu* (white teatfish), Barrang Lompo Island, Spermonde Archipelago

Source: Marshall Clark

Figure 10.9 A *'pengumpul teripang lokal'* (local trepang collector), with uncured trepang including *tripang nanas* (prickly redfish) (top), *tripang ballang ulu* (surf redfish) (middle) and *tripang susu* (white teatfish) (bottom), Kodingareng Lompo Island, Spermonde Archipelago

Source: Marshall Clark

Conclusion

This chapter has drawn attention to examples of what could be regarded as Makassar's sites that can be viewed as displaying important aspects of a Macassan tangible cultural heritage. Almost all of them provide fresh insights into the little-known local impact of the centuries of interaction between the trepangers of the Indonesian archipelago and Aboriginal communities of northern Australia; however, at none of the sites can satisfactory levels of general protection and management be demonstrated. One site in particular—the two-storey house said to have been made of ironwood from Arnhem Land in Jalan Maipa—has very recently been demolished to make way for the expansion of a luxury hotel. None of the sites has proper visitor reception and interpretative facilities, unless one takes into account the ubiquitous groups of interested neighbours and onlookers who are able to recount or embellish well-known oral history narratives.

Through an examination of the maritime and fisheries displays of the Terengganu State Museum in the Malaysian port city of Kuala Terengganu, this chapter has outlined what might be achieved in Makassar should a concerted effort be made to create a museumified or static form of cultural expression to showcase Makassar's rich maritime heritage; however, a negative comparison with a Malaysian institution does little to help explain Makassar's deeply layered Macassan history and heritage. Unlike economically advanced Malaysia, Indonesia might not yet be ready for its rich and continuous cultural heritage to be mothballed and museumised, for the simple reason that much of Indonesia's traditional heritage, such as fishing praus, is still in use. This is particularly the case in South Sulawesi, whose coastal communities are among Indonesia's poorest, where many fishing folk eke out a meagre existence on small fishing boats in primarily artisanal fisheries. In present-day Sulawesi, Makassar's maritime history is very much an ongoing cultural process that is still being lived on a daily basis.

If we move beyond the previously hegemonic Western understanding of cultural heritage conservation, in which 'cultural heritage resided mainly in great monuments and sites' (Taylor 2009, p. 14), it becomes evident that South Sulawesi's Macassan history is far from non-existent, especially if we consider Makassar's contemporary maritime culture and trepang fisheries. If we regard the contemporary trepang fishers, trepang collectors and wooden boatbuilders of southern Sulawesi as participants in Makassar's living history continuum then we can argue that Makassar's Macassan past has clearly not yet ended, just as the Makassar-based trepang fishers did not entirely cease their trepang collecting along the northern coast of Australia after the 1906-7 season. There is no doubt that trepang fishing continues in earnest in South Sulawesi and its environs, despite decreasing catch sizes. Many islands in the Spermonde Archipelago, offshore from Makassar, remain economically dependent on the international trepang trade. On these same islands there are numerous middle-aged trepangers—some of whom are captains or financiers of the current generation of trepang vessels—who are proud of the fact that they fished in Australian waters in the 1980s and 1990s, despite this illegal fishing resulting in detention and the destruction of their praus.

It is easy to question Indonesia's commitment to preserving its culture, heritage and traditions, as history has little honour. This chapter, however, has suggested that much of Indonesia's intangible cultural heritage is still in use, which adds layers of complexity to our understanding of Indonesia's heritage, especially when we compare it with the heritage of Malaysia and its preservation and management.

References

Adams, K. M. (2003) 'Museum/city/nation: negotiating identities in urban museums in Indonesia and Singapore', in R. Goh and B. Yeoh (eds), *Theorizing the Southeast Asian City as Text: Urban landscapes, cultural documents and interpretive experiences*, Singapore: World Scientific Publishing.

Adams, K. M. (2006) *Art as Politics: Re-crafting identities, tourism, and power in Tana Toraja, Indonesia*, Honolulu: University of Hawai'i Press.

Adams, K. M. (2010) 'The politics of heritage in Tana Toraja, Indonesia: interplaying the local and the global', *Indonesia and the Malay World*, 31 (89), pp. 91–107.

Andaya, L. Y. (2010) *Leaves of the Same Tree: Trade and ethnicity in the Straits of Melaka*, Singapore: NUS Press.

Behr, E. (1990) *Indonesia: A voyage through the archipelago*, Paris: Millet Weldon Owen Ltd.

Bharucha, R. (2000) 'Beyond the box: problematising the new Asia museum', *Third Text*, 52, pp. 11–19.

Burarrwanga, L. L. (2012) Memories of my Makassan family, Paper presented to Macassan History and Heritage: Building Understandings of Journeys, Encounters and Influences, 8–9 February, The Australian National University, Canberra.

Choo, P. (2008) 'Population status, fisheries and trade of sea cucumbers in Asia', in V. Toral-Granda, A. Lovotelli and M. Vasconcellos (eds), *Sea Cucumbers: A global review of fisheries and trade*, Rome: Food and Agriculture Organization of the United Nations.

Cooke, M. (1987) *Makassar and Northeast Arnhem Land: Missing links and living bridges*, Batchelor, NT: Educational Media Unit, Batchelor College.

Derks, W. (1996) '"If not to anything else": some reflections on modern Indonesian literature', *Bijdragen tot de Taal-, Land- en Volkenkunde*, 152 (3), pp. 341–52.

Derks, W. (2002) 'Sastra pedalaman: local and regional literary centres in Indonesia', in K. Foulcher and T. Day (eds), *Clearing a Space: Postcolonial readings of modern Indonesian literature*, Leiden: KITLV Press.

Ganter, R. (2006) *Mixed Relations: Asian/Aboriginal contact in north Australia*, Perth: University of Western Australia Press.

Greenough, P. (1993) 'Nation, economy and tradition displayed: the Indian Crafts Museum, New Delhi', in C. A. Breckenridge (ed.), *Consuming Modernity: Public culture in a South Asian world*, Minneapolis: University of Minnesota Press.

Henderson, J. (2005) 'Exhibiting cultures: Singapore's Asian Civilisations Museum', *International Journal of Heritage Studies*, 11 (3), pp. 183–95.

Hoffstaedter, G. (2008) 'Representing culture in Malaysian cultural theme parks: tensions and contradictions', *Anthropological Forum*, 18 (2), pp. 139–60.

Knaap, G. (2001) 'Manning the fleet: skippers, crews and shipowners in eighteenth-century Makassar', in E. Sedyawati and S. Zuhdi (eds), *Arung Samudra: Persembahan Memperingati Sembilan Windu A. B. Lapian*, Depok: Pusat Penilitian Kemasyarakatan dan Budaya & Lembaga Penelitian Universitas Indonesia.

Lloyd, K., S. Suchet-Pearson, S. Wright and L. Burarrwanga (2010) 'Stories of crossings and connections from Bawaka, north east Arnhem Land, Australia', *Social & Cultural Geography*, 11 (7), pp. 701–17.

Macknight, C. C. (1976) *The Voyage to Marege': Macassan Trepangers in northern Australia*, Carlton, Vic.: Melbourne University Press.

Macknight, C. C. (2008) 'Harvesting the memory: open beaches in Makassar and Arnhem Land', in P. Veth, P. Sutton and M. Neale (eds), *Strangers on the Shore: Early coastal contacts in Australia*, Canberra: National Museum of Australia.

Macknight, C. C. (2011) 'The view from Marege': Australian knowledge of Makassar and the impact of the trepang industry across two centuries', *Aboriginal History*, 35, pp. 121–43.

Malaysian National Commission for UNESCO (2008) *Malaysia: 50 years of membership in UNESCO*, Kuala Lumpur: NATCOM.

Meereboer, M. (1998) 'Fishing for credit: patronage and debt relations in the Spermonde Archipelago, Indonesia', in K. Robinson and M. Paeni (eds), *Living through Histories: Culture, history and social life in South Sulawesi*, Canberra: Department of Anthropology, Research School of Pacific and Asian Studies, The Australian National University.

Nor, M. A. M. (2011) 'Eclecticism and syncretic traditions: the making of Malay folk dance', in M. A. M. Nor and S. Buddidge (eds), *Sharing Identities: Celebrating dance in Malaysia*, London: Routledge.

Pemberton, J. (1994) *On the Subject of 'Java'*, Ithaca, NY, & London: Cornell University Press.

Peycam, P. (2012) 'Broadening intercultural dialogue', *The Newsletter*, 62, p. 3.

Raslan, K. (1996) *Ceritalah: Malaysia in transition*, Singapore: Times Books International.

Ricklefs, M. C., B. Lockhart, A. Lau, P. Reyes and M. Aung-Thwin (2010) *A New History of Southeast Asia*, Basingstoke, UK: Palgrave Macmillan.

Stephenson, P. (2007) *The Outsiders Within: Telling Australia's Indigenous–Asian story*, Sydney: UNSW Press.

Sutherland, H. (2000) 'Trepang and wangkang: the China trade of eighteenth-century Makassar c. 1720s–1840s', in R. Tol, K. van Dijk and G. Acciaioli (eds), *Authority and Enterprise among the Peoples of South Sulawesi*, Leiden: KITLV Press.

Taylor, K. (2009) 'Cultural landscapes and Asia: reconciling international and Southeast Asian regional values', *Landscape Research*, 34 (1), pp. 7–31.

Waterson, R. (2011) *Paths and Rivers: Sa'dan Toraja society in transformation*, Leiden: KITLV Press.

11. Traditional and 'modern' trepang fisheries on the border of the Indonesian and Australian fishing zones[1]

Dedi Supriadi Adhuri

Introduction: A history of trepang fisheries

Fishing for trepang is one of the oldest practices of maritime resource exploitation. Its story started in China, the country where trepang consumption was and still is common. In China, trepang is called *hai-sen* or sea ginseng. The first reference to *hai-sen* was found in a sixteenth-century work, the *Shih-wu pet-ts ao*, which outlined the use of trepang in relation to various substances of medical use (Macknight 1976, p. 7). Another book, the *Miscellanies of Five Items*, which was published in 1602, describes trepang as an aphrodisiac (Schwerdtner Máñez and Ferse 2010). Later in the same century, trepang is mentioned more frequently in Chinese literature. One could suggest that with this increase in familiarity the habit of using trepang has been progressively gaining popularity in China.

In terms of an explanation for the Chinese demand for trepang, it seems that the coastal waters of China did not have much trepang, and what was there was not of high quality (Macknight 1976, p. 8). At the same time, demand was increasing, and in the same century it outstripped domestic supply. Once it was clear that supply from China's mainland coastal waters could not meet the demand for trepang, expansion into external markets started in earnest. The expansion led to the exploitation of Southeast Asian waters and eventually to the coastlines of Australia and the Pacific Islands.

The development of trepang exploitation in Indonesia started not long after, thus by the 1720s trepang fisheries were relatively well established. This is shown both by the quantities of trepang being exported from Makassar, the

---

1 I thank The Australian National University's College of Arts and Social Sciences for sponsoring my six week visit to Canberra, where I was able to write the body of this chapter. I would like to express my thanks and appreciation to Dr Marshall Clark, who acted as my personal host and provided comments and corrections on several earlier versions of this chapter. Dr Jim Prescott has provided me with key information on the English and Latin names of the trepang discussed in this chapter. He also kindly shared important information on the Oelaba fishers. Dr Michelle Carnegie has helpfully commented on an earlier version of this chapter. Mr James Riwu accompanied me on my visit to Oelaba village in 2011 and I express my gratitude to him.

centre of the trepang trade in Indonesia (see Table 11.1), and by the broad level of trepang exploitation. Historical reports describe trepang fishing being carried out all over eastern Indonesia. Maluku (including Kei and Aru), South Sulawesi, Buton, Selayar, Spermonde Islands, Sumbawa, West Papua and Timor are noted by the Dutch and others for the presence of trepang fishing (Schwerdtner Máñez and Ferse 2010; Sutherland 2000).

Indonesian fishers also have a history of using what can be termed as Australian waters. These include those around Ashmore Reef, Scott Reef, Seringapatam Reef, Cartier Island and even further south to Marege' (Arnhem Land) and Kayu Jawa (the Kimberley), since at least the 1750s (Macknight 1976). The Indonesian fishers involved in trepang fishing in these areas were identified as Makassarese, Butonese, Bugis, Bajau and Madurese (Fox and Sen 2002). In the literature they are commonly labelled with the generic term 'Macassans'; but, in light of his reading of the official reports of the Vereenigde Oostindische Compagnie (VOC), or Dutch East India Company, Fox (1977) argues that it was not the Makassarese who first fished in Australian waters but rather the Bajau people, who reached Kupang on Timor Island in the 1720s. He notes that one of the reasons for the Bajau voyaging to Timor is to collect trepang. In fishing for the trepang, the Bajau did not stop at Timor but sailed south, where they 'accidentally' found Ashmore Reef. It was only in the 1750s that the Makassarese vessels were reported to have begun arriving en masse in the Timor Sea, sailing south–southeast from Makassar to collect trepang in the vicinity of Ashmore Reef. Also by accident, according to Flinders, they found trepang to be more abundant along the New Holland (mainland Australian) coast in the second half of the eighteenth century (Macknight 1976, p. 93). This was the beginning of the establishment of the Macassan trepang industry in Marege' and Kayu Jawa, an industry that lasted until the early twentieth century.

Table 11.1 Trepang exports from Makassar, 1717–1917

Years	Amount in tons
1717–26	157
1733–34	71
1766–69	640
1774–77	844
1786–89	1304
1796–97	154
1820s	~ 430
1832–34	< 568
1868–70	1504
1871–78	3478
1915–17	1637

Source: Modified from Schwerdtner Máñez and Ferse (2010, p. 4)

Political and economic development in Australia and the expansion of its marine territory drove the Macassans from the Australian coastal territories. For Ashmore Reef and its surrounding islands, the process of exclusion started with American whalers' discovery of large deposits of guano on islands in the northwest Kimberley region in the 1840s (Stacey 2007, p. 83). This discovery instigated competition between the Americans and the British, who had an interest in the guano business. In turn, this competition led to the annexation of Ashmore Reef and Cartier Island by the British in 1878 and 1909 respectively. Fisheries, especially trepang, became a contested resource. In 1909, for example, an Australian trepang businessman complained to the Secretary of State for the Colonies in London about fishers from the Dutch East Indies who were interfering with his trepang fishing operation (Bach 1955, p. 208).

The Macassan trepang industry in Arnhem Land and the Kimberley coast faced similar concerns. The emergence of an Australian-based trepang industry in the 1870s (Macknight 1976, pp. 101–3) made the presence of the Macassans in the territory awkward. Subsequently, the Australian Federal and local governments created several new regulations, eventually leading to the termination of the Macassan trepang industry in 1907 (Macknight 1976; Stacey 2007).

The expansion of Australian waters to 200 nautical miles from the coastline, declared in 1979, pushed Indonesian fishers further to the north. Subsequent agreements between the Indonesian and Australian governments concerning marine boundaries between the two countries, which were finalised in 1997, reaffirm the exclusion of Indonesian fishers from Australian waters. An exception to this is an area popularly called the MoU Box: the waters surrounding Ashmore Reef, Scott Reef, Seringapatam Reef and Cartier Island. In this area, Indonesian traditional fishers are allowed to conduct some fishing activities (see the next section for more detail).

Interestingly, however, in spite of these formal government agreements, trepang collecting in the border areas, legal and illegal (Fox 2009), has never completely ceased. For example, Figure 11.1, which shows the apprehension of Indonesian fishers fishing in Australian waters between 1997 and 2009, demonstrates that fishing activities in the border zone of the two countries continue until the present day. Of course, we also note that since 2006 the number of apprehensions has decreased significantly; but, we should note that this has taken place after the Australian Government, under the prime ministership of John Howard in particular, spent many additional millions of dollars to increase border operations. Additionally, in my visit to the two localities, which will be discussed shortly, I found that fishing activities were still taking place, at least until the end of 2010.

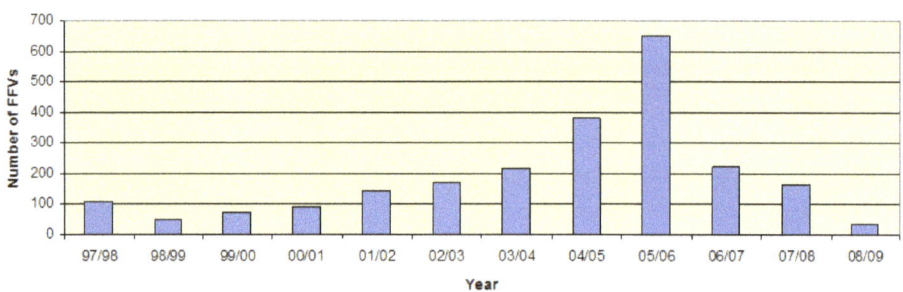

Figure 11.1 Apprehension of Indonesian Fishers in the Australian Fishing Zone (AFZ), 1997–2009

Source: Wilson (2009)

Who are these fishers? What are the characteristics of their fishing activities? What is their relation to the traditional voyages to Australian waters? These are important questions. Using the two fishing communities Oelaba on Rote and Oesapa in Kupang as examples, this chapter will discuss the characteristics of trepang fisheries that are currently operating along the border zone of Indonesia and Australia. These two communities embody a contrast between, on the one hand, 'traditional' trepang fishery practices and, on the other hand, 'modern' practices of trepang fishing. I will compare the socioeconomic characteristics of both communities, framed by the underlying technological differences between the two, as well as the management consequences.

Setting the stage: Defining 'traditional' and 'modern' fisheries

In 1974, the Indonesian and Australian governments signed an agreement concerning Indonesian fishers fishing in Australian waters. This memorandum of understanding (MoU), which is popularly known as 'the 1974 MoU', is an acknowledgment of the historical role of traditional fishing in Australian waters. The MoU states that the traditional fishers of Indonesia are allowed to fish within 12 nm of five small islands in the waters of northern Australia. This includes the waters around Ashmore Reef, Cartier Island, Scott Reef, Seringapatam Reef and Browse Island (see Figure 11.2). The MoU also notes that 'Indonesian fishermen will not be permitted to take turtles in Australian waters', but they are permitted to take 'trochus, bêche-de-mer [trepang], abalone, green snail, sponges and all molluscs' from the seabed adjacent to the five reefs and islets specified in the agreement.

11. Traditional and 'modern' trepang fisheries on the border of the Indonesian and Australian fishing zones

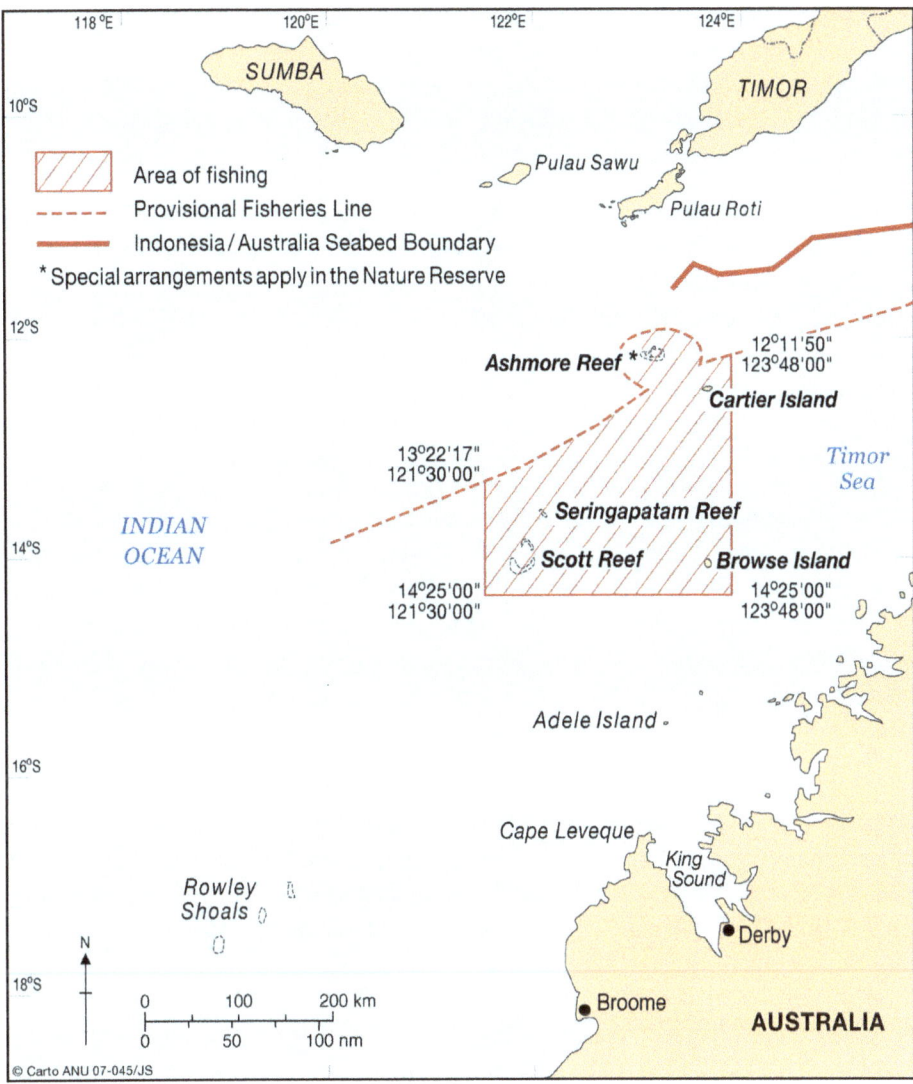

Figure 11.2 The MoU Box

Source: Stacey (2007, p. 202)

This agreement explicitly uses the term 'traditional fishermen' and provides its definition as follows: 'By "traditional fishermen" is meant the fishermen who have traditionally taken fish and sedentary organisms in Australian waters by methods which have been the tradition over decades of time.'[2]

---

2 This is the second attempt of the Australian Government to directly address Indonesian fishing in Australian waters. The first was in 1968, when a decision was made to permit traditional Indonesian fishing

In 1989, the definition of 'traditional fishermen' was clarified with some clauses of explanation. For instance: 'Access to the MOU area would continue to be limited to Indonesian traditional fishermen using *traditional methods* and *traditional vessels* consistent with the *tradition over decades of time*, which *does not include fishing methods or vessels using motors or engines*' (my emphasis).

This clarification means that the defining characters of tradition are: 1) the fishing methods, and 2) the fishing vessels. Both gear and vessels that are considered traditional are those that have been used over decades and are non-motorised. Interestingly, this agreement does not define who 'traditional' fishers are. So, it does not problematise whether they are those who used to work the Australian waters in the past, their descendants or just any Indonesian citizen. This means that the MoU Box has become an open-access area for thousands of Indonesian fishers who do not use motorised vessels and gear.

Both governments have revisited the 1974 MoU in light of how it has been utilised. In 1989, the two governments revised the agreement. The 1989 revision accommodates the fact that Ashmore Reef has been declared a National Nature Reserve since 1983. Subsequently, this area has been closed to any fishing activities. The revision also notes that Indonesian traditional fishers are allowed to fish in an area wider than the 12 nm mentioned in the 1974 MoU. A map showing the new spatial MoU Box was attached to the agreement.

Another area of concern is that 1974 MoU's definition of traditional fishers implies that fishers who do not possess the characteristics outlined above automatically fall into the categories of 'non-traditional' or 'modern' fishers. This means that fishers of this type are not allowed to access or exploit the MoU Box area or any other part of Australian waters, for that matter.

Outside the MoU Box area, the Indonesian and Australian governments have established a number of agreements that have led to fishing activities in the border area becoming quite complicated affairs. These agreements include regulations on the continental shelf and the Economic Exclusive Zones. The most recent agreement between the two countries, signed in 1997, states that both countries consent to the presence of an overlapping claim of the maritime border (Commonwealth of Australia 1997). It is agreed that in this area Indonesia has rights over the water column while Australia has rights over the seabed. Consequently, Indonesia has the right to manage the fisheries resources on the water column, but has no right to manage anything on the seabed. This includes sedentary resources that inhabit the seafloor such as trepang and trochus. These resources are under the management of Australian authorities.

---

to continue within the 12 nm territorial sea zone adjacent to Ashmore and Cartier islands, Seringapatam Reef, Scott Reef, Browse Island and Adele Island, providing operations were confined to a subsistence level (Stacey 2001). The first attempt, however, did not mention the terms 'tradition' or 'traditional' as in the MoU of 1974.

The remainder of this chapter will adopt the above definitions for its discussion of the two fisheries of Oelaba and Oesapa. Based on these definitions, the two fisheries can be categorised as two different forms of fishing practice. These definitions, by the way, continue to be used by the Australian authorities in protecting their marine territories.

The Oelaba-based trepang fishery

Oelaba is a sub-village of Oelua village situated on the north coast of western Rote (see Figure 11.3). By 1997 it was home to 685 people living in 143 households (Fox and Sen 2002). Carnegie (2008) notes that by 2004 the number of households had increased to 178; Carnegie also found that almost one-third (27 per cent) of Oelaba people were Rotinese Muslim households of mixed ethnic heritage. Considering the key themes of this book, it is important to note that the migratory ancestors of the Rotinese Muslims in Oelaba sub-village are from the three most prominent maritime trading groups in eastern Indonesia—namely, the Bugis, Butonese and Makassarese. Like the Macassans of centuries past, they are all originally from the island of Sulawesi (South and southeast Sulawesi to be precise). Together with the Bajau, these ethnic groups were those who established the trepang fisheries tradition.

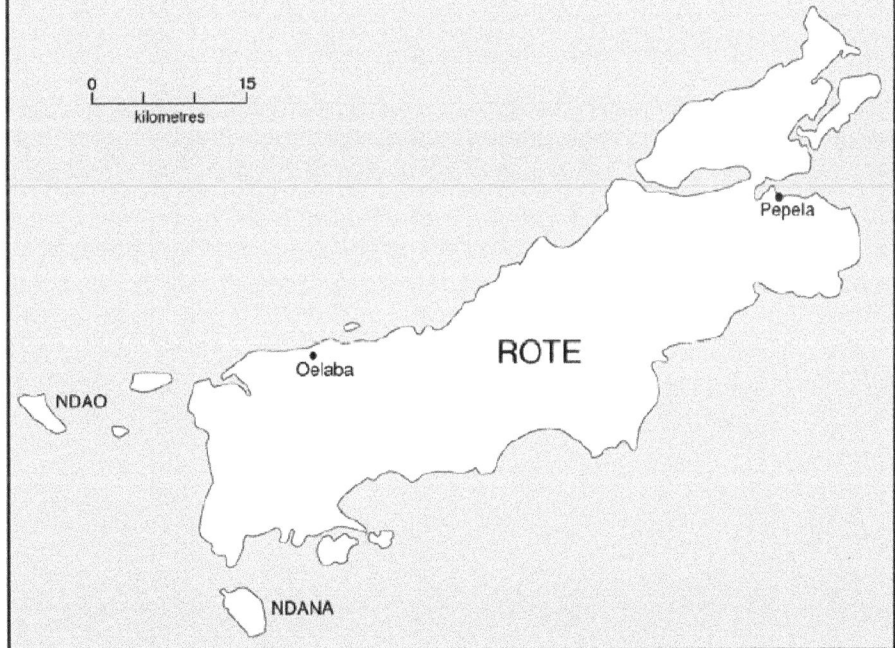

Figure 11.3 Rote Island

Source: Fox and Sen (2002, p. 22)

The primary livelihood of the Oelaba inhabitants was originally inter-island trade and sailing. In the 1980s the Oelaba people started to get involved in trepang fishing in the MoU Box. In this regard, Carnegie (2008, p. 212) notes:

> In response to this declaration of a special area set aside for any Indonesian in a non-motorised sailing boat to legally enter and extract valuable marine resources, such as trepang and trochus, in the 1980s a few Oelaba sailor-traders removed their boat motors and began sailing to the AFZ [Australian Fishing Zone].

The interest of Oelaba sailor-traders in becoming trepang fishers is also partly because the older players of the trepang fishery in the MoU Box region, such as the Macassan mixed-ethnics and the Bajau from Pepela (another village on Rote, see Figure 11.3), shifted their target species to shark fin, due to a rapid increase in the price of shark fin in the 1980s. A by-product of this shift is that it opened up a new opportunity for the Oelaba sailor-traders to fill a niche that became available when the Pepela fishers moved out of trepang gathering and into shark fishing. Subsequently, the number of boats from Oelaba journeying to the MoU Box has gradually increased over the years. In 2004, 39 sailing boats from a total of 42 in Oelaba sailed to the Australian waters (Carnegie 2008, p. 213).

The fishing practices of the Oelaba fishers can be regarded as 'traditional' insofar as the chosen fishing methods and vessel type align with the stated definition of a 'traditional' fishery, as outlined in the MoU Box agreement. Some of the vessels, known as *lambo*, used to have engines installed, but for the purpose of fishing in the MoU Box area the engines are systematically removed. Thus, the vessels that are between 10 and 20 gross tonnes have become what could be classed as 'sail-powered' boats. The fishing techniques and equipment used for trepang collection are also 'traditional' and in this sense quite simple. These include wading in shallow water collecting trepang barehanded, using *ladong* (a spear for catching trepang), or free diving. The last is mostly conducted by 'visiting' or 'invited' fishers from Alor, who are considered much better divers.[3] Additional equipment used includes torches, canoes and firewood for cooking and post-harvest processing (Figure 11.4). For the last process in particular, the fishers boil the trepang catch before drying it in the sun. All post-harvest processes are carried out on the boat.

---

3 As noted earlier, the Oelaba trepang fishers are not traditional free divers, rather they are traders and sailors. Even those who fish in the inshore waters conduct fishing from their canoes. Diving is not part of this fishing practice.

11. Traditional and 'modern' trepang fisheries on the border of the Indonesian and Australian fishing zones

Figure 11.4a Sailing *lambo*

Source: Michelle Carnegie

Figure 11.4b Some fishers are preparing their *lambo*

Source: Dedi Supriadi Adhuri

Figure 11.4c Fire wood for food and trepang post harvest cooking

Source: Dedi Supriadi Adhuri

Figure 11.4d Canoes for trepang collecting

Source: Dedi Supriadi Adhuri

As a result of 'sail power', Oelaba trepang fishing can only be carried out in certain seasons. In the earlier voyages to the MoU Box, fishers arranged mostly two trips in a year, usually between April–May and July–August. Since the closure of Ashmore Reef to fishing in 1988, most of the fishers can only consider one trip per year. Thus, they usually leave Oelaba in July/August, returning home in early October (Carnegie 2008).

In collecting trepang, either by wading or diving, Oelaba fishers do not conduct selective harvesting. They harvest all economically valuable trepang of any size. Carnegie (2008) documents about a dozen different species of trepang gathered by Oelaba fishers. These include *koro batu* (black teatfish, *Holothuria whitmaei*), *koro susu* (white teatfish, *Holothuria fuscogilva*), *tripang nanas* (prickly redfish, *Thelenota ananas*), *kasut* (surf redfish, *Actinopyga mauritiana*), *japung* (greenfish, *Stichopus chloronotus*), *cerak hitam* (lollyfish, *Holothuria atra*), *cerak merah* (pinkfish, *Holothuria edulis*), *bintik merah* (leopardfish, *Bohadschia argus*), and others. On being asked about the general trends of the harvest, Oelaba fishers commented that trepang stocks have been decreasing significantly over time. This is actually a strong indicator of over-exploitation, which is corroborated by research conducted by the Commonwealth Scientific and Industrial Research Organisation (CSIRO). In 1998, the CSIRO Division of Marine Resources conducted a survey in the MoU Box and found that 'the sedentary marine living resources on the shallow reefs were heavily depleted with the high-value species over-exploited and the lower value species probably either fully or over-exploited' (Skewes et al. 1999, p. iv).

Fishers are well aware of this trend, of course, and understand that continuous pressure on the available resources might well lead to the collapse of the trepang fisheries and their marine economy; however, increases in the price of trepang and the lack of other viable livelihood alternatives have led them to consistently consider trepang fishing as a still-viable livelihood. In thinking about possible solutions to this vicious circle, fishers live in the hope that wider fishing grounds will be opened for exploitation. Some consider going back to or intensifying their old activities in trading and sailing (that is, transporting cargo). In any case, for the latter form of employment in particular, they will need a small engine for their *lambo*, as sail-powered vessels are inappropriate for inter-island cargo transportation. Increased business competition and increasingly frequent extreme weather events, which are overwhelmingly blamed on global climate change, mean there is a need for better-equipped vessels, in terms of both safety and speed.

Oesapa-based trepang fishery

Oesapa village is a large *kelurahan* (village administrative unit) in the city of Kupang. It is located on the western end of Timor Island. In 2005, Oesapa's population numbered 25 813, comprising some 8001 households. The fishing centre is located in one corner of the village, close to the food and trade market. This is also the area where most fishing households are located. The majority of the population living here are migrants or descendants of migrants from South Sulawesi. In terms of ethnicity, they are either Bugis or Makassarese, or a combination of both. The settlement was established by the first generation of these migrants in 1994. Originally fishermen, or wives or dependants of fishermen, they migrated to Oesapa to further their livelihoods. Prior to the migration process, they fished for trepang in the coastal areas of their hometowns in South Sulawesi or in the waters of neighbouring islands. It was the endless search for better trepang resources that ultimately led to the move to Oesapa. The move was inspired by rumours that trepang were in abundance in the waters bordering Indonesia and Australia. When they checked the official map of the area, popularly known as 'Map No. 367', and saw the presence of a large number of reefs, indicating the ideal habitat for trepang, they were convinced that the rumours might be true. Based on their annual trepang catches, this rumour has indeed proven true.

Nonetheless, by definition, Oesapa fishers fall into the category of 'non-traditional' or 'modern' fishers. They use smaller boats compared with the size of the *lambo* used in Oelaba. Their boats, which are called *jolor* (Figure 11.5), weigh around 4–5 gross tonnes. These relatively small boats are equipped with two or three 23–26 hp engines (Figure 11.6). Although Oesapa fishers use a spear gun and fishing line, the main gear used is a set of air compressors (Figure 11.6).[4] Oesapa fishers also fish for fin-fish using a spear gun and line, but their primary fishing target is trepang. In search of the latter, they will dive as deep as their air hose can accommodate, which is close to 40 m.

---

4 According to one informant, the Oesapa had adopted the air compressor for fishing/diving in 1970s, in South Sulawesi, well before the move to Kupang.

11. Traditional and 'modern' trepang fisheries on the border of the Indonesian and Australian fishing zones

Figure 11.5 *'Jolor'*

Source: Dedi Supriadi Adhuri

Figure 11.6a The engine

Source: Dedi Supriadi Adhuri

Macassan History and Heritage

Figure 11.6b A fisher showing a spear and gun

Source: Dedi Supriadi Adhuri

Figure 11.6c A compressor

Source: Dedi Supriadi Adhuri

11. Traditional and 'modern' trepang fisheries on the border of the Indonesian and Australian fishing zones

Figure 11.6d Diving equipment

Source: Dedi Supriadi Adhuri

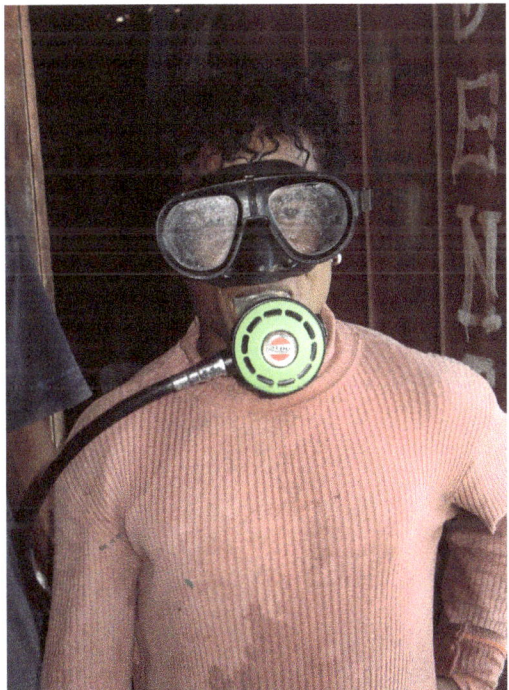

Figure 11.6e A fisher showing how to wear diving mask

Source: Dedi Supriadi Adhuri

Unlike with the *lambo* vessels in Oelaba, fishing trips in Oesapa do not depend on wind for power. Engines make it possible for them to go fishing at any time. Because they fish in comparatively small vessels, only very strong wind and waves constrain their fishing activities, as these threaten their safety. In this regard, they are acutely familiar with the '*musim angin*' (windy season) that falls between January–February and June–August. During these months, the wind blows strongly, causing strong waves. Thus, the sea is difficult and dangerous to navigate. Other months are known as *musim teduh* (calm season). This is the season when the Oesapa tend to go fishing because the sea is calm due to the absence or low levels of wind. Since their trips only last between four and seven days, during the calm season they can make as many as four trips a month. Oesapa fishers are lucky if they can make more than two trips a month during the windy season. The extreme weather during the windy season sometimes does not allow for even a single fishing trip.

It is interesting to note that while Oesapa fishers dive at deeper depths with the support of oxygen from the compressor, albeit with a higher risk of suffering decompression illnesses, they are careful to practise selective harvesting. Fishers commented that they only harvest large-sized trepang, and prioritise economically valuable species, such as *koro putih* (white teatfish, *Holothuria fuscogilva*) and *tripang nanas* (prickly redfish, *Thelenota ananas*). When conducting site visits in September 2011, observation revealed that the average individual size of their catch was 2.3 kg. This is calculated from the average size of the dried trepang, which is 700 g. The dried weight is usually around 30 per cent of the original (wet) weight. Although some trepang species, such as *tripang nanas* (prickly redfish, *Thelenota ananas*) grow faster, reaching a comparatively large size in a short time, more than 2 kg of wet catch is considered a very large individual size for trepang. Most probably it is a well-matured individual. Interviews and field observation found that Oesapa fishers catch several species of trepang. The most targeted species were *koro putih* (white teatfish, *Holothuria fuscogilva*), *tripang nanas* (prickly redfish, *Thelenota ananas*) and *tripang hitam* (black teatfish, *Holothuria whitmaei*). These are the largest and most expensive species. In the absence of these species, however, they also collect low-value species, but still tend to harvest relatively large specimens. Table 11.2 shows these targeted species and their prices in September 2011.

Unlike Oelaba fishers, whose fishing is specifically focused in the MoU Box, Oesapa trepang fishers cover much wider areas. Their fishing grounds include, on the one hand, a variety of reefs stretching from the west to the east of the Indonesia, Australia and Timor-Leste border; and, on the other, coastal areas of Timor, Rote and surrounding islands. The former area is the preferred fishing ground during the calm season. Fishing during the windy season, if the fishers manage to go out, is mostly conducted in the latter area. Fishing in the reefs on the border zone between Indonesia and Australia means that sometimes they are in the area of the overlapping claim of the two countries where the water column is under Indonesian authority and the seabed belongs to Australia. This effectively means that they often fish for trepang illegally. As mentioned earlier, the agreement between Indonesia and Australia stipulates that the seabed of this area is under the control of the Australian Government. Indonesian sea bed fishing without Australian permission is therefore considered illegal.

Table 11.2 Main target species and local market price

Species	Price per kg (Rp)	Species	Price per kg
koro putih (white teatfish, *Holothuria fuscogilva*)	550 000	*kuning* (elephant trunk fish, *Holothuria fuscopunctata*)	60 000
koro pake (?)	400 000	*gamat* (curryfish, *Stichopus hermanni*)	200 000
tripang nanas (prickly redfish, *Thelenota ananas*)	450 000	*bintik* (leopard fish, *Baradschia argus*)	150 000
tripang hitam (black teatfish, *Holothuria whitmaei*)	250 000	*donga* (?)	40 000

Source: Dedi Supriadi Adhuri

Many fishers in Oesapa have been visited by both Australian and Indonesian fisheries officers whose task it is to educate them on the regulations for fishing in these border areas. Some of them have a map, provided to them by either the Indonesian Marine and Fisheries Department's staff or the Australian officials who visited them for the purposes of 'socialising' the Indonesian and Australian agreement relating to fishing in the border zone. The fishers in possession of this map are then expected to have a good understanding that fishing for trepang in the area of overlapping claims is forbidden;[5] however, often the fishers concerned are at a loss to understand why in this area fishing for fin-fish is allowed while fishing for sedentary species such as trepang and trochus is forbidden. Under Indonesian fishing regulations, trepang and other sedentary species are considered and categorised as the same thing—that is, as a 'fish resource'. For many fishers, the bilateral agreement concerning the different regime of authorities and management over the water column and the seabed is particularly confusing. In fact, some argue that even if the seabed is under the jurisdiction of the Australian authorities, it is difficult to believe that the sedentary species can live on the seafloor without the water column above. So, as the argument goes, in relation to sedentary species in particular, it does not make sense to apply the two management regimes.

---

5 In the map distributed to the fishers, this area is shaded with an image of trepang crossed out, indicating that it is not allowed to be gathered in this zone.

Conclusion

Trepang fisheries along the border of Indonesia and Australia are certainly a social, economic and heritage 'tradition' worth honouring, appreciating and even conserving. Historical evidence demonstrates that these fisheries have existed for at least four centuries without much disruption. This tradition, by the way, has been handed down from one generation to the next. It entails a deep understanding of sailing and a depth of traditional ecological knowledge of marine species such as trepang and its habitat. In fact, in certain contexts, the traditional knowledge and skills of trepang fishers might exceed those of the scientists working on trepang. An Australian Fisheries Management Authority (AFMA) fisheries official, for example, has informed me that his expert team assessing the status of trepang in the MoU Box did not find many trepang in a certain transect plot; however, when he asked Oelaba fishers to do the same survey, they were able to gather many more trepang than his highly qualified Australian team. As argued throughout this book, the Macassan trepang tradition has also contributed to much cultural exchange between different groups of people, the products of which might not exist without the trepang and the Macassan trepang industry in particular. Economically, present-day trepang fisheries are the source of livelihoods for many people from different places in Indonesia. Of course, this industry has also created competition, conflict and other socio-ecological problems; but the negatives should not overshadow the positives.

Unfortunately, the construction of the modern Australian and Indonesian political states and economic systems has led to most people thinking primarily of the political and economic interests of their own state and their own fellow citizens, even if this is at the cost of their nearest neighbours. Thus, in this context, the word 'tradition' has become an instrument for the 'politics of exclusion' (Campbell and Wilson 1993). The implementation of this conception to the Oelaba people, who are regarded as the embodiment of 'traditional' fishers in comparison with the Oesapa community, who are formally identified as 'non-traditional' or 'modern' fishers, is a case in point. Little can be said or done in regards to this, as it is what state regulations and agreements say it is.

Having examined the trepang fisheries in the two communities, however, the policy and its implementation do not always accord with the reality. As it stands, formal regulations suggest that Oelaba and Oesapa fishers represent two distinct or unrelated fisheries, which implies that they are either traditional or contemporary fishers. Is this the case in reality? We should agree that Oelaba fishers fall into the category of 'traditional' fishers concerning the fishing methods and vessels they use; however, they only became trepang fishers in the 1980s. This means that historically they do not share the heritage of those who for decades have used traditional boats and gear to fish in Australian waters. In fact, they were even not fishers when the term of 'traditional fishermen' was formally defined through the signing of the MoU in 1974. Of course, we may argue that by birthright they might be part of a Macassan heritage. Their South Sulawesi-based hereditary lineage certainly suggests that they are the descendants of, at least partly, the Bugis, Makassarese and Butonese who initially established the Macassan trepang fishery in Australian waters in centuries past. But, if this argument is valid, it should also be applied to the Oesapa fishers who are almost 100 per cent Bugis and Makassarese and thus by rights can be labelled latter-day Macassans. They might well be direct descendants of those involved in the Makassar–Marege' voyages. Or, at least, since they have been fishers for the majority of their professional lives, it could be argued that they are culturally living embodiments of the Macassan tradition.

Finally, it is worth noting that formally one of the reasons for the declaration of the MoU Box and accompanying regulations relating to the border area is the need to establish a better process of transnational fisheries management. In that context, to some extent, we can judge whether 'traditional' trepang fisheries represented by the Oelaba fishery are performing better than those of the contemporary Oesapa. On the one hand, the fact that Oelaba fishers can only exploit the MoU Box seasonally, based on the direction of the wind, is good, at least from a management perspective. It acts as natural closed and opened seasons for the fishery in question. This can reduce pressure on the marine resource as well as the associated ecosystem. On the other hand, non-selective harvesting during the collection time, which usually lasts for months, might produce a countering negative function to the closed-season benefit. This means the absence of pressure during the closed season might be overridden by the exploitative pressure during the harvesting season. Tellingly, the fact that the harvest has decreased significantly over time indicates that the traditional fishing practice is not sustainable.

In contrast with the Oelaba, the selective harvest conducted by Oesapa fishers theoretically might produce a better result for the sustainability of both the marine resources in question and the fishers' fishing economy. In saying this, however, I do not argue that contemporary fishing is necessarily better than traditional methods. The point is that both practices contain positive and negative elements. Thus, the formulation of better management should be based on a strong understanding of both the impact and the historical contours of both practices. Such an understanding would suggest that the exclusion and/or inclusion of either practice—based on the type of fishing vessel or gear used—from the MoU and surrounding area might not be the best choice for both the people and the resources concerned. As many key stakeholders would agree, a thorough and comprehensive understanding of the entire fishing practice and the closely related socioeconomic context of the people concerned is urgently needed.

References

Bach, J. P. S. (1955) *The Pearling Industry of Australia: An account of its social and economic development*, Canberra: Commonwealth of Australia.

Campbell, B. and B. V. E. Wilson (1993) *The Politics of Exclusion: Indonesian fishing in the Australian Fishing Zone*, Perth: Indian Ocean Centre for Peace Studies & the Australian Centre for International Agricultural Research.

Carnegie, M. A. (2008) Place-based livelihoods and post-development challenges in eastern Indonesia, Unpublished dissertation, The Australian National University, Canberra.

Commonwealth of Australia (1997) *Australia–Indonesia Maritime Delimitation Treaty, Twelfth Report*, Canberra: Parliament of the Commonwealth of Australia.

Earl, G. W. (1937) *The Eastern Seas: Or voyages and adventures in the Indian archipelago in 1832–33–34*, London.

Fox, J. J. (1977) 'Notes on the southern voyages and settlements of the Sama-Bajau', *Bijdragen Tot de Taal-, Land- en Volkenkunde*, 133 (4), pp. 459–65.

Fox, J. J. and S. Sen (2002) *A study of the socio-economic issues facing traditional Indonesian fishers who access the MOU Box*, A report for Environment Australia, Canberra, <http://rspas.anu.edu.au/people/personal/foxxj_rspas/Fishermen_MOU_BOX.pdf> [accessed 14 January 2012].

Fox, J. J (2009) Legal and Illegal Indonesian Fishing in Australian Waters. In R. Cribb and M. Ford (eds) *Indonesia beyond the Water's Edge: Managing an Archipelagic State*. Singapore: Institute of Southeast Asian Studies (ISEAS), pp. 195-220.

Johannes, R. E. and M. Riepen (1995) *Environmental, economic and social implications of the live reef fish trade in Asia and the western Pacific*, Report funded by The Nature Conservancy, the South Pacific Forum Fisheries Agency & Pew Scholarship in Conservation and the Environment.

Macknight, C. C. (1976) *The Voyage to Marege': Macassan trepangers in northern Australia*, Carlton, Vic.: Melbourne University Press.

Sadovy, Y. and M. Liu (2004) *Report on current status and exploitation history of reef fish spawning aggregations in eastern Indonesia*, Western Pacific Fisher Survey Series Vol. 6, Hong Kong: Society for the Conservation of Reef Fish Aggregations.

Schwerdtner Máñez, K. and S. C. A. Ferse (2010) 'The history of Makassan trepang fishing and trade', *PLoS ONE*, 5 (6), p. e11346, <doi:10.1371/journal.pone.0011346>

Skewes, T. D, D. M. Dennis, D. R. Jacobs, S. R. Gordon, T. J. Taranto, M. Haywood, C. R. Pitcher, G. P. Smith, D. Milton and I. R. Poiner (1999) *Survey and Stock Size Estimates of the Shallow Reef (0–15 M Deep) and Shoal Area (15–50 M Deep) Marine Resources and Habitat Mapping within the Timor Seas MOU74 Box. Volume 1: Stock estimates and status*, Canberra: CSIRO.

Stacey, N. (2001) Crossing borders: implications of the Memorandum of Understanding on Bajo fishing activity in northern Australian waters, Paper presented at Understanding the Cultural and Natural Heritage Values and Management Challenges of the Ashmore Region, 4–6 April, Darwin.

Stacey, N. (2007) *Boats to Burn: Bajo fishing activity in the Australian fishing zone*, Asia-Pacific Environment Monograph 2, Canberra: ANU E Press.

Sutherland, H. (2000) 'Trepang and wangkang: the China trade of eighteenth-century Makassar c. 1720s–1840s', *Bijdragen tot de Taal-, Land- en Volkenkunde* (BKI), 156, pp. 451–72.

Wilson, R. (2009) Reducing illegal fishing in the region—an Australian experience, PowerPoint presentation at Regional Plan of Action meeting, Manado, Indonesia.

12. Travelling the 'Malay Road': Recognising the heritage significance of the Macassan maritime trade route

Sandy Blair and Nicholas Hall

The 'Malay Road', just off the northeastern tip of Arnhem Land, was part of the historical route followed by annual fleets from the port of Makassar in what is now South Sulawesi, Indonesia. The fleets sailed to the northern Australian coastline, seeking edible *Holothuria*,[1] commonly known as trepang or sea cucumber. As mentioned throughout this volume, these marine invertebrates of the echinoderm family were prized for their culinary and medicinal values in Chinese markets. This extensive maritime tradition and trading connection linked Australia, Sulawesi and China and long predated European settlement of Australia. Recent research based on the dating of Aboriginal rock art depictions of the early praus, or wooden boats, used extensively in this trade, suggests the connection may be at least 400 years old (Taçon et al. 2010, p. 8).

This chapter explores the tangible and intangible evidence of the trade in the context of how the extended cultural exchange and connections between Indonesia and the Aboriginal people of northern Australia might be recognised in the contemporary setting of cultural, heritage and economic development approaches and practices. The cultural connections that have arisen from the trade have been enduring and are manifest in a range of personal, educational and arts activities today. The heritage sites that are connected to the trade in northern Australia, South Sulawesi and at points along the way are subject to ongoing research, creating new understandings and knowledge of the activities around the trade itself. Recognition of the significance of these sites is being pursued at both state and national levels. Meanwhile, Aboriginal groups are retelling the stories of this cross-cultural exchange in art, film and through the development of new tourism products that reinterpret the ideas of the trade into contemporary contexts.

This chapter raises the possibility of seeking greater recognition for the heritage of this trade and exchange and its potential to be recognised as a cultural route of outstanding universal value under the UNESCO World Heritage Convention. In 1992, the World Heritage Convention became the first international legal instrument to recognise and protect cultural landscapes of outstanding

---

1 In the shallow coastal waters of island Southeast Asia and adjacent Australian waters, 80–100 species are known, up to half of which have commercial value; see Schwerdtner Máñez and Ferse (2010, p. 1).

universal value (Lennon 2012, p. 47). In 2005, the concept was widened to include cultural routes and itineraries, and an international scientific committee has been established to promote research and world heritage inscriptions in this area: the Scientific Committee on Cultural Routes and Itineraries (ICOMOS 2012). The new category highlights long-distance routes and journeys, such as those associated with trade or pilgrimage, which have linked people, countries, regions or even continents for long periods. Little work has been done to date on the recognition of maritime trading routes on a regional or global scale or on communicating their values as universal cultural heritage.

The Malay Road

On Thursday, 17 February 1803, as he rounded Cape Wilberforce, having completed the survey of the Gulf of Carpentaria, the navigator Matthew Flinders recorded in his journal an encounter with six praus and their captain:

> The chief of the six prows was a short, elderly man named 'Pobassoo';[2] he said there were upon the coast, in different divisions, sixty prows, and that 'Salloo' was the commander in chief. These people were Mahometans…
>
> [Friday, 18 February]…[F]ive other prows steered into the road from the S.W. anchoring near the former six…At daylight they got under sail and steered through the narrow passage between Cape Wilberforce and Bromby's Isles, and afterwards directed their course south-eastward into the Gulph of Carpentaria.
>
> [Saturday, 19 February]…According to Pobassoo, sixty prows belonging to the Rajah of Boni and carrying a thousand men, had left Macassar with the north-west monsoon, two months before…The object of their expedition was a certain marine animal called 'trepang'…Pobassoo had made six or seven voyages from Macassar to this coast, within the preceding twenty years, and he was one of the first who came…
>
> This road was the first rendezvous for his division, to take in water previously to going into the Gulph…Pobassoo even stopped one day longer at my desire, than he had intended, for the north-west monsoon, he said, would not blow quite a month longer and he was rather late. (Flinders 1814, pp. 228–34)

---

2 According to Macknight (1969, p. 67), Flinders writes 'Pobassoo' for the Makassarese name 'Pu' Baso''.

12. Travelling the 'Malay Road': Recognising the heritage significance of the Macassan maritime trade route

Impressed by the large number of praus he met at the rendezvous point for the trepang fleet, which was a sheltered stretch of water near the Wessel and English Company's Islands just off the northeastern tip of Arnhem Land, Flinders named it in his journal the 'Malay Road'. The ship's artist, William Westall, has depicted the fleet of praus anchored in the Malay Road, as viewed from Pobassoo's Island (Figure 12.1).

Figure 12.1 *'View of Malay Road from Pobassoo's Island'*. Painting by W. Westall, artist on Matthew Flinders' Voyage to *Terra Australis*, 1803. Engraved by Samuel Middiman. Location is The English Company Islands, Northern Territory.

Source: National Library of Australia, PIC 52269 LOC Westall Box 16

In his journal, Flinders has also provided a firsthand account of his extended interview with Pobassoo, communicating through Williams,[3] his Javanese cook, to find out details of Pobassoo's voyage and many aspects of the trepang trade (see Thomas, this volume). Westall also sketched Pobassoo himself, as well as details of the exotic and unfamiliar 'prows' (praus).

---

3   Flinders' journal describes Williams as being 'from the island of Java', though in his published account he uses the more general racial classifier of 'Malay' (see Flinders 1814, p. 229).

Figure 12.2 *The English Company's Islands, Pobassoo, a Malay chief*. Drawing by William Westall, 1803

Source: National Library of Australia, PIC R4366 LOC Westall Box 12

12. Travelling the 'Malay Road': Recognising the heritage significance of the Macassan maritime trade route

The area where Flinders encountered the Macassan fleet, and what he referred to as the 'Malay Road', is shown in Figure 12.3.

This area of northeastern Arnhem Land is a channel between the mainland and the English Company's Islands, which provides a well-defined linear path, relatively protected from the open ocean. When Flinders marked the place where the praus were anchored the 'Malay Road', he was using it in the seafaring sense of a place where ships ride in a sheltered piece of water near the shore; however, the Malay Road is also symbolic of the more extensive trading route and its repeated journeys back and forth along a defined pathway, more akin to a road or a busy highway on land.

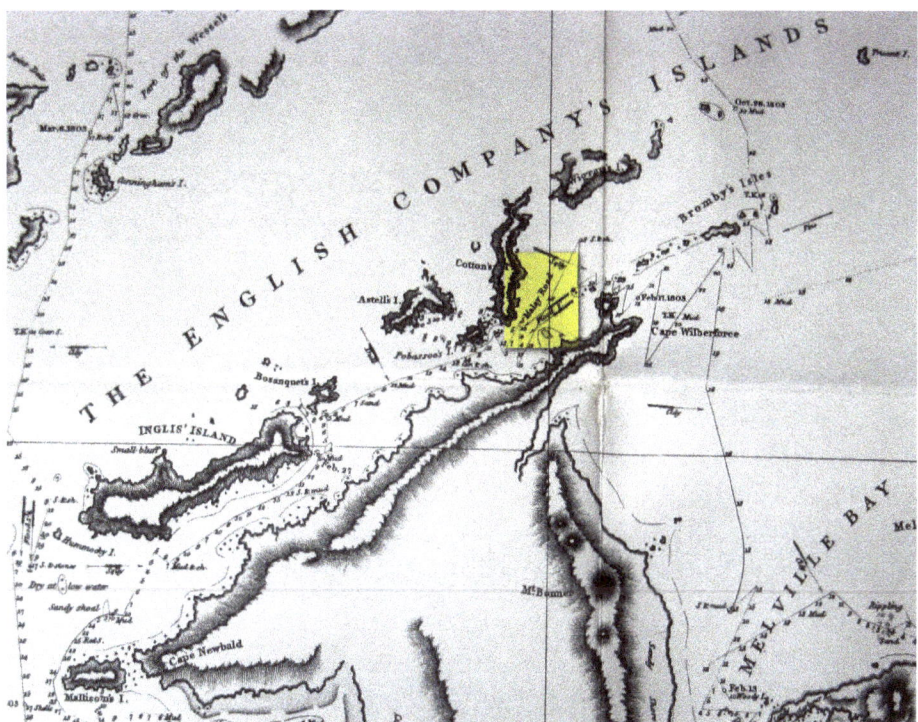

Figure 12.3 The location of Flinders' 'Malay Road'

Source: After McIntosh (2006); based on Flinders' chart 'North West Side of the Gulf of Carpentaria, 1803', in Flinders (1814, Atlas)

Flinders described the men he met on the praus as 'Malays', a term often used by European observers to describe the trepangers (Macknight 1976, p. 17; Sutherland 2004, p. 92). Distinct from our current use of the term 'Malay', which refers to a particular ethnic group centred in present-day Malaysia (Milner 2008), the seafarers who travelled to northern Australia, we now know from considerable research, were of diverse backgrounds and origins that reflect the historical role and maritime history of Sulawesi. Amongst the crews were predominantly Makassarese, Bugis and Bajau, as well as crewmembers from various other racial groups in the Malay and Indonesian archipelagos (Macknight 1976, p. 18). As outlined in the opening chapter (see Clark and May, this volume), the term 'Macassans' has come to be the encompassing one for all those who came on the annual fleet of praus to the northern Australian coastline. They most intensively worked the section of the Arnhem Land coast known to them as Marege', until the economic conditions for the trade changed and it was finally closed by the South Australian Government after the 1906–07 season (Macknight 1976).

The trade: Makassar, China and the trepang fishery

The Malay Road was part of a much wider intercultural trading route, carrying substantial seaborne traffic from at least the eighteenth century and possibly earlier.

The route immediately to the north of Australia was determined partly by the effect of the prevailing winds across the Timor Sea, but extended much further north, to East Asia and China in particular. The trade links to Australia's north provide an important historical link of Australia to its region. While there is much talk of Australia's new links to Asian economies, Australia's trade connections with China are not quite as new as contemporary commentators lead most Australians to believe (Walker and Sobocinska 2012). China's demand for new sources of trepang emerged from the late seventeenth century (Sutherland 2004, pp. 98–9). Maritime expansion and commercial development by Muslim traders working the trade into China spread throughout Southeast Asia into the Indo-Malay archipelago. The port city of Makassar was captured by the Dutch in 1669 and was established as a centre for Dutch trade and as a colonial outpost.

The timing and impetus for the initial development of the trepang trade remain matters of much debate (see, for example, Macknight 2008, pp. 136–7); however, new research into the records of the Dutch East India Company has filled in many of the details of the ships, skippers and commodity trading from eighteenth-century Makassar (Knaap and Sutherland 2004). Ready access to the trepang-rich southeastern seas enabled certain ethnic groups who had lost access to the more-profitable spice trade through the new Dutch monopoly to re-engage in local and regional trade by tapping the new and rapidly expanding market for trepang in China. The productive trepang fisheries in the Gulf of Carpentaria and more generally on the northwest coast of New Holland were called by the Chinese Lam-Hai' (Crawford 1967, p. 441). Makassar benefited in this local and regional trade from its central position at the intersection of many routes. Northern Australia became the southernmost limit of this trade (Knaap and Sutherland 2004, pp. 148, 246; Macknight 2008, p. 137).

The Macassans came on yearly return visits, setting up temporary villages and processing sites at sheltered beaches along the coast. The Arnhem Land coast offered a long series of suitable anchorages, running parallel, or nearly so, with the direction of the monsoons and relatively free of unwelcome control by government or other interests, at least until the 1880s (Macknight 1976, p. 49). Extensive archaeological evidence at sites such as Anuru Bay, including what are almost certainly Macassan burials, as well as the distinctive rock-line processing sites where trepang were boiled in stone fireplaces, offer tangible proof of the Macassan industry, its industrial processing methods and the density of related sites in particular locations along the Arnhem Land coast (Macknight 1976, pp. 61–82; Theden-Ringl et al. 2011, pp. 41–8). The sole reason for Macassans travelling to Marege' was commercial: focusing on the collection and processing (smoking and drying) of trepang. Processed trepang was returned to Makassar, and from there exported to China. While not of the highest quality, Marege' 'chalk fish' or 'white trepang', known as 'koro susu', was very abundant and of consistent quality such that it commended reasonable prices when processed skilfully (this including being buried in sand to remove the calcareous deposits in the skin that gave it its chalky appearance). It was also referred to as *'tripang Marege''* (Schwerdtner Máñez and Ferse 2010, p. 5; Macknight 1976, pp. 7, 40). There appears to be only opportunistic collection of other products by prau crew: besides trepang, the Macassans also imported to Sulawesi timber (ironwood, cypress pine, sandalwood), pearl, pearl shell and tortoise shell. Items such as these were often collected and traded by Aboriginal people in exchange for cloth and various items made of iron (tomahawks and knives), glass and ceramics, food (rice, cocoa), alcohol and drug substances such as betel nut, opium and tobacco (Macknight 1976, pp. 40, 84; Wurramarrba 1986, pp. 1, 3; Brady, this volume).

Tripang Marege' made up the largest part of Macassan exports and of the total imports into China (Macknight 1976, pp. 14–16; Schwerdtner Máñez and Ferse 2010, p. 5). The trepang industry in Australian waters was comparatively large and well organised. At the height of the trade, as many as 60 praus carrying between 1000 and 2000 Macassans spent four to five months of the year gathering trepang. The product fetched considerable amounts of money in Makassar for the fleet financiers, who enjoyed high social standing in their community (Macknight 1976, p. 19). Shipping to southern China was handled by the Chinese businessmen living in Makassar. Most voyages were financed and outfitted by merchants who supplied basic items like rice, tamarind fruit, *'kajang'* (awning mats made from palm leaves), *'atap'* (mats similar to *kajang*, made of nipa palm leaves), rattan, '*karoro*' (palm-leaf sail cloth), iron pots for cooking, '*parring*' bamboos for building, and so on (Macknight 1976, p. 20). At the height of the trade from the 1770s, an annual junk sailed directly from Xiamen, or Amoy, in southeast China, to Makassar to collect the trepang (Knaap and Sutherland 2004, pp. 148–9).

Figure 12.4 The route of the trepang trade from Makassar north to China and south to Australia

Source: Peter Johnson

The experience of the journey of the Macassan traders to Marege' is of considerable interest. Recent research into the navigation skills of the Bugis of South Sulawesi helps to explain the success of the Macassans in undertaking these difficult and often dangerous journeys year after year (Ammarell 1999, p. 1). Bugis seafaring capability, developed over centuries of inter-island trade, was based on an indigenous system of non-instrument navigation by which fishing boats and trading ships could be guided along often treacherous coastlines and across broad stretches of open sea (Ammarell 1999, pp. 1–8). Of particular importance was an intimate knowledge of the wind, which propelled their ships and determined the ship's course. As well, knowledge of stars, currents, wave patterns and the behaviours of various sea animals and birds was crucial to safe navigation in these difficult and sometimes dangerous waters. The Macassans drew on this rich seafaring knowledge and practice to sail without any navigational instruments to guide them other than simple compasses or telescopes, although Dutch maps and charts were available. Navigation was possible because of the personal knowledge and skill of the master of the prau, so they could successfully navigate their praus in a southeasterly direction, having learnt by oral tradition. Many could remember details of the coastline years after they sailed (Macknight 1976, p. 35; see also Daeng Sarro's account in Macknight 1969, pp. 180–7).

Indonesian praus were frequently described and drawn by early Europeans, often seaman themselves, who were intrigued by the unfamiliar craft with its great rectangular sails, as well as the use of bamboo, rattan and other seemingly flimsy local materials in the rigging and superstructure. These craft and other Macassan objects are also depicted frequently in Aboriginal rock art along the northern Australian coastline (May et al. 2010, pp. 57–65; Clarke and Frederick 2008, pp. 148–64).

The praus left Makassar with the onset of the northwest monsoon in late December or early January (Macknight 1976, pp. 33–5). The total trip from Makassar was about 1600 km and often took approximately two weeks. The crossing from Makassar to Timor took about eight days, while the 500 km crossing from Timor to Melville Island (immediately to the north of Darwin) took four days. Early visits were haphazard and poorly coordinated but as the industry became more organised, so did their visits. They aimed to strike the Australian coast in the vicinity of the Cobourg Peninsula to the northeast of Darwin and then work slowly eastwards. During these summer months of the wet season, several praus usually worked together in one locality for a few days or even weeks. When the dugout canoes, from which the trepang was collected, had combed the immediate vicinity of the processing camp, the bamboo smokehouses were dismantled and the praus moved on. By April and the change of the monsoon, the fleet was scattered around eastern Arnhem Land, Groote Eylandt and down into the bottom of the Gulf of Carpentaria. With the dry southeasterly wind behind them, all then turned back to Makassar (Macknight 1976, p. 37).

According to oral tradition, the Macassans regarded the voyage to northern Australia as a long and adventurous one. Marege' was the farthest south and east of the areas they normally visited, with many differences from the more familiar islands to the north. As Macknight points out, among the novelties and perhaps the dangers of the coast were the local people (1976, p. 83). While there were also contacts with the Kimberley coast, as Macknight points out, this trade has always been more complex, in regard of both the products collected and the home ports of the vessels involved. This well-defined industry came to an end when the last prau returned from the Arnhem Land coast in early 1907. Nevertheless, there have also been varied and sporadic visits to this coast throughout the twentieth century (Macknight 1976, pp. 133–6).

The route of connections

This route of intercultural trade, together with the journeys, encounters and influences it has encompassed over centuries and which still continue, has created many cultural resonances both in Makassar and among the Indigenous peoples of northern Australia. The effects of such interactions have been manifested across many fields including language, art and music, religion, health and economic life. As well, the memory of the Macassan presence is still strong, particularly for the communities along the coast of Arnhem Land.

Some of the most compelling accounts we have today of the Macassan traders and their close relationship with Aboriginal people come from the Yolngu of northeast Arnhem Land. The Macassans had mainly friendly relations with the Yolngu: the same boats returned each year to the same places and their crews established continuing relations with the people who lived there. Yolngu were employed to work collecting and preparing the trepang. They learnt to communicate with the Macassans, and a trade language developed that survived long after the trade was halted. Yolngu would travel with the Macassans along the coast, with some even returning with them to spend the dry season in Sulawesi. The captains of the Macassan boats developed close relationships with particular local Indigenous leaders, which were reflected in an exchange of names. These were passed on, and Yolngu are still able to identify names of Macassan origin (Morphy 2004).

There are also many Malay, Bugis and Makassarese loan words in Yolngu languages and other items of material culture from Macassan times (Evans 1992). Yolngu obtained dugout canoes from Macassans and, with the benefits of iron tools, began to manufacture them for themselves (Morphy 2004). The vessels were much more stable and seaworthy than bark canoes (Mitchell 1996, p. 184). The Yolngu learnt how to work iron from the Macassan traders and trade with them would have been one of the main sources of metal for use in shovel-nose spears that then provided Yolngu with a valuable commodity for trade with inland groups (Allen 2011).

Cross-cultural interaction has its dark forms and inevitably with Macassans came disease. Smallpox epidemics had a devastating effect on local communities, although it remains unclear as to the scale of impact this caused (Campbell 2002; Macknight 2008, p. 138). Better understood is the fact that Macassan influence has been manifested in the social, spiritual, symbolic and ceremonial lives of the Yolngu in intricate and complex ways. There is a particular parallel made between mortuary rituals and farewelling the Macassans for the return journey. Morphy describes in detail how ceremonies associated with the concluding stages of Yolngu rituals contain multiple and juxtaposed layers of symbolism that cross-referenced Macassan activities with the ancestral past (Morphy 1998, pp. 212–18). He indicates that as such ceremonies manifest a conflation of the past, the Macassan influences continue to be reinterpreted in ceremonial contexts in new ways into the present.

Flags, sails, anchors, masts and the wind itself that brought the Macassans have been incorporated into Yolngu daily and ritual life. Items such as daggers, swords and flags had particular roles in South Sulawesi villages as sacred heirlooms that were powerful symbols of unity and solidarity (Rössler 1990, p. 300; Röttger-Rössler 2000, pp. 521–2). Yolngu *'bungul'* (ceremonial dances) and *'manikay'* (ceremonial songs) that deal with Macassan themes also make reference to these items (Palmer 2007), and flags have come to play a prominent and highly symbolic role for Yolngu. Today, communities across the north and east coasts of Arnhem Land have their own local flags, and proudly fly flags and display them. They appear in many rituals and are used to effect in contemporary political statements (McIntosh 2011). In Blue Mud Bay, *'Bawu'* is an image of the sails of the Macassan ships. *Bawu* appears in local ritual and bark paintings and is used as a Mardarrpa and Mangalili clan design (Mununggurr 2010). The two horizontal bands of white and blue make the flag that is flown by these clans. The flag was used in symbolic fashion when it was planted in the tidal zone offshore from the community of Yilpara at the time of the successful sea rights case in the High Court of Australia in July 2008. The High Court decision established that the intertidal water lying over Aboriginal land should not be treated differently from the land itself, and clan leaders saw the flag as a fitting symbol of this victory.

Figure 12.5 *Bawu*, the flag that represents the Macassan sail, which is also the symbol for two clans in the Blue Mud Bay region of east Arnhem Land

Photo: Nicholas Hall, 2008

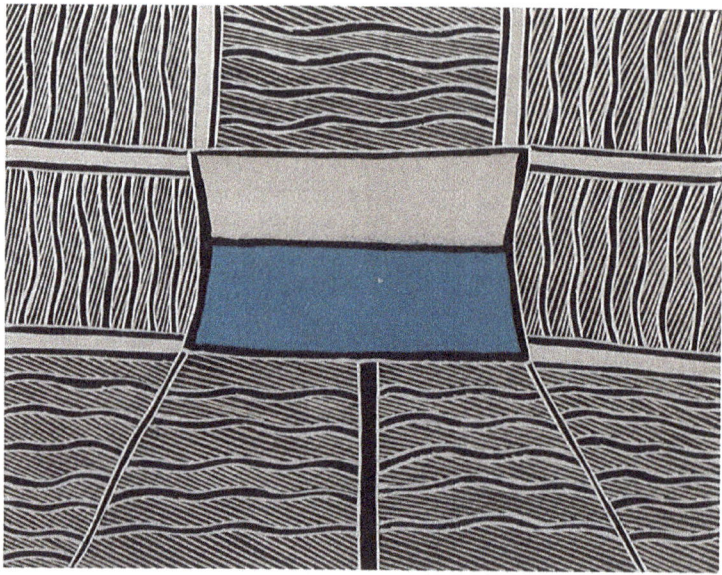

Figure 12.6 An image of *Bawu* in the form of the Macassan sail by Yolngu artist Marrnyula Mununggurr

Source: Mununggurr (2010)

Archaeological evidence confirms a close relationship between Macassans and Aboriginal groups, with camps located in close proximity and Macassan goods present in Yolngu sites that have been researched and documented. The influence of these encounters and relationships flows into the present. An ongoing debate connected to the trepang trade is about Aboriginal agency and the extent to which they controlled and directed relations with the Macassans (see Russell 2004). An example of this is through negotiating to protect and secure their own interests and the influence this continues to have on contemporary events. Russell makes a case that 'in some places Aborigines did assert a right to exclude Macassan fishers, and that the history of Macassan and Aboriginal interactions justifies a rethink of the basis for sea claims for Aboriginal people'. Russell argues that 'if Macassan fishing formed part of a network of negotiated arrangements in the eighteenth and nineteenth centuries, this provides a good basis for the restitution of similar negotiated arrangements in the twenty-first' (Russell 2004, p. 15). The sea rights cases determined in the High Court of Australia, in relation to both Croker Island and Blue Mud Bay, documented and highlighted the importance of the Macassans in the historical memory of the people of these areas. In the High Court cases, evidence was brought forward about the way in which a cultural legacy of trade and negotiation is a part of recognising traditional rights of agency and responsibility (Russell 2004, p. 15).

Ian McIntosh (2006) has also argued that the current Yolngu vision of intercultural diplomacy is based on former negotiated partnerships, which could be considered as treaties. His informant, Warramirri elder David Burrumarra, describes ceremonies linked to a Dreaming entity, Birrinydji (loosely based on a Macassan boat captain and traditional iron-maker), who united Yolngu and the very earliest Macassan visitors, the Bayini and Wurrumala. According to McIntosh, 'this mirrors the fundamental principle of intermarrying moieties, bringing together the very best from both Aboriginal and non-Aboriginal worlds, and is as relevant today as during the heyday of trepangers' (McIntosh 2006, pp. 153–72).

The connections the trade generated are reflected across different aspects of culture and society, in tangible and intangible forms. They go back prior to European records in Australia and have endured even after the historical trade itself. Moreover, Yolngu returned to Makassar in the past and such visits continue sporadically today. Recognition of the heritage significance of the trade and route itself needs to include not only the historical contexts and values but also the contemporary connections and influences in northern Australia as well as in Sulawesi.

Macassan History and Heritage

What does the route of connections mean today?

The Macassan contact with northern Australia as it was through the trepang trade is no longer, yet its influence still resonates and has enduring and strong contemporary social significance. Both Indonesian and Arnhem Land Aboriginal cultures maintain, celebrate and explore their cultural contact and connections in present-day stories and memories. This is done in relation to specific places through family connections, visits and exchanges, ongoing cultural practices and artistic expression. There has been a string of cross-cultural exchanges since the 1980s. In 1986, 10 students from Batchelor College in Darwin visited Makassar and, in 1988, there was a bicentennial project to create a replica of a Macassan prau, the *Hati Marege*, which now resides in the Museum and Art Gallery of the Northern Territory in Darwin (see Ganter, this volume). In 1993, Indigenous artist Johnny Bulunbulun, well-known for his paintings of Macassan themes, led a group from Maningrida to Makassar, which was known at the time as Ujung Pandang. In 1996, an opera, *The Trepang Project*, was developed with input from both Aboriginal and Makassar-based artists and musicians (see Ganter, this volume). This musical theatre project was performed in both Darwin and Makassar (Palmer 2007; Stephenson 2007, pp. 40–57; Macknight 2008, pp. 141–2). Musicians from Makassar have also performed at the Garma Festival in east Arnhem Land in 2005 (Thomas 2005).

Another aspect of contemporary reinterpretation of the Macassan trade and retelling of its narratives has been the conception and trial of a new tourism product taking visitors on a nine-day voyage by sea from Darwin to Nhulunbuy. The 'Across the Top: Macassan Voyage' was a niche cultural tourism product intentionally created to provide an opportunity for Bininj and Yolngu traditional owners (and emerging tourism businesses) along the Arnhem coast to greet travellers coming from the sea. The voyage stopped at various communities along the coast for them to tell their stories of Macassan encounters in their own way. A series of resource materials for the voyagers was prepared with contributions from researchers and traditional owners. The boat carried 10 passengers and four crew and moved along the coast as Macassans might have; at each stop different narratives, places and influences of the trade were encountered, building a larger picture of the context of the trade as the voyage progressed. The visitors had the experience of approaching by sea and appreciating the seas and winds for themselves. A stated aim of the tour was for the economic aspect of the payments for guiding and local cultural knowledge being means of recreating a form of maritime economic activity and a 'trade' commensurate with that of the past. The reinterpretation of the context from historical to the present was a natural way of creating significance for and in the activity itself. The 'Across the

Top: Macassan Voyage' was one way of celebrating the significance of the route while demonstrating how heritage values can be used to create tourism products and experiences as cultural productions with resonance and local meaning.

There is increasing interest in recognising the heritage places associated with that part of the route associated with Australia. The Northern Territory Government, for instance, has recently assessed the Djulirri rock art site in the Wellington Ranges on the Arnhem Land coast for inclusion on the Northern Territory Heritage Register for its significance as a pictorial document of observations and encounters, including the prominent Macassan contact images of boats, people and material culture such as Macassan daggers. There are many places of significance connected to the route (see, for example, May et al 2010, pp. 57–65). The Malay Road we have mentioned specifically here is an example. There are other places that contain tangible evidence or key components of the stories of the trade and connections that lie along the route, including South Sulawesi (see Clark, this volume). A more comprehensive listing of places and intangible values connected to the route in its entirety would be an important next step in recognition of the significance of the route. It would be a critical research tool to further document the associations with the trade and its broader significance in local, national, regional and international terms. A heritage approach would have a role to play in thinking of the tangible and intangible aspects, the sum of knowledge and how the ongoing aspects of the connections may be more widely understood and celebrated. The project would be a fitting engagement between Australia and Indonesia and assist in placing the history of Australia's northern coast and seas rightfully into the context of regional trade and exchange—a much different perspective to the usual conceptions of Australia's maritime and settlement links to Europe. Recognising the heritage of the Macassan route helps us to look at Australia not as an isolated continent a long way from 'home' but as one historically connected to the region, with the sea as a contact zone, a place of exchange (Macknight 2008, pp. 139–44; Balint 2012, pp. 345–65).

As suggested earlier in this chapter, the new world heritage category of 'cultural routes' offers one opportunity to recognise and celebrate the intercultural heritage of this route in an international setting. Routes and journeys have often created remarkable cross-cultural exchanges and influences—for example, the Pilgrim Routes of Santiago Compostela in France and Spain, entered on the World Heritage List in 1993 and 1998, or the more recently inscribed Camino Real de Tierra Adentro (the Royal Inland Road, or silver route) connecting Mexico City to Texas and New Mexico. While these routes are well known, to date there has been little work on understanding the heritage values of maritime trading routes on a global scale. Table 12.1 looks at some of the defining features of a cultural route, and considers how they might apply to the Macassan trading route with China and northern Australia (ICOMOS 2008, pp. 3–5).

Exploring the possibility of a world heritage nomination to recognise the heritage values as a collaborative project between Australia, Indonesia and perhaps also China may be one option for the future. Such a project would present many challenges (see Clark, this volume), not least because the route crosses territorial, social and cultural boundaries. Like the 'China Silk Road', already on the world heritage tentative list, the Macassan route has both land and sea components, and a network of related sub-routes. It would require researchers to document and assess the wide range of tangible and intangible heritage values and aspects associated with the proposed cultural route. There are also challenging management issues associated with sites along what remains today a remote coastline, as many sites of former Macassan contact are suffering heavily from natural and human impacts. Yet Aboriginal ranger groups are eager to incorporate meaningful cultural heritage work in their land and sea management programs (see, for example, Marika and Roeger 2012, pp. 119–31). A Macassan-themed project documenting stories and sites and looking after them would be a valuable addition. Such a project needs vision, context and practical support across a wide range of possible partners including local communities, government, researchers and heritage practitioners. Hence more than just an inclusion on a list is needed for heritage practice to play a useful role. A strategic and integrated approach is needed to understand the contribution and interplay of tangible and intangible heritage in this cross-cultural context.

Many maritime historians have envisaged the sea as the greatest highway of all—with imprints of long, lonely and difficult journeys, especially in the age of sail (Powell 2010, p. 1). The Macassan trepang trade is part of this long tradition of seaborne journeying to seek adventure and new resources in a wider world, through connections with different cultures and lands. This route of intercultural connections situates Australia in the Southeast Asian region in ways that other travel routes do not, those that emphasise connections to Europe and the remoteness and distance of the colonies. The Malay Road is presented at the beginning of this chapter as a small 'porthole' into the people, places and stories of this route. The broader story we present is of an intercultural and international route that symbolises the complex connections and seas in our region. We will only understand it with multiple perspectives.

Table 12.1 World Heritage cultural route category: Defining features and preliminary application to Malay Road

Cultural route defining feature	Macassan trepang route
Different types, for example, religion (pilgrimage), trade (silk, salt, slaves), military (crusades)	Intercultural maritime trade route linking Indonesia, China and Indigenous Australia
Interactive movement of peoples as well as exchange of goods and ideas, knowledge and values between peoples, countries, regions or continents over significant period	Eighteenth-century trading route based on marine products especially trepang collected along northern Australian coastline by fleets of praus from Makassar, then traded with China. Some evidence suggests the trading relationship predates the eighteenth century, with other forms of contact prior to trepang trading. Significant cultural exchange involving material and social-symbolic aspects over hundreds of years. Has significant contemporary cultural expression and reinterpretation through art, music and ongoing cultural practices.
Reflects cross-fertilisation of cultures in both tangible and intangible aspects of heritage	Tangible aspects include: Rock art and bark painting depictions of Macassan praus and trading goods Archaeological remains of beach camps and processing sites on northern Australian coastline Technology of dugout canoes and working of iron learnt from Macassans. Intangible aspects include: Language, placenames in northern Australia Influence on cultural practice of Yolngu in many areas Expression in art, music and other cultural forms Oral narratives Macassan traditional navigation practices and knowledge associated with riding the monsoon winds to Australia.
Must combine cultural exchanges with journeys, compared with those that only represent a physical act of travel, such as railway lines	Extensive evidence from many sources of cultural exchange over a long period, including Aboriginal bark painting and rock art, archaeological remains of Macassan campsites, linguistic evidence of word borrowings and ethnographic evidence of changes in cultural practices.
Interaction with the natural environment in all of its diversity is often important	Winds, sea, currents, wave patterns, maritime ecology, coastal geomorphology, terrestrial fresh water.

Cultural route defining feature	Macassan trepang route
Must be described and delineated to its full extent, including boundaries, component parts, setting	The route is a 1600 km sea crossing from the port of Makassar in central Indonesia to the northern coastline of Australia (and perhaps to China). Stopping points/features along the way. Sites in South Sulawesi. Sites along northern Australian coast.
Does the cultural route as a whole entity (rather than individual components or features) have Outstanding Universal Value?	The Malay Road meets World Heritage criteria.

Source: Sandy Blair

References

Allen, H. (2011) 'Thompson's spears: innovation and change in east Arnhem Land projectile technology', in Y. Musharbach and M. Barber (eds), *Ethnography and the Production of Anthropological Knowledge: Essays in honour of Nicolas Peterson*, Canberra: ANU E Press.

Ammarell, G. (1999) *Bugis Navigation*, New Haven, Conn.: Yale University Southeast Asia Studies.

Balint, R. (2012) 'Epilogue: the yellow sea', in D. Walker and A. Sobocinska (eds), *Australia's Asia: From yellow peril to Asian century*, Perth: University of Western Australia Press, pp. 345–65.

Burarrwanga, L. (2009) Memories of my Makassan family, Unpublished manuscript.

Campbell, J. (2002) *Invisible Invaders: Smallpox and other diseases in Aboriginal Australia 1780–1880*, Carlton South, Vic.: Melbourne University Press.

Cawte, J. (1996) *The Healers of Arnhem Land*, Sydney: UNSW Press.

Clarke, A. and U. Frederick (2008) 'The mark of marvellous ideas: Groote Eylandt rock art and the performance of cross-cultural relations', in P. Veth, P. Sutton and M. Neale (eds), *Strangers on the Shore: Early coastal contacts in Australia*, Canberra: National Museum of Australia.

Crawford, J. (1967 [1820]) *History of the Indian Archipelago*, London: Frank Cass & Co.

Evans, N. (1992) 'Macassan loan words in Top End languages', *Australian Journal of Linguistics*, 12 (1), pp. 45–91.

Flinders, M. (1814) *A Voyage to Terra Australis…in the Years 1801, 1802 and 1803, in Two Volumes with an Atlas*, vol. II, London: G. W. Nicol [Australian Facsimile Editions No. 37].

International Council on Monuments and Sites (ICOMOS) (2008) *The ICOMOS Charter on Cultural Routes*, Sixteenth General Assembly, Quebec, pp. 1–11, <http://www.international.icomos.org/charters/culturalroutes_e.pdf> [accessed 27 July 2012].

International Council on Monuments and Sites (ICOMOS) (2012) Scientific Committee on Cultural Routes and Itineraries, Paris, <http://www.icomos-ciic.org/> [accessed 25 July 2012].

Knaap, G. and H. Sutherland (2004) *Monsoon Traders: Ships, skippers and commodities in eighteenth-century Makassar*, Leiden: KITLV Press.

Lennon, J. (2012) 'Cultural landscape management: international influences', in K. Taylor and J. L. Lennon, *Managing Cultural Landscapes*, London & New York: Routledge.

McIntosh, I. (2006) 'A treaty with the Macassans? Burrumarra and the Dholtji ideal', *The Asia Pacific Journal of Anthropology*, 7 (2), pp. 153–72.

McIntosh, I. (2008) 'Pre-Macassan at Dholtji?: exploring one of north-east Arnhem Land's great conundrums', in P. Veth, P. Sutton and M. Neale (eds), *Strangers on the Shore: Early coastal contacts in Australia*, Canberra: National Museum of Australia, pp. 165–80.

McIntosh, I. (2011) 'Missing the revolution! Negotiating disclosure on the pre-Macassans (Bayini) in north-east Arnhem Land', in M. Thomas and M. Neale (eds), *Exploring the Legacy of the 1948 Arnhem Land Expedition*, Canberra: ANU E Press.

Macknight, C. (2008) 'Harvesting the memory: open beaches in Makassar and Arnhem Land', in P. Veth, P. Sutton and M. Neale (eds), *Strangers on the Shore: Early coastal contacts in Australia*, Canberra: National Museum of Australia, pp. 133–47.

Macknight, C. C. (ed.) (1969) *The Farthest Coast. A selection of writings relating to the history of the northern coast of Australia*, Carlton, Vic.: Melbourne University Press.

Macknight, C. C. (1976) *The Voyage to Marege': Macassan trepangers in northern Australia*, Carlton, Vic.: Melbourne University Press.

Marika, M. and S. Roeger (2012) 'Dhimurru wind bring change', in J. Altman and S. Kerins (eds), *People on Country: Vital landscapes, Indigenous futures*, Sydney: Federation Press, pp. 119–31.

May, S. K., P. S. C. Taçon, D. Wesley and M. Travers (2010) 'Painting history: Indigenous observations and depictions of the "Other" in northwestern Arnhem Land, Australia', *Australian Archaeology*, (71) (December), pp. 57–65.

Milner, A. (2008) *The Malays*, Hoboken, NJ: Wiley-Blackwell.

Mitchell, S. (1996) 'Dugongs and dugouts, sharptacks and shellbacks: Macassan contact and Aboriginal marine hunting on the Cobourg Peninsula, north western Arnhem Land', *Indo-Pacific Prehistory Association Bulletin 15*, (Chiang Mai Papers, vol. 2), pp. 181–91.

Morphy, H. (1998) *Aboriginal Art*, New York: Phaidon.

Morphy, H. (2004) An anthropological report on the Yolngu people of Blue Mud Bay, in relation to their claim to native title in land and sea, Unpublished report to the Northern Land Council.

Morphy, H. and F. Morphy (2006) 'Tasting the waters. Discriminating identities in the waters of Blue Mud Bay', *Journal of Material Culture*, 11 (1–2), pp. 67–85.

Morphy, H. and F. Morphy (2009) 'The Blue Mud Bay case: refraction through saltwater country', *Dialogue of the Academy of Social Science in Australia*, 28 (1), pp. 15–25.

Mununggurr, M. (2010) 'Artist statement', in A. Cameron (ed.), *Djalkiri: We are standing on their names*, Darwin: Nomad Art Productions.

Palmer, L. (2007) 'Negotiating the ritual and social order through spectacle: the (re)production of Macassan/Yolngu histories', *Anthropological Forum*, 17 (1), pp. 1–20.

Powell, A. (2010) *Northern Voyages. Australia's monsoon coast in maritime history*, Melbourne: Australian Scholarly Publishing.

Rössler, M. (1990) 'Striving for modesty: fundamentals of the religion and social organization of the Makassarese Patuntung', *Bijdragen tot de Taal-, Land- en Volkenkunde*, 146, pp. 289–324.

Röttger-Rössler, B. (2000) 'Shared responsibility: some aspects of gender and authority in Makassar society', *Bijdragen tot de Taal-, Land- en Volkenkunde*, 156 (3), pp. 521–38.

Russell, D. (2004) 'Aboriginal–Makassan interactions in the eighteenth and nineteenth centuries in northern Australia and contemporary sea rights claims', *Australian Aboriginal Studies*, 1, pp. 3–17.

Stephenson, P. (2007) *The Outsiders Within. Telling Australia's Indigenous–Asian story*, Sydney: UNSW Press.

Sutherland, H. (2004) 'Trade, court and company', in *Hof en handel: Aziatische vorsten en de VOC, 1620–1720*, Leiden: KITLV, pp. 85–112.

Schwerdtner Máñez, K. and S. Ferse (2010) 'The history of Makassan trepang fishing and trade', *PLoS ONE*, 5 (6), pp. 1–8, <www.plosone.org> [accessed 27 July 2012].

Taçon, P. S. C., S. K. May, S. J. Fallon, M. Travers and D. Wesley, (2010) 'A minimum age for early depictions of Southeast Asian praus', *Australian Archaeology*, (71) (December), pp. 1–10.

Theden-Ringl, F., J. N. Fenner, D. Wesley and R. Lamilami (2011) 'Buried on foreign shores: isotope analysis of the origins of human remains recovered from a Macassan site in Arnhem Land', *Australian Archaeology*, 73, pp. 41–8.

Thomas, M. (2005) Sound recording of Addul Muin Daeng Mile and Halilintar Lathief, <http://trove.nla.gov.au/work/20932387?selectedversion=NBD40222288> [accessed 27 July 2012].

United Nations Educational, Scientific and Cultural Organisation (UNESCO) (2011) *World Heritage Centre, Operational Guidelines for the Implementation of the World Heritage Convention*, WHC 11/01, November, Paris: UNESCO, Annex 3, pp. 87–94, <http://whc.unesco.org/en/conventiontext/> [accessed 25 July 2012].

Walker, D. and A. Sobocinska (2012) 'Introduction: Australia's Asia', *Australia's Asia: From yellow peril to Asian century*, Perth: University of Western Australia Press.

Wurramarrba, C. G. (1986) 'Macassar story collected by J. Stokes', in L. Hercus and P. Sutton (eds) *This is What Happened*, Canberra: Australian Institute of Aboriginal Studies, pp. 1–3.

Contributors

Dedi Supriadi Adhuri is Senior Researcher, Research Center for Society and Culture, Indonesian Institute of Sciences.

Sandy Blair is Program Coordinator, Institute for Professional Practice in Heritage and the Arts, The Australian National University.

Rebecca Bilous is a PhD candidate, Department of Environment and Geography, Macquarie University.

Maggie Brady is Fellow at the Centre for Aboriginal Economic Policy Research, The Australian National University.

Marshall Clark is Senior Lecturer at the Institute for Professional Practice in Heritage and the Arts, Research School of Humanities and the Arts, The Australian National University.

Nicholas Hall is Director, Stepwise Heritage and Tourism.

Sally K. May is Senior Lecturer at the School of Archaeology and Anthropology, Research School of Humanities and the Arts, The Australian National University.

Regina Ganter is Professor, School of Humanities, Griffith University.

Campbell Macknight is Professor Emeritus of the University of Tasmania and Fellow, Research School of Asia and the Pacific, The Australian National University.

Ian S. McIntosh is Director of International Partnerships and Adjunct Professor of Anthropology, Indiana University–Purdue University at Indianapolis.

Anthony Reid is Emeritus Professor and Visiting Fellow, Department of Political & Social Change, School of International, Political & Strategic Studies, The Australian National University.

Paul S. C. Taçon is Chair in Rock Art Research and Professor of Anthropology and Archaeology in the School of Humanities, Griffith University. He is also Director of Griffith University's Place, Evolution and Rock Art Heritage Unit (PERAHU).

Paul Thomas is Coordinator of Indonesian Studies and lecturer in Translation Studies, School of Languages, Cultures and Linguistics, Monash University.

Index

1948 American–Australian Scientific Expedition to Arnhem Land 23, 116, 117
Aboriginal 1, 111, 118, 119, 132, 220
   affairs 115
   art 136, 205, 213, 221
   conflict with outsiders 89
   divers 45
   female divers 44
   history 12, 27, 28, 61
   industry 27
   informants 10, 23, 27
   life-world 102
   –Macassan contact 1, 2, 4, 5, 6, 13–14, 62, 107–14, 116, 117, 118, 119–20, 128, 129, 162, 179, 214, 217, 218
   non-Aboriginal 95, 103, 217
   relations with outsiders 10, 12, 14, 22n.3, 55, 61, 86, 127, 128, 134, 153, 205, 214
   religion 95, 141
   rituals 59
   society 97, 108, 136
   studies 6
   trade with outsiders 57, 107, 134, 135, 141, 142, 211, 221
   see also Indigenous Australian, language—Aboriginal
Aborigines 13, 87, 95, 111, 113, 114, 115, 116, 117, 118, 120, 167
   and disease 28
   and drugs 14, 141, 142, 144–7, 149, 151, 152, 153, 154
   and Dutch 24
   and Islam 12, 57–64
   and native title 61, 64, 95, 215, 217
   communication with 80
   contact with trepangers 7, 23, 26, 27, 141
   in Macassar 2, 5, 23, 32, 60, 135, 152, 162, 163, 165, 166, 167, 169
   outsider relations with 86, 115
   speaking Malay 70, 87

Adelaide 84
Adele Island 187n.2
Afghans 12, 55, 56
Africa 41, 70n.1, 144
agriculture 42, 44
Albinia Island 27
alcohol 14, 59, 134, 141, 142, 143, 144, 147, 150, 211
   see also arrack, drugs
Ambon 47, 49, 71, 78, 85
Ambonese 71, 78
America 42, 110, 112, 185
Amoy, *see* Xiamen
anthropology 6, 14, 55, 95, 97, 102, 106, 110, 111, 115, 116, 117, 119, 127n.2, 147
Anuru Bay 3, 27, 128, 145, 211
aquaculture 32, 33
Arab 128
Arabic 58, 59, 61, 84, 144
Arafura Sea 6, 11, 12, 41, 47, 98
'Arafura zone' 43, 45
archaeology 2, 3, 5, 6, 11, 13, 24–8, 42, 56, 106, 128, 145, 162, 211, 217, 221
arrack 14, 45, 142–4, 154
art 4, 5, 6, 61, 63, 148, 160, 207, 214, 216, 218, 221
   galleries 32
   Islamic 57
   see also Aboriginal—art, painting, rock art
artefacts 5, 26, 141, 142, 150, 160
arts 69
Aru Islands 21n.2, 43, 45, 47, 144, 168, 184
Ashmore Reef 47, 60, 184, 185, 186, 188, 193
Asia 12, 30, 42, 136, 210
   see also East Asia, Southeast Asia
Asian 3, 4, 8, 12, 20, 49, 55, 56, 64, 69, 134, 144, 168
Asia-Pacific 10
Asiatic 72, 90
Australia 48, 58, 70, 71, 77, 79, 87, 109, 110–20, 128, 141, 144, 210, 212, 219
   –Indonesia relations 1, 7, 46, 48, 52, 61, 69, 89, 162, 219, 220

see also Commonwealth—
Australian, New Holland, visitors to
Australia, visits to Australia
Australian
fishing zones 7n.2, 14–15, 183–202
history 1, 4, 11, 12, 14, 22, 27, 28,
29, 47, 55–64, 114, 134
waters 7, 8, 14, 184, 185, 186, 188,
189, 190, 194, 198–9, 200, 201,
205n.1, 211
Australian Fisheries Management
Authority (AFMA) 9, 200
Australian Geographic 13, 108, 110, 111,
112, 118, 120
Australian Government 8, 9, 10, 22, 50,
57, 64, 88, 100, 185, 186, 187n.2,
188, 199
see also Commonwealth—Australian
Australian MoU Box 14, 15, 185, 187,
188, 190, 193, 200, 201
Australian National Travel Association
110, 111
Austronesians 43, 44, 77
axes 99, 134, 149

Bajau 11, 21, 47, 184, 189, 190, 210
Bajau Laut ('Sea Gypsies') 5, 21
Bajo (Bajau) 1, 5
Bajoe 31
Balanda (non-Aboriginal) 63, 103
Bali 48
Balikpapan 49
Banda Archipelago 43, 101
Banjarmasin 51
Banks, Joseph 150
Barker, Captain Collet 70, 80, 81, 82, 89
Barrang Lompo 33, 166, 170, 177, 178
Barunga 60, 142
Batavia, see Jakarta
Batchelor College 61, 62, 218
Bathurst Island 118
Baudin, Nicolas 143
bayini 4, 5, 24, 96, 98–104, 148n.8, 217
Bednall, Colin 113, 114
beeswax 2, 3, 127, 129, 136
Beijing 63
Bentinck Island 27

Berndt, Ronald 4, 149
Berndts, Ronald and Catherine 23, 25, 27,
100, 107, 116, 144
betel nut 14, 46, 141, 144–5, 148, 149,
154, 211
Bininj 132, 218
Blue Mud Bay 114, 215, 216, 217
Bonerate 31, 43
borders, see maritime borders, northern
Australia—borders
Borneo 49, 50, 51, 128
Borroloola 154
Botany Bay 62
Bowen Straits 60, 71, 75, 85, 86, 87–8
Brisbane, Governor 76
Britain 50, 115
British 21, 22, 28, 46, 50, 51, 55, 58, 60,
62, 63, 64, 71, 72, 77, 78, 79, 81, 82,
87, 88, 89, 109, 128, 134, 141, 148,
151, 185
see also English
British East India Company 58, 72
Broome 46, 47
Brown, Robert 73, 74
Browse Island 186, 187n.2
Buginese 11
Bugis 2, 11, 21, 31, 46, 47, 58, 75, 80,
81n.20, 84n.31, 95, 141, 148n.8,
151, 159, 161, 171–5, 184, 189, 194,
201, 210, 212, 214
buildings
in art 129, 133, 134
smokehouse 25, 133, 213
Bukulatjpi 99–100, 101, 102, 103
Bulunbulun, John 5–6, 62, 63, 218
Burarrwanga, Laklak 107, 165, 166, 169
Burdon, Amanda 119, 120
Burrumarra, David 13, 59, 61, 95, 96,
98–104, 217
Butlin, Noel 28n.10
Buton 21, 184
Butonese 1, 11, 47, 184, 189, 201

Cadell, Francis 46
Caledon Bay 26, 114, 115, 116
Cape Arnhem 102
Cape Londonderry 25

Cape of Good Hope 72
Cape Town 72
Cape Wilberforce 59, 87, 206
Cape York 115
Captain Maliwa/Daeng Mallewa 166
Cartier Island 184, 185, 186, 187n.2
Cartier Reef 60
Catholic, *see* religion—Catholic
Ceram 43, 145
Ceramese 46
ceramics 26, 62, 211
ceremonial 147, 149, 160n.3, 215
ceremonies 24, 25, 58, 59, 60, 62, 100, 101, 142, 215, 217
China 2, 6, 8, 10, 15, 20, 21, 26, 30, 31, 32, 43, 45, 47, 60, 63, 128, 145, 150, 152, 159, 171, 175, 183, 205, 210–14, 219, 220, 221, 222
Chinese 2, 5, 6, 8, 20, 21, 31, 32, 33, 43, 44, 45, 46, 63, 73n.6, 128, 152, 153, 154, 169, 170, 172, 183, 205, 210, 211
Christianity 44, 50, 56, 58, 60, 95
    see also religion
Clark, Manning 28
Cobb, Joan 118
Cobourg Peninsula 22, 77, 80, 83, 84, 86, 141n.1, 213
cognitive dissonance 99–100, 102
Cohen, John 52
colonial 12, 13, 22, 24, 29, 48, 49, 50, 56, 69, 70, 84, 88, 109, 110, 114, 160, 210
    Australia 10, 22
    Makassar 6
    Malaya 51
    post-colonial 160, 172
colonisation 57, 58, 60, 64, 109, 136
Commonwealth Fisheries Association 8
Commonwealth Scientific and Industrial Research Organisation (CSIRO) 193
Commonwealth, Australian 12, 60, 86, 87, 88, 100, 115
    see also Australian Government
Conlon, Alf 50, 51
Cook, James 144
cosmology 5, 57, 58–60, 142

Croker Island 64, 149n.11, 217
cross-cultural exchange 134, 135, 136, 205, 215, 218, 219, 220, 221
cultural exchange 6, 15, 64, 69, 70, 80, 200, 205, 218, 219, 221
cultural memory 108–10
cultural routes, *see* routes
Cunningham, Allan 76, 89, 90

Dadirringka rock shelter 3
Daeng Sarro 88, 213
daggers 131, 149, 215, 219
    badik 131, 135
    keris 149, 171
    see also knives, swords
Dalrymple, Alexander 21,58
dance 59–60, 62, 63, 96, 100, 101, 102, 103, 142, 146, 160, 215
Darwin 9, 63, 64, 82, 83, 84, 85, 87, 113, 150, 213, 218
de Hans, Tingha 12, 13, 70, 82–8, 89
del Castillo, Francisco 46
Denpasar 161
Dhuwa 96
Dieng Riolo 80
dingo 99, 102, 103, 136
diplomacy
    Australian 12, 57, 62, 64
    British 88
    intercultural 217
    with Macassans 77–82, 84
disease 28n.10, 99, 144, 215
divers 46, 47, 190
    Aboriginal 44, 46
    Japanese 12, 46, 47
    Oelaba 190, 193
    Oesapa 194, 198, 194n.4
    pearl 12
    Sama Bajau 45
    see also pearling
diving 46, 197
Djakapura, *see* Singapore
Djang'kawu 4, 5
Dobo 43, 45
'Dobson rings' 27
Dobson, Graeme 27
dog, *see* dingo

Dougherty, Ivan 51
Dreaming 96, 98, 101, 102, 103, 119, 217
drugs 14, 141–53, 211
  see also alcohol, betel nut, opium, smoking, tobacco
Drysdale Island, see Yirringa
d'Urville, Dumont 144, 150
Dutch 9–10, 12, 19, 21, 22, 24, 26, 28, 43, 44, 45, 47, 48, 49, 51, 63, 71, 72, 76–9, 81, 84, 86, 87, 88, 113, 116, 128, 142, 145, 149n.11, 151n.14, 184, 210, 213
Dutch East India Company (Vereenigde Oostindische Compagnie, VOC) 19, 21, 22, 26, 29, 30, 168, 184, 210
Dutch East Indies 10, 45, 48, 49, 161, 185

Earl, George Windsor 70, 77, 82
East Asia 1, 8, 9, 19, 33, 48, 210
Economic Exclusive Zones 188
Elcho Island 62, 63, 96, 166
England 46
English 19, 29, 48, 81, 144, 145
  see also British, language—English
English Company's Islands 87, 95, 207, 208, 209
Entrance Island 2
Eurasia 41, 42, 43, 44
Evatt, H. V. (Doc) 50

Ferguson, Glennys 77, 78
Filipino 12, 46
First Fleet 62, 141
flags 59, 62, 100, 142, 169, 215, 216
  see also symbols
Flinders, Matthew 21, 24, 29, 30, 47, 70, 71–6, 77, 79, 89, 95, 116, 127, 184, 206, 207, 209
Flores 42, 128
Food and Agriculture Organization (FAO) 33
Forrest, Thomas 21
Fort Dundas 77, 141n.1
France 219
French 22, 58, 77, 144, 150, 152

Galiwin'ku 62, 63, 95, 96
Garma Festival 63, 218
Garngarr/Garnggar 165, 166, 167
Gillen, Frank 153, 154
gold 44
Gondwana 41
Goram 43, 145
Goulburn Island 134
Gowa 58, 61, 130, 167, 168, 172
graves 167–70, 169
Gray, Fred 5
Groote Eylandt 3, 23, 25, 26, 27, 118, 213
Gulf of Carpentaria 5, 22n.3, 25, 64, 101, 146, 153, 206, 209, 210, 213
Gumatj-Burarrwanga 98
Gunano/Kunano 166

Hall, V. C. 116
Hati Marege (Heart of Marege) 32, 62, 96, 218
Heritage Act 2012 (NT) 162
High Court of Australia 215, 217
Holland 47, 49
  see also Netherlands
Holmes, Cecil 117
Holmes, Charles 111
Hong Kong 83
Howard Island 102
Howard, John 9, 57, 185
Husein Daeng Rangka 61, 62, 63

Iban, Candido 46
Idriess, Ion L. 113, 115
Immigration Restriction Act 1901 (Cwlth) 12, 47
India 41, 79, 82n.23, 109, 136, 144, 160n.2
Indian 172
Indian Ocean 19
Indigenous Australian 64, 71, 97, 111, 113, 114, 115, 117, 118, 119–20, 135, 136
  cultural exchange 12, 69, 70
  culture 89
  non-Indigenous 120
  see also Aboriginal, Aborigines

Indonesia 1, 6, 7, 12, 14, 32, 48, 51, 52, 56, 64, 107, 112, 160, 161, 162, 171, 173, 175, 179, 180, 186, 194, 198, 199, 200, 205, 219, 220, 221, 222
  East 49, 50
  eastern 41–52, 57, 81n.20, 162, 167, 168, 184, 189
  see also Australia–Indonesia relations
Indonesian, see language—Indonesian
Indonesian archipelago 7, 20, 22, 29, 55, 57, 69, 79, 88, 143, 148, 161, 171, 175, 179, 205
Indonesian Government 186, 188, 200
Indonesian Marine and Fisheries Department 199
Investigator 29, 70–1, 73, 74, 80
Iranun 46
iron 101, 147, 153, 211, 212, 214, 217, 221
  see also metal
iron ore 44
ironwood, see timber—ironwood
Islam 11, 29, 56, 57, 58, 59, 60, 72, 79, 150
  Mohammedans 50, 150n.13
  Muslims 12, 29, 43, 55–61, 64, 77, 79, 162, 163, 170, 189, 210

Jakarta (Batavia) 48, 72, 160n.3, 161
Jalan Maipa 163–7, 179
Japan 9. 19, 20, 47, 48, 49, 51, 103, 113, 114
Japanese divers, see divers—Japanese
Java 41, 49, 51, 72, 75, 128, 145, 148, 160n.3, 171, 175, 207n.3
Javanese 46, 70, 72, 75, 171, 207
  see also language—Javanese
Java Sea 43
Jones, Charles Lloyd 111

Kalimantan (Indonesian Borneo) 49, 51, 168
Kayu Jawa, see Kimberley
Kei 118, 168, 184
Kimberley (Kayu Jawa) 1, 2, 7, 15, 21, 22, 25, 44, 58, 127, 184, 185, 214
King, Phillip Parker 75, 89, 144

Kingdom of Johor 172
knives 45, 59, 99, 101, 107, 131, 134, 135, 149, 153, 211
  see also daggers, swords
Kodingareng Lompo 60, 169, 170, 177
Korea 20n.1
Krakatau 41
Kuala Lumpur 8, 160
Kuala Lumpur Handcraft Museum 160
Kuala Terengganu 159, 171, 179
Kupang 21, 22n.3, 76, 83, 85, 88, 184, 186, 194

Lamilami, Lazarus 25
Lamilami, Ronald 127n.1, 129
Land Rights Act 1976 (NT) 61
language 13, 24, 61, 62, 69–90, 142, 151, 214, 221
  Aboriginal 1, 24, 25, 61, 69, 83, 86, 88, 129, 151
  Austronesian 77
  Bugis 2, 58
  Dutch 48
  English 57, 58, 72, 79, 83, 84, 88, 166, 172
  European 22
  foreign 58, 141
  German 52
  Indonesian 1, 2, 8, 11, 57, 59, 61, 63, 69
  Javanese 75, 76, 151
  Macassan 60
  'Makasar' 24, 31, 84n.31, 151
  Makassarese 24, 58, 59, 81n.20, 84n.31, 141, 142, 148, 151, 206n.2, 214
  Malay 2, 48, 51, 58, 59, 63, 70, 72–5, 77, 79, 81–5, 87, 89, 151, 154, 171, 172, 214
  non-Yolngu 148n.8
  Papuan 43
  Sinhalese 79
  South Sulawesi 24
  Tamil 79
  Warramiri 104
  Yolngu 58, 61, 101, 151, 214
  Yolngumatha 59, 61, 62, 63

Laurasia 41
Leku 101
Lela 101
Limmen Bight 25
Lombok 168
Long Island 42
Luki 101

Macassan contact, *see* Aboriginal–Macassan contact
Macassan visits to Australia, *see* visits to Australia—by Macassans
Macassar, *see* Aborigines in Macassar
Macassar Well 25
McArthur, General Douglas 51
McCarthy, Fred 23, 25, 117
McGuinness, Rory 118
Macknight, Campbell 3, 4, 10, 11, 47, 58, 61, 106–7, 154
MacLean, Donald 113, 118
Madura 128
Madurese 183
Makarrwola, Harry 95, 102
'Makasar', *see* language—'Makasar'
Makassarese 2, 11, 80, 159, 172, 173, 174, 175, 184, 189, 194, 201, 210
   see also language—'Makasar', language—Makassarese
Malarrak 128–35
Malay Archipelago 58, 79, 82n.23, 171, 210
Malay Peninsula 171, 172
'Malay Road' 95, 205, 206–7, 209, 210, 219, 220, 221, 222
Malaya 51
Malays 8, 12, 46, 51, 55, 56, 69, 71–5, 77, 78, 80, 83, 85, 86, 112, 113, 116, 117, 118, 127n.2, 146, 149ns7–8, 154, 160, 171, 172, 173, 208, 209, 210
   see also language—Malay
Malaysia 6, 8, 51, 159, 160, 161, 170, 171, 172, 173, 175, 179, 180, 209
Maluku 43, 44, 45, 184
Mangngellai Daeng Maro 166
Manikay 59, 215
Maningrida 62, 63, 218

Mansjur Muhayang 62, 63
Marege' 1, 11, 14, 21, 29, 30n.12, 62, 162, 184, 201, 210, 211, 212, 213
maritime borders 7, 8, 14, 185–8, 194, 198–201
Maryanageene 86
Matjuwi Burrawanga 62
Mattjuwi, Charlie 98, 166
Mauritius 73
Melbourne 6, 50, 56, 63
Melbourne Museum 5, 32
Melville Bay 60, 61, 100
Melville Island 77, 141n.1, 213
Melville, H. S. 133
metal 2, 99, 135, 147, 150, 151, 152, 214
   see also iron
Methodist, *see* religion—Methodist
Milingimbi 25, 61, 63, 95
mining 6, 44, 152, 153
Misool 44
missions, *see* religion—missions
Mountford, Charles P. 23, 116, 117
Muis Daeng Tarrang 29
Museum and Art Gallery of the Northern Territory 32, 218
Museum Victoria 57
music 59, 63, 214, 218, 221
   see also song
Muslims, *see* Islam—Muslims
myths 4, 5, 43, 44, 58, 64, 97, 99, 102, 103, 109, 116, 120

nakhoda 72, 73, 74, 77, 79, 80, 81, 84, 85, 88
Namarnyilk, Jimmy Galareya 131
National Geographic 13, 107n.1, 108, 110, 112, 115, 116
National Geographic Society 112
National Museum of Australia 4, 32, 57
native title, *see* Aborigines—and native title
Netherlands 48, 50, 63
   see also Holland
Netherlands Indies Civil Administration (NICA) 51
   see also Dutch East Indies
New Delhi 160n.2

New Guinea 41, 42, 128
New Holland (Australia) 58, 79, 184, 210
New South Wales 28, 56, 71, 77, 78, 79
New Zealand 111
Nhulunbuy 100, 218
North America 41
   see also America
northern Australia 9, 12, 28, 32, 33, 40, 47, 113, 128, 213
   borders 7, 8
   coastline 6, 13, 141, 159, 162, 205, 219, 222
   communities 1, 7, 13, 62, 135, 162, 165, 179, 205, 214, 217
   contact with 11, 58, 118, 209
   European settlements in 22, 69, 77, 81–2
   first voyages to 5
   history of 2, 129
   Macassan contact with 1, 57, 107, 213, 218
   trade with 6, 211, 219
   trepang fishery 6, 9, 186
   trepang industry 19, 21, 26, 30, 87, 108, 179, 210, 221
Northern Territory 22, 28, 32, 60, 61, 62, 71, 83, 89, 114, 127, 152, 162, 167, 207, 218, 219
   see also 'Top End'
Northern Territory Museum 96
Nusa Tenggara Timur 41

Oelaba 15, 182n.1, 186, 189, 190, 193, 194, 198, 200, 201
Oenpelli 133
Oesapa 15, 186, 189, 194, 198, 199, 200, 201
Onin Peninsula 44
Oodeen 12, 13, 71, 77–83, 85, 88, 89
opera, *see* song—opera
opium 141, 149, 150, 151, 152, 153, 154, 211
'othering' 108, 109, 110, 112, 113, 114, 118, 119

Pacific Islands 8, 12, 111, 183
Pacific Ocean 22, 29, 48–9, 51, 55, 144

painting 3, 4, 5, 32, 62, 63, 117, 118, 127–36, 147, 148, 207, 215, 218, 221
   see also art
Palmerston, *see* Darwin
Paotere Harbour 161, 173, 174
Papua 43, 44, 46, 49
Papua New Guinea 42
pearl shell 2, 12, 44, 45, 46, 134, 144, 211
pearling 47, 82, 84, 87, 114
   see also divers
pearls 12, 44, 45, 46, 47, 134, 211
Pellew Group 25
Philippines 47
Phillip, Captain Arthur 141
Pieterzoon, Pieter 21n.2
Pilbara 25
Pires, Tomé 19
Pobassoo (Pu' Baso') 29, 30, 73, 74, 75, 95, 206, 207, 208
Pobassoo's Island 207
Port Bradshaw (Yalangbara) 4, 5, 25, 27
Port Essington 60, 70, 77, 82, 133, 134, 141n.1, 152
Port Jackson 71, 74
Port Raffles 79
Portuguese 19, 58, 73n.6, 128, 145, 151n.14
pottery 107
   shards 3, 13, 96
prehistory 27, 28, 41, 42
pre-Macassans 4, 5, 13, 95, 96, 100, 101, 102
   see also bayini
psychology 100, 108
Pu' Baso', *see* Pobassoo
Puddu Daeng Tompo 167

Queensland 29, 31, 47, 56, 101, 110, 127, 145

radiocarbon dates 3, 26, 127
Raffles Bay 141n.1, 151
Raffles, Sir Thomas 75
Ratulangie, Dr 51, 52
religion 55, 56, 69, 79, 80, 89, 95, 101, 141, 214, 221
   Catholic 58, 167

Methodist 94
missions 4, 58, 60, 95, 111, 117, 118, 120, 134
pagan 50, 57
see also Aboriginal—religion, Christianity, Islam
religious
    ceremonies 58, 150n.13
    conversion 58
    music 59
Robinson, E. O. 84, 85, 86, 89
rock art 3, 14, 25, 104, 127–9, 131, 133–6, 142, 148, 205, 213, 219, 221
Rote 15, 21, 44, 47, 85, 128, 143, 186, 189, 190, 198
routes 5, 44
    cultural 15, 162, 205, 206, 219, 220, 221, 222
    intercultural 210, 214
    maritime trading 15, 162, 205–20, 221, 222
    Muslim trading 43
    shipping 47
Royal Geographical Society 115
Rudd, Kevin 57

Sabah 50
Sahul 11, 41, 42, 43
Sama Bajau 1, 45, 47
sandalwood, *see* timber—sandalwood
Scientific Committee on Cultural Routes and Itineraries 15, 206
Scott Reef 60, 184, 185, 186
Searcy, Alfred 84, 85, 86, 148n.8, 149, 151–2
Selayar 184
Seringapatam Reef 184, 185, 186
sexuality 8, 97, 100, 145
Shanghai 31
Shark Bay 45
Singapore 101, 161, 171, 175
smallpox, *see* disease
Smith, Dick 111
smoking 14, 59, 101, 107, 129, 142, 145–8, 152, 153, 154
    of trepang 5, 8, 25, 133, 211, 213
    opium 150, 151, 152, 153, 154
    see also tobacco

Smyth, Captain Henry 80, 89
sociology 108
song 59, 63, 101, 142, 146, 215
    opera 32, 63, 218
    see also music
South Africa 72
South America 40
South Australia 2, 82, 84, 86, 88, 153, 210
South China Sea 32
South Goulburn Island 25, 27, 145
South Korea 175
South Wellesley Group 27
Southeast Asia 1, 3, 6, 19, 20, 23, 26, 31, 32, 33, 41, 46, 47, 57, 95, 101, 120, 127, 128, 130, 133, 134, 135, 144, 145, 154, 159, 167, 183, 205n.1, 210, 220
Spain 219
Spanish 45, 128
Speelman, Cornelis 19
Spencer, Baldwin 153
Spermonde Archipelago 6, 60, 166, 169, 173, 174, 175, 177, 178, 180, 184
spices 43, 44, 168, 210
Spillett, Peter 61, 62
Sri Lanka 71, 72, 77, 78, 82
Stephen's Island 96, 98
Stretton, William George 87
Sultan Abdurrazak Jalaluddin 30–1
Sultan Ahmad as-Salih 30
Sulu 31, 43, 45, 47
Sulu Sea 43
Sumatra 42, 51, 166, 171
Sumbawa 42, 184
Sunda 11, 41, 42, 43
Surabaya 85, 161, 175
Susilo Bambang Yudhoyono 174
Swan River Settlement 77
swords 45, 59, 100, 101, 131, 166, 215
    see also daggers, knives
symbols 5, 59, 63, 75, 101, 209, 215, 216, 220, 221
    see also flags

Taiwan 20n.1
tamarind trees 13, 96, 103, 107, 211
Tambora 42
Tanah Toraja 162

Tanimbar 43, 74n.7
Tarakan 49
technology 42, 46, 89, 99, 103, 120, 174, 186, 221
Terengganu State Museum 159, 171–3, 179
Ternate 43
terra nullius 13, 108, 109, 113, 115, 116, 120
The Geographical Journal 115
Thomson, Donald 23, 107, 115, 116, 117, 146, 147, 154
Tidore 43, 44
timber 211
    cypress pine 211
    ironwood 2, 134, 163, 164, 167, 179, 211
    sandalwood 44, 211
    see also tamarind trees
Timor 21, 44, 46, 47, 49, 64, 71, 74, 83, 85, 128, 143, 184, 194, 198, 213
Timor Sea 6, 7, 9, 14, 22, 44, 184, 210
Tindale, Norman 10, 23
Tiwi Islands 22
tobacco 14, 45, 134, 141, 142, 144, 145–7, 148–54, 211
    see also smoking
'Top End' 5–7, 9, 62, 118, 127
    see also Northern Territory
Torres Strait 29, 44, 148n.7
trade, *see* Aboriginal—trade with outsiders, northern Australia—trade with
trading routes, *see* routes
tuberculosis, *see* disease
Tuckfield, Trevor 117
turtle 21, 134, 186

Unbirri 96, 97, 98–104
United Kingdom 87n.42
United Nations Educational, Scientific and Cultural Organisation (UNESCO) 15, 162, 163, 170
    World Heritage Convention 15, 205
    World Heritage List 162
    World Heritage Committee 162
Unusu Daeng Remba 163–6

Using (Husein) Daeng Rangka 22, 61, 163, 166

Vereenigde Oostindische Compagnie, *see* Dutch East India Company
Vietnam 20n.1, 171
violence 85, 86, 114, 115, 116, 119, 120
visitors to Australia
    contemporary 60, 61, 62, 217, 218
    evidence of 3
    lack of 44
    maritime 149
    rejection of 102
    to Arnhem Land 32
    to Gulf of Carpentaria 25
    to Kimberley 21
    to Northern Territory 22
visits to Australia
    by Asians 2
    by Bajau 1, 47
    by Europeans 150
    by Indonesians 55, 56, 57, 60, 88
    by Macassans 1, 2, 55, 69, 100, 107, 113, 116, 118, 127, 134, 135, 211, 217
    by Malays 146
    by Muslims 56, 57, 58, 60
    by Southeast Asians 95, 128, 134, 135
    by trepangers 85, 86, 101, 213, 214
    see also Aboriginal—visits to Macassar, Aborigines—in Macassar

Walkabout 13, 108, 110–19
Wallace Line 41, 42, 45
Wallace, Alfred Russell 45, 46, 143, 144, 145
Wandjuk Marika 4, 61
Wang Gungwu 20
Wangurri 95, 100, 103
Warner, Lloyd 23, 25, 95, 102, 142, 146, 148n.8, 154
Warramiri 95, 96, 99, 100, 101, 103, 104
Weber Line 41
Wellesley Islands 22, 25, 27
Wellington Range 3, 27, 128, 129, 136, 219

Wessel Islands 99, 102, 207
West Papua 184
Westall, William 73, 207, 208
Western Australia 7, 77
Willey, Keith 118
Williams, Abraham 12, 70–5, 80, 81, 83, 85, 88, 89, 207
Wobalinna Island 25
Wurrawurrawoi 27

xenophobia 12, 57
Xiamen (Amoy) 31, 212

Yalangbara, *see* Port Bradshaw
Yalangbara: Art of the Djang'kawu 4, 5, 6
Yirringa (Drysdale Island) 98, 99
Yirritja 96, 100, 101, 102
Yirrkala 4, 27, 60, 62, 95, 117, 147n.6, 149
Yolngu 5, 12, 13, 56, 58–62, 64, 95–105, 107, 119, 141, 142, 145, 147, 148n.8, 151, 152, 165, 214, 215, 216, 217, 218, 221
    see also language—Yolngu, language—Yolngumatha
Yolngumatha, *see* language—Yolngumatha
Yothu Yindi 63, 103
Yunupingu, Mandawuy 103

Zhou Xiaoping 5, 63

www.ingramcontent.com/pod-product-compliance
Lightning Source LLC
Chambersburg PA
CBHW040935240426
43670CB00033B/2981